The Sleep of Reason

The James Bulger Case

DAVID JAMES SMITH

FABER & FABER

For Petal

First published in 1994 by Century,
an imprint of Penguin Random House UK

This paperback edition first published in 2017
by Faber & Faber Ltd
Bloomsbury House, 74–77 Great Russell Street
London WC1B 3DA

This paperback edition first published in the USA in 2017

Typeset by Faber & Faber Ltd
Printed in England by CPI Group (UK) Ltd, Croydon, CRO 4YY

A CIP record for this book
is available from the British Library

ISBN 978–0–571–34056–9

The Sleep of Reason

David James Smith was born in South London and wrote for *Esquire* before joining the *Sunday Times Magazine*, for whom he travelled around the world writing cover stories, investigative articles, reportage and profiles, winning several awards for his feature writing. An article for the *Magazine* led to his second book, *All About Jill: The Life and Death of Jill Dando* (2002). The acclaimed *Supper with the Crippens* followed in 2005, then came *One Morning in Sarajevo: 28 June 1914* (2008), a reconstruction of the assassination of Archduke Franz Ferdinand. *Young Mandela*, his influential biography of the early life of Nelson Mandela, was published in 2010. More recently, David has served as a commissioner at the Criminal Cases Review Commission investigating miscarriages of justice.

Further praise for *The Sleep of Reason*:

'After twenty-five years, the murder of James Bulger continues to haunt Britain with so many unanswered questions. *The Sleep of Reason* is an honest and sincere attempt to try to understand this most tragic of cases.' David Peace

'Painstakingly researched . . . avoids prescriptive comment and prurient flash . . . makes a persuasive case for the humanity of the two children.' *New Statesman*

'Compelling and compassionate.' *Times Educational Supplement*

Hold childhood in reverence, and do not be in any hurry to judge it for good or ill. Leave exceptional cases to show themselves, let their qualities be tested and confirmed, before special methods are adopted. Give nature time to work before you take over her business, lest you interfere with her dealings. You assert that you know the value of time and are afraid to waste it. You fail to perceive that it is a greater waste of time to use it ill than to do nothing, and that a child ill taught is further from virtue than a child who has learnt nothing at all. You are afraid to see him spending his early years doing nothing. What! Is it nothing to be happy, nothing to run and jump all day? He will never be so busy again all his life long. Plato, in his *Republic*, which is considered so stern, teaches the children only through festivals, games, songs, and amusements. It seems as if he had accomplished his purpose when he taught them to be happy; and Seneca, speaking of the Roman lads in olden days, says, 'They were always on their feet, they were never taught anything which kept them sitting.' Were they any the worse for it in manhood? Do not be afraid, therefore, of this so-called idleness. What would you think of a man who refused to sleep lest he should waste part of his life? You would say, 'He is mad; he is not enjoying his life, he is robbing himself of part of it; to avoid sleep he is hastening his death.' Remember that these two cases are alike, and that *childhood is the sleep of reason*. The apparent ease with which children learn is their ruin. You fail to see that this very facility proves that they are not learning. Their shining, polished brain reflects, as in a mirror, the things you show them, but nothing sinks in. The child remembers the words and the ideas are reflected back; his hearers understand them, but to him they are meaningless. Although memory and reason are wholly different faculties, the one does not really develop apart from the other. Before the age of reason the child receives images, not ideas; and there is this difference between them: images are merely the pictures of external objects, while ideas are notions about those objects determined by their relations.

from *Emile* by Jean-Jacques Rousseau, 1762

Acknowledgements

The people who deserve most thanks for any merit in this book had better remain anonymous. They wanted to see the story told truly and without prejudice. They gave me their trust and confidence, and their friendship. Neither money nor favours were ever asked for, offered or given. Many other people on Merseyside were willing to give me their time and cooperation, despite the sensitivity of the subject. I owe them all a thank-you. Merseyside Police offered considerable assistance, within the limits of their own concern about the disclosure of evidence in advance of the trial, when the bulk of this book was researched and written. I'm grateful to all the officers who helped me, but special thanks are due to Jim Fitzsimmons, Albert Kirby, Brian Whitby and Ray Simpson. I've characterised one or two police officers in the book. This doesn't mean they solved the case on their own. I hope readers will see them as representative of the many officers involved in the inquiry. Thanks also to Dominic Lloyd and Jason Lee of Paul Rooney and Co., solicitors for Robert Thompson, and to Sean Sexton who represents the family of James Bulger. I was grateful for the advice and support of the editor of this book, Mark Booth, and my friends Dominic Ozanne and John Pickering. Dominic, more than anyone, contributed to the structure and shape of the narrative. Thanks, randomly, to Jane Gregory, Georgina Capel, Julian Browne, Tim Hulse, Rosie Boycott and Sue Douglas. Thanks to Jamie Bruce, because he deserves it. Some time before James Bulger died, I met Dr Gwyneth Boswell of the University of East Anglia who had produced a report for the Prince's Trust about young people who commit serious crimes. Gwyneth and the report taught me a great deal and, in a way, her insight was a starting point for *The Sleep of Reason*. But my best and wisest ally, as usual, was Petal, who listened, read, transcribed, and tolerated my complete absorption in the case. I wanted to acknowledge the anguish of the parents and wider family of James Bulger. I hope they will appreciate the spirit in which this book was written, and forgive me when I also acknowledge the suffering of the two boys who were responsible for the killing, and their families.

Note

Everything in this book is true to the best of my knowledge. This is a work of non-fiction, and there is no imagining, invention or embellishment of what happened. There have been some changes of names to protect identities in accordance with the orders of the trial judge.

Preface

James Bulger is buried at Kirkdale Cemetery in Liverpool, which is just about midway between Kirkby, where he lived, and Walton, where he was killed by two ten-year-old boys, Jon Venables and Robert Thompson, in February 1993. At his death he was a month short of his third birthday. When I last visited the grave in the early spring of 1996 the substantial white headstone had been inlaid with James's photograph – an enduring image of a cherubic son, all blond hair and toothy grin. The inscription betrayed nothing of his fate: 'Goodnight and God bless, little innocent babe.' The plot and surrounding area were scattered with toys and flowers, one bouquet left with a card signed 'From a father in Reading: The pain of mourning never goes, the reason for your loss, only God knows.'

God knows, indeed, why James Bulger died. It is as true now as it was then that the murder has never really been explained and the motive for the crime remains a mystery. This book, the result of considerable research and a painstaking, sometimes distressing assembly of the facts, was my attempt to offer some insight and understanding.

I had gone to Liverpool within a few weeks of the murder, rented a small house there for the duration and soon found myself at the heart of the case, well connected to some of the participants. *The Sleep of Reason* was first published a year later in 1994 and, such was the interest in this case, it went on to be reproduced in numerous editions and translations around the world.

By that spring of 1996, when I went to pay homage at the cemetery, I was getting ready to write a lengthy new magazine article. I was still in contact with Ann Thompson, the mother of Robert, who was then three years into his detention and still only thirteen years old. Ann had knitted bonnets – helmets, she called them – for my newborn daughter, whom I had brought to see her. As we sat talking in her home, the phone rang and it was Robert calling from his secure unit. Ann told him I was there and offered me the phone to speak to him. I held up a flat hand in refusal – that conversation would have got both of us into trouble – and later, when I dropped Ann at the unit for a visit she pointed out the distant figure of Robert, who stood watching from a window.

When my article appeared it described something of Ann's life – she would often sit watching television clips of Denise Bulger, the mother of the victim, which she had recorded on video. She would imagine going on television herself, setting the world to rights, saying things that really were better left unsaid – 'If that child had been wearing reins this would never have happened' was one – and generally letting everyone know how much she cared for and believed in her son and was suffering on his behalf. Ann Thompson had suffered a lot over the years and felt all that suffering acutely.

She had left Liverpool and was living with her family under an assumed name, but she went about in a state of perpetual dread at being unmasked – the guilt and fear were so powerful they seemed visible to her. I said it was as if she felt she had a neon sign on her head: Mother of Bulger Killer. Missing her home, she would become maudlin, listening to Daniel O'Donnell songs such as 'The Leaving of Liverpool', and reminded herself of her old life by cooking scouse, which I described as a one-pot dish made with cheap cuts of meat. I also referred to Ann's VHS player as a 'tired old video recorder'. She was upset and thought I had patronised her and, after a difficult phone call our contact came to an end. It was a tricky relationship and, perhaps because I liked and respected her in spite of everything, I had often worried that I was simply exploiting her for my journalism. I knew that Ann was always grateful and relieved not to be judged by the people she met and I could see from the start that her own wretched childhood had left her vulnerable and poorly prepared to become a caring adult.

But, of course, the case had provoked a great deal of judgement, not just of Ann and the parents of Jon Venables but of their sons, too. From the beginning I had tried to encourage the view that James Bulger's murder was a tragedy for three families, but that was not how most people thought, and both politicians and the media seemed keen to exacerbate the furore it had caused. Some police officers would claim to have looked into Robert and Jon's eyes and seen evil lurking there. (Probably they were looking at fear and trauma in two small children.) The *Sun* newspaper printed a coupon which over 20,000 readers took the trouble to cut out and complete and post to the then Home Secretary, Michael Howard: 'Dear Home Secretary, I agree with Ralph and Denise Bulger that the boys who killed their son James should stay in jail for life.'

In fact, as I later discovered, life was not long enough for Howard: he had wanted them to serve a tariff – a minimum sentence – of twenty years, which was two lifetimes for ten-year-olds. He was restrained by advisers and instead set the tariff at fifteen years, still nearly double the recommendation of the trial judge, who had said that eight years would do. Howard's mistake – and his undoing – was to admit that he had taken note of *Sun* readers in reaching his decision. In late 1999 the European Court of Human Rights concluded that he had been wrong to take public opinion into account. The decision should have been left to the judiciary.

The European Court also concluded that the two boys' human rights had been infringed by putting them on trial in an adult court – Preston Crown Court – in October 1993. They were so very clearly too young to cope with such a traumatic experience, on top of the horrors of their crime. But compassion for them was in short supply. Both boys would recall the feeling of being stared at in court: Venables had counted in his head to avoid listening, while Thompson had determined never to betray his feelings to those around him during the trial.

I would later learn just how disturbing it has been for Jon Venables, who asked his parents if they thought James was in the courtroom too. No, his mother had told him, James was in heaven. Venables then asked if they thought James could hear what was being said in the courtroom. At the end of each day in court he had taken his clothes off, saying he could 'smell the baby' on them or 'could smell James like a baby smell'. He wanted the clothes he had worn in court thrown away when the case was over. Venables' remorse was so great that he imagined a baby James growing inside him, waiting to be reborn.

Throughout the trial the two boys' identities were protected by court order; they were known simply as Child A and Child B. Following their conviction, the judge succumbed to media pressure and agreed they could be named – a decision that had far-reaching implications the judge could not have foreseen. Had he been able to, he might have taken a different decision. The boys' lawyers have since argued that the naming of them greatly added to their trauma. It also gave focus, and impetus, to the public mood for vengeance, and helped to create a very real threat to their lives, in perpetuity.

As the years progressed through their sentences, I would often hear of people who claimed to have encountered them in secure units up and down the country. A friend training to be a probation officer had a lecturer who had met one of them in Devon. Someone else had met one of them in Essex. They were here, there and everywhere. It was a kind of absurd sideshow, born of their notoriety, I suppose. But as I well knew, they had never actually gone anywhere. Venables had been sent to Red Bank in Newton-le-Willows after he was charged, Thompson had been taken to Barton Moss in Greater Manchester, and that was where they remained, every night for the next eight years.

They started out as the youngest members of their enclosed communities and ended up the eldest, serving far longer sentences than everyone else, kept on beyond the normal time at which they might have been expected to be transferred to Young Offenders' Institutions. YOIs are tougher establishments and there were rumours that staff and inmates couldn't wait to get their hands on Thompson and Venables. Staying put, they were apparently transformed from frightened, disturbed children into functioning young adults. They achieved GCSEs and enjoyed graduated mobility, making escorted trips back into the world where they had the chance to compensate for the lack of freedom that might otherwise have meant they could never have the opportunity to lead normal lives. Still, at the time of their release neither Thompson nor Venables had ever made an unaccompanied trip on a bus or bought something in a shop.

The European Court judgment meant they could be freed in 2001 and a series of parole hearings took place with initial assessments for both boys that February, followed by longer hearings six months later. There was some alarm over Thompson when a psychologist claimed to have found evidence of psychopathic personality traits during testing of him. The tests were meant to be done on adults but the results could not be ignored and a new expert report was called for. It echoed an additional concern that Thompson had manipulated the long-term relationship with the psychiatrist who had worked with him during his time at Barton Moss. Thompson had so persuaded her of his anxiety at being betrayed to the media that she never wrote down anything but the barest details of their sessions. As the psychiatrist might have anticipated, this was setting up a serious problem, both for her professional credibility and Thompson's future release. In the absence of in-depth reports, what were the parole board supposed to work with as evidence of Thompson's redemption and understanding and remorse for his crime?

The new expert was very thorough and Thompson was now more open. The expert dismissed any suggestion that Thompson was a psychopath but at the same time he talked Thompson through the offence and gave an interpretive account of how and why James Bulger died which has a ring of authenticity about it. The psychologist appeared to agree with the manager of Barton Moss, who described Thompson as one of the most normally adjusted people in his circumstances. Thompson had never shown any trait of dishonesty and had never, despite occasional opportunities at the unit, abused alcohol or drugs. In eight years he had never needed to be significantly disciplined or punished.

Thompson was described in the new report as a child who had learnt to disengage emotionally as a result of earlier traumas, in particular his father leaving home when he was six, but also the violence he had seen at home before and after – especially the sight of his mother lying injured after being attacked by his father, when he was unable to go to her out of fear of his father. With his father gone and his mother struggling to cope, Thompson found himself among a pack of like-minded children in similar circumstances, going shoplifting, truanting, vandalising and breaking into cars. There was never a chosen victim for these crimes, never a plan, never any violence. There was a group dynamic or proposals idly adopted, and a kind of obligation to act on the impulses of the others. Thompson, on his own account, said he only went home when it was late and he hoped the house was asleep. He was 'an urban feral child'.

Although the psychologist's report was about Thompson, there were clear parallels with Venables, who had problems at home with conflict between his parents, siblings with learning difficulties, bullying by his peers and a wider family context of domestic violence and alcohol abuse. Thompson always maintained it was Venables who said, on the way to the Strand shopping centre in Bootle on 12 February 1993: 'Let's get a kid lost.' There was no other premeditation. Thompson claimed he was not interested but went along with the abduction of James Bulger and didn't do anything to stop it, and so accepted his own full responsibility for the crime, even though he could not clearly remember everything that happened.

There was increasing tension after the abduction as they could not decide what to do with the child and did not know how to 'get rid' of the child without being found out. The child's distress increased the tension and fear between them. The final assault – the killing of James on the railway line at Walton with stones and sticks and paint and a heavy metal 'fishplate' – had been 'a chaotic destruction' of the source of the boys' fear. The psychologist likened those moments to the climax of the novel *Lord of the Flies*, 'where one troublesome child is objectified or dehumanised by the others and then killed in a frenzied attack'. This was just a hypothesis, but if it was right it could have been triggered by the unusual combination of those two boys being together, being poorly socialised, having no sense of responsibility for inhibiting the behaviour of the other, and being able to 'emotionally disengage' because of their past experiences.

The psychologist noted comments from staff at Barton Moss about the limited feedback from his therapy sessions and the way Thompson had set the terms of his therapy. This had resulted in staff hearing nothing further when one of them had passed on to the therapist a disclosure from Thompson that he had been sexually abused in childhood. Neither the psychologist nor the staff at Barton Moss knew anything more about the abuse, but those references to it in the psychologist's report obliged the therapist and Thompson to describe it to the parole board.

Meanwhile, although it was not a race, all the indications appeared to be that Venables had made even swifter advances towards rehabilitation. In 1997 his therapist could say he had made exceptional progress in both his personal development and acknowledgment of the enormity of his offence. Around the same time, staff at Red Bank reported that he had become a role model for others in the unit and he had matured into an amiable young man. His recent behaviour had been exemplary. That fitted the widely held view of the two co-murderers, that Thompson was the more thuggish and likely ringleader and Venables the innocent led astray. I had always thought that was a complete misreading of what we knew. If anything, it was the other way around and Venables had seemed to me to be the more disturbed of the pair.

But by now there was a consensus that Venables posed a low risk or no risk at all to the public, although it was also recognised that the shame and remorse he felt at his crime would be with him for ever. So while Thompson was wrestling with his past as a victim of abuse, Venables appeared to be gliding towards a viable future. The two were released in June 2001 and both lived in semi-independent units specially prepared for them in the grounds of the secure units, before moving to live with full independence, some time later. They both took on assumed names and lived with the protection of a far-reaching injunction put in place at the High Court by Dame Elizabeth Butler-Sloss, largely in response to plausible evidence that there were people who would like to find them and kill them or, at the very least, cause them harm.

As we later learned, Jon Venables' new identity required intensive policing and a year to set up, at a cost of over £250,000. He needed everything from passports to examination certificates and medical records – not even his GP knew who he really was. A 'legacy life' – a false past – had to be created for him, and presumably for Thompson too. It is hard to imagine how difficult it must be to live within such a phoney construct. The pressure, you have to conclude, must be immense. In 2006 I wrote that both young men had been living quiet settled lives over the five years since their release. How little I knew. Unbeknown to anyone, including his army of minders reaching right into the heart of government, Jon Venables had terrible unresolved problems – issues I now believe he must have kept hidden throughout his time in custody – and was descending into a life of chaos and criminality.

In the first place, as I disclosed in an article in the *Sunday Times Magazine* in 2011, Venables is believed to have had a brief sexual relationship with a female member of staff at Red Bank, not long before his release. This was, at the least, an abuse of power by the woman, and appears to have reflected an unstable period at Red Bank with poor management being recorded during inspections. Such an incident must have had a profound effect on Venables who, as was observed by his psychiatrist, had been through an abnormal psychosexual development during his adolescence, never free to explore his sexuality as other young men would in the outside world. You wonder, though, at the extent to which that incident shaped the offence that took him back to prison in February 2010, after a long period of instability and increasing abuse of drugs and alcohol.

Venables had seemed settled at first, after his release, under close supervision by the probation service. Both he and Thompson were subject to strict conditions of release, preventing them from visiting Merseyside and associating with children. Venables studied and later worked, but he began to struggle with debt and isolation. Significantly, he spent a lot of time alone on the Internet. His probation officer wondered what games he was playing. In fact, for at least two years before his recall to prison he had been collecting videos and still images of child pornography and in some cases sharing them. Some of the images were among the most obscene available. He had also masqueraded on the Internet as a mother who, together with her husband, was abusing her child and now offering the child for sale to others to abuse. He had expressed a specific interest in looking at images of parents abusing their own children.

How he managed to behave like that for at least two years, while supposedly being one of the most closely supervised individuals ever freed on life licence, has never been fully explained. An investigation into the whole affair, by former civil servant Sir David Omand, seemed superficial and all too ready to blame Venables himself. Others ought to have been culpable too, especially when so many warning signs were missed.

Venables admitted the child pornography offences and received a two-year prison sentence. He became eligible for parole, once more, in July 2011, by which time his new identity had allegedly been widely disclosed on the Internet: another burden, in addition to the honest talking he will have been obliged to do, finally, in relation to his paedophile activities. It now seems probable that, like his co-accused Robert Thompson, Jon Venables may have been the victim of child sexual abuse before the murder of James Bulger.

But that is not something known or proven. Like so much about this case, it exists only in the realms of speculation and, I like to think, emphasises the importance of continuing to review and examine one of the most significant crimes in modern history.

David James Smith,
September 2011

Introduction

The first time I met Albert Kirby, the officer who led the investigation into the killing of James Bulger, I said that it was not a unique case. He said it *was* unique: the two boys were the youngest ever to have been accused of murder. He had never encountered anything like it, and hoped he never would again.

Albert was articulating the mood of the moment and a sentiment that was widely shared. A unique case born of a lawless generation. It was a symbol of the age, of declining standards, loss of values, lack of respect, breakdown of the family, too many single mothers, failure of the Welfare State, collapse of society, moral vacuum . . . moral panic.

If the boys were guilty, what had possessed them to commit such a terrible crime? Were they evil, born bad, led on by adults, influenced by violence on television, desensitising computer games, video nasties? Were they playing a game that went wrong, were they lords of the flies acting out the wickedness of children (the latent cruelty in us all), or were they just plain possessed? These theories were offered less as speculation than as statements of fact. Many people, it seemed, needed to explain James Bulger's death to themselves and to others. And if there was no ready explanation, what then?

Only two people can provide an understanding. Barely eleven years old now, they are unlikely to be able to do this for many years, and unlikely to achieve such an understanding without psychiatric help.

Such limited research as exists in this area suggests that most young people who commit serious crimes – murder, manslaughter, rape, arson – have one thing in common. They have been abused physically or sexually, or both, and emotionally, in childhood. Not all young people who commit serious crimes have been abused. And not all young people who have been abused commit serious crimes. But the pattern is there.

Many people find this idea risible or lame. They detect the making of excuses. They think kids pretend they've been beaten to get off the hook. A good slap never did *them* any harm. Anyone who has seen or experienced the effects of this kind of abuse, or spent time observing and listening to young offenders, will not be so dismissive.

Perhaps it is not the two boys who are unhappy products of the television age, but the global audience that watched the security video footage of the child's abduction and were provoked by unprecedented media coverage to unprecedented reactions of shock and horror.

The sad truth is that similar cases have happened in Britain in recent times, in not so recent times, and long, long ago. Children have killed, periodically, in the past and who then attributed the killings to wider social ills, or took them to be an emblem of decay? Where was the national debate? What Prime Minister of the day stood to declare, as John Major did in February 1993, that 'We must condemn a little more, and understand a little less'?

By way of recovering a perspective, this book begins with a catalogue of all the British cases I have been able to find of killings, or alleged killings, by children. With the exception of the first boy, the last child to be hanged, all were under the age of fourteen. The older records are the fruit of someone else's research: in 1973 Patrick Wilson, spurred on perhaps by the Mary Bell case, wrote *Children Who Kill*, a book long since out of print. The more recent examples I found filed in the news library of the *Sunday Times*.

The age of criminal responsibility in Britain was fixed at ten years by the 1963 revision of the Children and Young Persons Act. When implemented 30 years earlier, this Act had raised the minimum age to eight from seven, at which it had been fixed since the middle ages.

The law has also determined that a child becomes a young person on his or her fourteenth birthday. Between the ages of ten and fourteen children are presumed to be *doli incapax*, which literally means incapable of doing wrong. In practice, this means that the law presumes they are unable to understand the seriousness of their actions. To obtain a conviction the prosecution must rebut this presumption, proving to the court's satisfaction that the child would have known the action to be seriously wrong, and not just mischievous or naughty.

In March 1831 John Any Bird Bell, aged fourteen, robbed and cut the throat of a thirteen-year-old boy who was collecting money for his father. Tried at Maidstone, Bell was found guilty of murder after two minutes' discussion by the jury, who did not leave the box. The jury made a recommendation for mercy, on account of the dreadful state of ignorance he was in and the barbarous manner in which he had been brought up by his parents. The judge said it was his imperative duty to pass the death sentence. Bell was sentenced on a Friday and hanged on the Monday morning, outside Maidstone Gaol. Before he dropped, Bell cried, 'All you people take heed by me!' This to the crowd of 5000 who had come to see him go. There were 52 hangings in Britain that year. Bell was the last child to be hanged.

The earliest recorded killing by a child under the age of fourteen was in 1748, when William York, aged ten, was living in a Suffolk workhouse and sharing a bed with a five-year-old girl. He cut the girl with a knife and a billhook after she had fouled the bed, and stated in his confession that the devil put him up to committing the deed. Found guilty of murder and sentenced to death, York was granted a Royal pardon on condition that he enlist immediately in the Navy.

In 1778 at Huntingdon three girls aged eight, nine and ten were tried for the murder of a three-year-old girl. It was said that 'the manner in which they committed this act was by fixing three pins at the end of a stick, which they thrust into the child's body, which lacerated the private parts and soon turned to a mortification of which she languished for a few days and then died'. The girls were found to be *doli incapax* and acquitted.

In 1847 in Hackney, a twelve-year-old, William Allnut Brown, stole ten sovereigns from his home, fired a gun near his grandfather, then poisoned the old man with his own arsenic. Brown was said to be a sickly and difficult boy. He was charged with murder and found guilty by the jury despite a plea of insanity. He was sentenced to death but reprieved.

In 1854, Alice Levick, aged ten, was living with an aunt and caring for the aunt's baby. She was sent on an errand with the baby to collect some knives and forks. When found by a group of men, she was crying and carrying the baby, whose throat had been cut. She said a stranger had come up behind her in the woods and killed the baby. The inquest jury returned a verdict of wilful murder by Levick, but she was acquitted at her subsequent trial.

In 1855, in Liverpool, nine small boys were playing 'cap on back', a kind of leapfrog, in a brickfield. There was an argument over fair play between Alfred Fitz, aged nine, and a seven-year-old. Fitz hit the other boy with a half-brick. When he fell down, Fitz hit him again. Fitz called to John Breen, also aged nine, 'Let's throw him into the canal, or else we'll be cotched.' They carried the seven-year-old 40 yards to the Leeds–Liverpool Canal and threw him in, while the others watched. They all stood there until the boy disappeared. The body was found four days later in Stanley Dock. Fitz and Breen were tried for murder at Liverpool Crown Court. They were found guilty of manslaughter and sentenced to twelve months at Liverpool Gaol where, the judge said, they would have a schoolmaster and a chaplain to instruct them, and be taught to earn their living.

In 1861, near Stockport, a two-year-old disappeared while

playing near his home. His body was found the next day, a mile away in a field near Love Lane, face down in a brook and naked except for his clogs. A woman said she had seen two boys aged about eight walking with a child who was crying. One of the boys had been leading the child by the hand. She had asked them where they were going, and they had said they were going down Love Lane. Another woman had seen them in the field, when the child was naked. She asked what they were doing with the child undressed, but they ignored her and moved away. Her son said he saw one of the boys hit the child with a twig.

James Bradley and Peter Barratt, both aged eight, were interviewed by a police officer. They admitted undressing the child, pushing him into the water and hitting him with sticks until he was dead. They referred to the child only as 'it'. At Chester Assizes they became the youngest children to have faced a murder trial and the death sentence. Defence counsel said, 'it must have happened in boyish mischief, they being unable to know right from wrong'. They were found guilty of manslaughter and sentenced to one month in gaol, and five years in a reformatory.

In 1861, in County Durham, John Little, aged twelve and employed to do odd jobs at a farm, shot a young woman housekeeper with his master's shotgun after an argument. He was charged with manslaughter, but acquitted on evidence that he did not understand firearms.

In 1881, in Carlisle, a thirteen-year-old girl was employed by a farming family to look after their three children. The two-year-old drowned suddenly, without explanation, and, not long after, the family's baby drowned in some mud. At first the girl claimed a man had snatched the baby from her, but eventually she admitted, 'I took the baby and put it in and nobody helped me.' She was charged with murder and found guilty, with a recommendation to mercy. The death sentence was passed, then commuted to life imprisonment. No charge was ever brought over the death of the two-year-old.

In 1920, in London, a boy aged seven told a child he would drown him if the child did not hand over his toy aeroplane. When the child refused the boy pushed him into the canal and kicked his hands away while he tried to climb up the bank, until he drowned. The inquest returned a verdict of accidental death, and the truth only emerged later, when the boy was sent to a psychologist for the treatment of rages. There was no trial, and the boy was placed in care.

In 1921, in Redbourn, Hertfordshire, a boy aged thirteen beat his next-door neighbour to death with a hammer and a poker, while trying to steal money from her home. He climbed into a well to drown himself, but changed his mind and climbed out again. He was found guilty of murder and sentenced to be detained at His Majesty's pleasure.

In 1938 a four-year-old girl disappeared while playing near her home. Her body was found the following morning in the conservatory of the house next door by the widowed mother of five children who lived there. The girl had been sexually assaulted and strangled. The widow's 13-year-old son was questioned and denied involvement until his mother told him to tell the truth. He then admitted telling the girl to undress, and strangling her when she began to cry. He was said to be 'retarded' and a frequent truant. The trial considered whether or not the boy knew that what he was doing was 'seriously and gravely wrong'. He was acquitted, and placed in an Approved School.

In 1947, in a Welsh mining village, a four-year-old boy disappeared while out playing, and was found later that evening, drowned in the nearby river, his hands and ankles bound together. Three weeks after the killing, the boy's nine-year-old playmate was questioned by police and said, 'I tied him up with the cords of his shoes and threw him off the manhole into the river and he was drowned. I went home and was afraid to tell anyone.' When charged, he replied, 'I won't do it again.'

He was acquitted of murder but found guilty of manslaughter, and ordered to be detained for ten years.

In 1947, in a Northern coastal town, a woman left her baby in a pram outside her husband's shop while she was serving. When the pram and baby disappeared, a search was made and the baby was found drowned in a water-filled pit. A nine-year-old boy was questioned and admitted, 'I took the pram from outside the shop. There was a baby in the pram and I threw it in the water. I just wanted to do it.' The boy pleaded not guilty to murder but guilty of manslaughter, and was ordered to be detained for a maximum of five years.

In 1961, in a West London suburb, a twelve-year-old boy killed his 53-year-old mother with a knife after an argument, allegedly over a bacon sandwich. The boy was the youngest of three and home life was said to be 'not entirely happy'. His parents had separated and reunited. At the time of the killing, his father, a taxi driver, was in hospital. Mother and son were said to quarrel frequently because of the boy's violent temper. He was allowed to plead not guilty to murder and guilty to manslaughter, and was placed in the care of his local authority.

In 1967, in Crewe, a boy of ten was charged with murder after the stabbing of another ten-year-old boy in a school playground. The result of this charge is unknown. In Wakefield, a boy aged twelve was sentenced to seven years' detention after pleading not guilty to murder but guilty of the manslaughter of a seven-year-old he drowned in a stream.

In 1968, in Islington, the coroner recorded a verdict of accidental death on a seven-month-old baby which had been battered to death. A pair of earrings were found in the baby's eyes. The coroner said that two brothers, aged four and three, would have faced trial for murder if they had been older.

In 1968, in Newcastle, Mary Bell, aged eleven, and Norma Bell, aged thirteen, a neighbour but no relation, faced trial for the murder of a boy aged four and another boy aged three, whom they were accused of strangling. The first boy had been killed the day before Mary Bell's eleventh birthday, the second two months later. Both girls pleaded not guilty to murder but, after hearing their evidence at the trial, the jury found Norma not guilty and Mary guilty of manslaughter on the grounds of diminished responsibility. Mary Bell was sentenced to detention for life. She was released in 1980, a week before her 23rd birthday, refusing at the time to change her name. She is now the mother of a ten-year-old child, living under a new name, with an injunction preventing its publication.

In 1972, in South Yorkshire, an eleven-year-old boy pleaded not guilty to the murder of a six-year-old he was said to have drowned. The accused was said to have suffered 'organic brain damage', and was acquitted after the judge directed the jury not to convict unless they were sure the boy knew that what he was doing was wrong. In Dundee, a girl aged thirteen was found guilty of killing a three-year-old girl she had suffocated while the child was in her care. She was sentenced to be detained for ten years.

In 1973, in Portsmouth, a boy aged twelve stabbed his mother and pleaded guilty to manslaughter. He was freed by the court after evidence that he had been under pressure from his parents over his schoolwork. He was placed on a three-year supervision order at his boarding school.

In 1973, in Liverpool, an eleven-year-old boy pleaded guilty to the manslaughter of a two-year-old child. He had hit the boy accidentally while throwing stones. Too scared to take him home, he held the child down in a pool of rainwater until he drowned. The boy was placed in the care of the local authority.

In 1975, in Sheffield, a thirteen-year-old boy beat an elderly woman to death with an iron bar. The boy lived near the woman, and sometimes ran errands for her. He had entered her flat to steal money for fireworks. He pleaded guilty to murder and was sentenced to be detained during Her Majesty's pleasure.

In 1975, in east London, a boy of thirteen pleaded not guilty to the murder of a two-year-old girl, and the attempted murder of her five-year-old sister. He had stabbed the girls while they watched television alone in their flat. He told the police he was always getting the blame for teaching the girls to swear. He was found guilty of manslaughter and attempted murder, and sentenced to be detained for fourteen years.

In 1976, in Dunfermline, a thirteen-year-old boy stabbed and strangled a twelve-year-old girl. He later said he had joined the girl while she was fishing, believing her to be a boy. After urinating in some bushes, in full view of the girl, he had discovered she was female, and attacked her in anger and embarrassment. The boy admitted the murder and was ordered to be detained during Her Majesty's pleasure.

In 1977, in Peckham, a twelve-year-old boy was the youngest of four people who attacked and killed a homeless man in a derelict house. One teenager was convicted of manslaughter, and the other three defendants were found guilty of murder. The twelve-year-old boy was ordered to be detained indefinitely.

In 1978, in Wolverhampton, two boys aged four and six were alleged to have beaten to death an 84-year-old woman who lived alone in a flat. They were said to be among a group of local children who had previously been pestering and taunting the woman in her home. They were too young to face criminal charges.

In 1979, in Leicester, a nine-year-old boy admitted to police that he had killed his eight-month-old sister by attacking her with a penknife and a ballpoint pen as she lay in her cot. The boy was too young to face criminal charges.

In 1982, in Birkenhead, a boy aged nine killed a twelve-year-old boy who died after a single stab wound during an argument in the street near their homes. The nine-year-old said the stabbing was accidental. Although this was disputed at the inquest, the coroner recorded an open verdict after declaring that the twelve-year-old had been unlawfully killed.

The nine-year-old boy was too young to face criminal charges.

In 1986, in Sussex, a girl aged five was with a friend when she allegedly took a three-week-old baby from his pram and swung the baby by his legs against a wall. The baby was killed, but the girls were too young to face criminal charges.

In 1988, in Borehamwood, a twelve-year-old boy abducted a two-year-old girl from a playground and walked her just over a mile to a railway embankment where he pushed her face into soft ground until she suffocated. They had been seen by a total of seventeen people during the 40-minute walk following the abduction. The boy had no history of violence and no previous convictions. His parents were separated, and he was in care at the time of the offence. He was convicted of the abduction and killing of the child, and ordered to be detained during Her Majesty's pleasure.

In 1990, in Glasgow, a twelve-year-old boy drowned a three-year-old child after beating his head against stones in a stream. The boy was said to have come from a 'fairly sad' family background. Cleared of murder but found guilty of culpable homicide, he was ordered to be detained indefinitely.

In 1992, in Northumberland, an eleven-year-old girl killed the eighteen-month-old child she was babysitting. When the baby would not stop crying, the girl beat him against the bars of his cot, and then suffocated the child by placing her hand over his mouth and nose. The girl was convicted of manslaughter.

I

Jon was late leaving for school. His mother was hurrying him out of the door a few minutes before nine, checking he'd got the note she'd written for the teacher in which she asked if it would be all right for Jon to bring the gerbils home for next week's half-term holiday.

Now, Jon headed for the walkways under the flyover. He vanished into the bushes in the middle of the roundabout, re-emerging without his school bag, the black one with red stripes on the handle that usually contained his wildlife books, his wrestling magazines and his PE kit. The bushes were Jon's preferred hiding place for the bag.

He met Bobby at the top of the village, by the church. Bobby was with his kid brother, Ryan. He had already called for Gummy Gee, who was staying off school with a belly ache. Gummy told Bobby he'd got the runs.

Jon and Bobby didn't say much to each other.

'You sagging?'

'Yeah.'

Ryan didn't want to sag. He wanted to go to school. Yesterday Jon had offered him two quid if he would sag today, but Ryan wasn't having any of it. He wanted to go to school. Friday was pottery day, and Ryan liked pottery. So they left him to make his own way down Bedford Road, and Jon and Bobby disappeared down the entries to avoid being spotted as they passed the school.

They were seen anyway by their 5R classmate Nicola. She told Miss Rigg, who marked two red circles by their names in the register, and mentioned the boys' apparent truancy to the head teacher on the way to assembly.

Last night, after the pupils had gone home, Miss Rigg had

moved Jon's desk to the back of the class. He had been particularly awkward yesterday, the worst she'd ever seen him, in fact; fidgety and excitable, as if barely able to contain himself, while the class made electrical circuits with batteries and light bulbs. She had remarked on it to her colleagues and had determined to do better with him today.

After assembly the head teacher, Irene Slack, spoke to Nicola, who confirmed that she had seen Jon and Bobby down an entry by the off licence, running in the opposite direction to school. Miss Slack called the Education Welfare Office, and tried to phone Jon's mother. No answer.

Jon and Bobby were on their way down Breeze Hill and out of Walton, past the reservoir, the Mons pub, Smiley's Tyre and Exhaust Centre, straight on to Merton Road and into the heart of Bootle, crossing Stanley Road, over the canal and round the back to the Strand entrance by the bus terminal. It was about two miles.

As they went along, they talked about robbing and sagging. Jon wondered what would happen if they got caught by a teacher or a policeman. Bobby said they'd probably end up in the police station.

They were both in school uniform, or most of it. Black trousers, white shirt, grey V-necked jumper, blue and yellow striped tie. Both boys were wearing their brogies. Bobby was wearing his black jacket with the green trim and the blue patches. Jon's jacket was mustard-coloured and plain, and not long bought from Dunn's.

Jon had a bowl 'ead haircut, Bobby a Number 2 crop, straight through with the shears. Jon was four feet and eight inches tall. Bobby was shorter by two inches. They were both ten years old, their birthdays two weeks apart in August.

When the shop assistant in Clinton Cards noticed the uniforms, she called out from behind the till. Bobby and Jon stood there, looking at the extensive selection of trolls on display. Bobby, who liked trolls, would have robbed one or two, if he could.

'You off school then?'

'Yeah, it's Baker's Day,' Bobby said.

'Do you mean Inset Day?'

'No. Half-term.'

What school did they go to? St Mary's. Where was that? Walton. At this, Jon gave Bobby a stamp with his foot. 'We're with our mum,' said Bobby, and with that they left the card shop.

Bobby stole a toy soldier from Superdrug. It was a clockwork sniper, which slithered along the floor when wound up. Bobby took it on the escalators, and tried to make it crawl along the rubber handrail. When the sniper fell or was thrown down on the escalating steps, a woman shopper told them off. They should be more careful. The escalator might get jammed. Bobby and Jon ignored her.

The woman was sitting on a bench outside Boots a few minutes later, waiting for her mother-in-law, when she saw Bobby and Jon again. They were walking out of the Strand's department store, TJ Hughes, followed by a small child. They were all laughing, the two older boys running forward, stopping and turning as the child ran towards them laughing. The woman watched as the child's mother appeared, in a bit of a panic as she called her son back and scolded him. The two older boys just seemed to melt away.

Bobby and Jon had left the escalator and gone into TJ Hughes, lurking round the bag counters, trying to rob the rucksacks, gloves and bumbags.

Mrs Power had been shopping with her three-year-old daughter and her two-year-old son. Mrs Power had been looking at sweatshirts; nearby, her two children turned their attention to the purses on display. She noticed the two boys, Bobby and Jon, kneeling there too, opening and closing purses as if playing with her children.

When she had chosen a sweatshirt, Mrs Power went to collect

her children. She overheard Jon say, 'Thommo, take one of these.' Bobby was still kneeling by the purses. Both froze as she approached and took her two children to the till.

There was a queue at the till, and Mrs Power's children wandered off again. Mrs Power retrieved them again, and yet again they wandered off. The daughter reappeared on her own.

'Where's your brother?'

'Gone outside with the boys.'

Mrs Power checked the purse counter before going to the store entrance, where she saw her son, a few yards in front of her, walking towards Bobby and Jon. Jon stood by one of the Strand's mirrored posts, beckoning the lad to him.

Mrs Power shouted, and her son stopped. 'Go back to your mum,' Jon said, and he went. While Mrs Power gave him a scolding, Jon and Bobby crossed into Mothercare. Camera 8 of the Strand's closed-circuit television security system recorded them there, at 12.34.34.

2

Ralph and Denise Bulger usually went to bed late, and got up late in the morning. Last night had been no different. Their two-year-old son, James, had fallen asleep on the settee just before midnight, and they had left him there until Ralph picked him up at about half past one, when they all went to bed.

Denise, who was 25, liked to keep James by her side. She was the first to concede that she was very protective. Not long before their Register Office marriage three years ago, the couple's first pregnancy had resulted in the stillbirth of a baby daughter they remembered as Kirsty. They had been together three years when Ralph proposed, on the day the pregnancy was lost. Denise reasoned that it was this loss which had made her so over-attached to James. She did not like him going out with her relatives or friends, and did not want him to go to playschool. He went to bed when she did, and got up when his mother got up.

On Friday morning, the Bulgers were awake and out of bed at about 10.30. Denise was washing in the bathroom and James followed her in, wanting the loo. She organised his breakfast, a bowl of Frosties, and he sat eating them by the fire in the living room with his father.

When they all left the one-bedroomed maisonette at midday, Denise was, as usual, on her way to her mother's with James. Ralph walked with them through Kirkby, but carried on to visit Denise's brother, Paul. At 26, Ralph was one of the long-term unemployed. He reckoned he'd been on seventeen training and job creation schemes, not one of which had created a job. Today he was giving Paul a hand putting some furniture together. Ralph, as he sometimes said, was a jack of all trades, a jobber without a job. He could do anything – given the opportunity.

Denise's mum was out, but one of Denise's sisters was there and the television was on, showing *Neighbours*. James played with the sister's daughter, Antonia, as a succession of relatives passed in and out. Denise was the second youngest of thirteen children, her mother having been one of ten. The core of the family was in Kirkby, and John, Denise, Paul and the others were always in and out of their mother's home.

Paul's partner, Nicola Bailey, was looking after John's three-year-old, Vanessa, that day. She called in to ask Denise to go with her to the Strand. Nicola wanted to change some underwear at TJ Hughes, but had no baby seat in her car. Denise could help her out by sitting in the back with Vanessa. James always liked the drive in Nicola's car, so Denise said she'd go along for the ride, and Nicola said she'd pop back in half an hour to collect them.

At about a quarter past two Nicola, Denise and the two children, settled now in the B Reg., burgundy Ford Orion, drove

15

through Walton and past the prison to the Strand. They parked on the ground floor of the multi-storey car park, went up the steps to cross the bridge, and entered the shopping centre through Woolworths. Camera 16 recorded them there, at 14.30.34.

Coming out onto the concourse from Woolworths, Denise and Nicola decided to give James and Vanessa a 20p ride on a children's mechanical seesaw. Then they all went into TJ Hughes so that Nicola could exchange her underwear.

While she was doing this, Denise could see and hear James and Vanessa playing around inside the store. James went to the door, lost sight of his mum and shouted in fright. Denise went over and picked him up, carrying him as they left the shop.

James was almost exactly two years and eleven months old. He would be three on 16 March. He had fair skin and light brown, almost blond hair. He had a full set of baby teeth and his eyes were blue, with a tinge of brown in the right eye.

He was dressed that day in a blue waterproofed, cotton anorak with quilted lining and a hood, which Denise had bought from In Shops in Kirkby. Beneath the anorak was a grey tracksuit, with white stripes down the legs, and beneath the tracksuit was a white T shirt with blue stripes on the back, and green stripes on the front around the word 'Noddy'. On his feet were a pair of white Puma trainers, and around his neck was a blue woollen scarf with yellow stripes, illustrated with a white cat's face, and with a white bobble at either end.

3

Jon and Bobby were darting in and out of the shops, pinching here and there, then mostly just throwing the stuff away, to make room in their pockets for the next lot of booty. Bobby was after a boxed troll in TJ Hughes, until a security guard told them to leave. Jon robbed a couple of felt-tipped pens, and left them lying on a display cooker.

They investigated the computer games and equipment in Tandy, Rumbelows, Dixons and Woolworths. The assistant in Tandy showed Jon some cheats for the Segas and told him how to put songs on the Commodores. They left Tandy with a four-pack of Evergreen AA-sized 1.5v batteries.

It was no fun in Woolworths, because you couldn't play with the computers. Jon and Bobby looked at the Thunderbird toys, but Bobby was unimpressed. They were stringy things, he said, and not worth the trouble of thieving.

Across Stanley Road from the Strand, next, to mess around in MacDonalds and the Bradford and Bingley Building Society next door. The Society's branch manager asked them what they were doing. Bobby said they were waiting for their mum. When they began clambering over the chairs, the branch manager suggested they go and wait in MacDonalds. Bobby said they'd already been thrown out of there, but Jon said, 'Come on, let's go,' so they left the branch manager in peace and ran down to the Kwikkie to rob some Chocolate Dips and Iced Gems. Back on Stanley Road they again bumped into the branch manager, who was on his way to lunch, and Bobby asked him for 20p. The branch manager said no, and carried on walking.

They went back into the Strand through Lunn Poly, pausing to pretend they were big holiday spenders, until Jon pinched a pen off the counter and knocked over a stapler, provoking an assistant to order them out.

Another pen went missing from Rathbones the bakers, just opposite Clinton Cards. The boys were back in the card shop, the assistant watching them carefully this time as they loitered by the trolls, when a middle-aged woman came in.

'Come on, where's the pen you took off the lady in Rathbones?'

Bobby tapped his pockets. 'What pen, I haven't got a pen.'

The woman said she'd get the police, so Bobby plucked the pen from his pocket and handed it over. The woman told the assistant to watch those two, and the assistant told Jon and Bobby to leave.

Round by the main square they started playing with the fire hydrant door on the pillar, opening and closing it as they shouted and laughed. A four-year-old boy approached and asked what they were doing, but was called away by his elder brother.

Jon said his mouth was dead upset, it was saying it was dying for a drink, so they went into Tesco, where Jon had to empty out his coat to make room for some cartons of yogurt, milk-shake and Ambrosia rice. Bobby got some too. Outside, they sat and ate on some scaffolding.

There was a stall in the main square of the Strand, set up as part of a mental health campaign to promote awareness of the effects of tranquillisers and sleeping pills. The stall carried a display of books, leaflets and audio cassettes. It attracted the attention of Jon and Bobby, who picked up a book called *Back To Life*, about the ways to withdraw from tranquillisers.

The stall was being run by a mother and daughter, who were talking to an elderly woman shopper. When they saw Jon and Bobby, the mother told them to put the book down, that it would be of no interest to them. The boys made a pretend grab at some of the other literature, and the elderly woman told them to get away and stop being so cheeky. You should be in school, she said. Jon and Bobby teased the woman, tapping her on the back and running away as she turned; tap and run, tap and run. When the woman finally struck out, swinging her bag and shouting, they ran off, calling out some abuse which was lost to the woman's partial deafness.

Bobby wanted to show Jon the talking troll in Toymaster, but when they got to the shop entrance, they were turned away by an assistant who said they couldn't come in without their parents. The boys waited, and ran in while she was serving, running out again with some tins of Humbrol enamel paint, Azure Blue and Antique Bronze.

They began playing football with a tin on the walkway. The

tin cracked against the glass shopfronts, and skidded around the feet of the shoppers. The boys retrieved it when it began to spill paint. The other, the Antique Bronze, rolled into the corner by Tym's the butchers, where it was found by a man who had cycled to the Strand on his bike. He took the paint home, to repair the chip on his Toby jug.

4

Denise had carried James as she walked from TJ Hughes with Nicola and Vanessa, and crossed into Sayers where they bought a sausage roll each for the two children.

Denise put her son down then, broke the sausage roll in half to make it manageable, and handed it back to James, who ate it as he walked in front of Denise through the centre.

In Marks and Spencer, James and Vanessa were given a ride round in a shopping trolley, while Nicola bought a few bits of food. Outside Marks, down the slope, James ran off ahead, and an elderly woman had to stop him clambering alone on to the escalator.

Denise took hold of James, only letting go when they were inside Ethel Austin, the children's clothing shop, where James was immediately struck by one of the baby suits being thrown down by an assistant standing on a chair. James began laughing and throwing the suits around the shop, and Denise marched him outside, waiting for Nicola and Vanessa.

James started walking around again, but Denise did not like the look of the scruffily dressed man who was sitting on a bench watching him. She held James's hand as Nicola and Vanessa came out of Ethel Austin's, and they all went across to Tesco.

Now James was on the move, kicking an empty box around,

helping himself to some Smarties and a carton of apple juice, and generally making mischief. Denise became self-conscious, thinking everyone must be watching them, and they left after Nicola had bought some sugar.

James was told off and given a smack on the legs. Nicola went into Superdrug to buy some sweets for Vanessa. This time, Denise stayed outside. Then they turned the corner towards Tym's the butchers. Camera 10 recorded them there at 15.37.51.

A. R. Tym's is a popular butchers, which regularly displays luminous orange signs offering the day's bargains: Natural Roast Lamb 69 qtr; Nat Honey Roast Ham 69 qtr; Danish Top Quality Bacon Ribs 99 lb; 4 Saus Rolls £1-00; We Do Traditional Cooked Meats For Your Special Occasions.

It was quieter than usual when Denise and Nicola went in, which was just as well, Denise thought, since James was playing up. She got her money out of her purse, ready to pay for the meat. Nicola, who was holding Vanessa, looked round and saw James at the entrance playing with the butt of a cigarette which was still alight. She turned to the counter to be served as Denise paid up and went out. Then Denise was back in the shop, panicking.

'Where's James?'

'He's only just outside,' said Nicola.

5

Jon and Bobby had finished their skirmishes with the tins of paint. They were outside TJ Hughes, next to the sweet barrow, which was closed, and which they had been eyeing with a view to robbing some sweets. They were facing A. R. Tym's.

They saw a little boy in a blue anorak outside the butchers.

James was still eating his Smarties. It was Jon's idea to approach him.

'Come on, baby.'

James followed, and Jon took his hand as they walked back towards TJ Hughes. A woman who had just finished work in a shoe shop noticed them as she passed. She smiled at James because he reminded her of a nephew.

They went into TJ Hughes and walked through the store, then up the stairs. Leaving the store, they turned left into the walkway by Sayers that led to the main square. A woman who was sitting in Sayers, having a quiet drink while she waited for her bus, looked up and thought her grandson was walking past. A little boy with blond hair, skipping as he went along. The woman realised it wasn't her grandson, and wondered momentarily why the little boy was on his own. She was reassured when he was joined by two older boys who seemed to call the child. He skipped to join them.

'Come on, baby.'

Bobby was walking just in front of Jon, who was holding James's hand as they made their way past Mothercare towards Marks and Spencer and the entrance to the Strand. Camera 8: 15.42.32.

6

'He's only just outside,' said Nicola.

Denise went back out, while Nicola finished being served. Denise came back.

'I can't find him outside.'

She went back to the door, as one of the shop assistants realised something was happening.

'What's wrong?'

'The little boy's gone missing from outside.'

The shop assistant told her to go to security and report it. Denise didn't know where security was. The shop assistant told her. Round to the right, on the far side, by the back entrance.

Denise and Nicola ran out, heading for security. They looked into a couple of shops, Superdrug and a stationers, asking around as they went. 'Has anybody seen a little boy?'

It was about quarter to four when Denise reached the security office with Nicola and Vanessa. She was very upset now, as she spoke to the guard on duty in the control room. James was the day's first reported missing child. They were common enough to be unremarkable, and were almost always found within 15 to 20 minutes. Friday had been a quiet day all round, at the Strand. The fire alarm activated at Dixons at half past one had turned out to be the staff making toast for lunch.

The guard took a description of James and where he had last been seen, then relayed the details by tannoy throughout the precinct. Denise and Nicola went off to search and came back about five minutes later, asking the guard to repeat the tannoy message. He had been looking through the security cameras but had seen nothing. He repeated the tannoy message as Denise and Nicola went off again.

The guard received a phone call from TJ Hughes. Denise was there. Had the child been found yet? No. The guard passed on James's description for the store's own internal tannoy system.

Denise returned to the office shortly before a quarter past four, with an in-store security officer from TJ Hughes. Any news? No. The Strand's guard then phoned Marsh Lane Police Station, around the corner, to report a missing child, and made his own entry in the Strand's Site Book: '16.15: Child missing on Precinct approx. 30 minutes. Police informed and given description. Police will attend a.s.a.p.'

7

James was carried the first few yards along Stanley Road, away
from the Strand. It was a clumsy hold, like a bear hug, with
James clasped to his carrier's chest. A taxi driver saw this, and
laughed at the older boy's inexperience with children. When
James was put down again, on the pavement between the Post
Office and the bridge over the canal, he began crying.

'Are you all right? You were told not to run,' one of the boys
said, loud enough for passers-by to hear.

'I want my mum,' said James.

They turned off Stanley Road, past the railings, and down the
slope towards the canal towpath. Jon was holding James's hand,
with Bobby beside them. A woman came out of the Post Office,
where she had just paid her mother's telephone bill. She saw the
three boys, and thought they seemed in a hurry. She watched
as James wandered ahead, and was ushered back. She thought
James looked confused, and that the two boys were too young
to be in charge of a child. They must be brothers, or relatives,
she told herself.

Down by the canal, Jon and Bobby went under the bridge
and sat James on the guard rail that separated the towpath from
the water. They talked about pushing him into the canal. Then
one of them picked James up, and dropped him to the ground
head first. His forehead was grazed and he began crying.

Jon and Bobby ran back up the slope, leaving James by the
canal crying. A woman walking over the bridge towards the
Strand heard his distress and looked down. She saw James
standing there crying, and presumed he must be with the other
children, a group of three or four, whom she saw further along
the towpath. Kids were always playing there.

When Jon and Bobby went back for James he was already walking up the path towards them. 'Come on, baby.' They put up the hood of his anorak, to conceal the cut on his forehead. One of them carried him across Stanley Road at the pedestrian crossing, and put him down again on the other side. A passer-by noticed them and, despite the hood, she saw the mark on James's forehead. She thought James seemed distressed, though he was no longer crying. She walked on, slightly uneasy, then decided to go back for another look. The three boys had disappeared.

They had turned off the main road, down Park Street, past the Jehovah's Witnesses' hall. They turned right at the bottom, and left again at the Jawbone Tavern. They walked through the car park of a block of flats, lifted James over a wall, and emerged on to Merton Road through the grounds of an architect's office. Jon and Bobby were now on the route they had taken earlier to the Strand, heading back to Walton.

The 67a double-decker bus to Bootle was waiting at the Breeze Hill roundabout as Jon and Bobby crossed there, by Smiley's Tyre and Exhaust Centre. A woman sitting downstairs, at the front of the bus, looked over to her right. She saw Christchurch on the corner, and noticed its sign, 'You don't have to be on your knees to pray.' She saw two boys holding a child between them, swinging him by the hands as they walked. She noticed one of the boys lose his grip just as the bus pulled away, obscuring her view.

Jon and Bobby did not turn directly on to Breeze Hill, but took the left fork at the roundabout, up Oxford Road. It took them past the offices of AMEC Building, a construction firm which had a security camera trained on its car park, facing the road.

Three young women, teenagers, were walking up from Bootle, behind the three boys. A driver from a local dry-cleaning company noticed them as he passed in his van. He saw their short skirts and black tights and thought they looked fit. As he glanced round the driver caught sight of Jon and Bobby, pulling at James's arms, as if trying to make him move. James looked red-faced and puffy, and the driver could see he was crying. He watched as Bobby gave James a persuasive kick in the ribs. The driver muttered to himself in disgust. 'You're going to be a scally.'

The young women did not see this, but one of them did watch Jon and Bobby walking ahead, holding James between them by his hands.

The other two teenagers barely noticed the boys; their attention was diverted by a lad they knew from school who was cycling past on his racer, head down, speeding up the incline of Oxford Road. He cycled straight into the back of a Nissan hatchback that was parked there. The two young women who had been watching him laughed, and laughed even louder when they realised their friend had missed the collision. She had been too busy watching the three boys.

The cyclist saw the three women as he got up and dusted himself down. He saw Jon and Bobby, but did not see James. Jon saw the three teenagers laughing. Bobby had seen the cyclist hit the car.

They led James from Oxford Road through to Breeze Hill, and idled there at the railings by the bus stop. It seemed to the woman driving past with her husband in a Ford Orion that they were playing a game; Bobby at the railings, and Jon back down the hill, apparently chasing James towards Bobby. The hood of James's anorak was still covering his head.

James began crying as they crossed Breeze Hill by the Mons at the junction with Southport Road.

'I want my mum.' Crying. 'I want my mum . . . I want my mum.'

He ran forward, and a driver who was stopped at the lights thought he was going to walk into the road. Then Bobby stepped forward and picked James up, turning him away from the road. The driver saw that James was crying, and presumed he was upset at not being allowed to run free.

Jon and Bobby were both holding James by the hand as they

crossed the central reservation, watched by a motorist on his way to a plumbing job in Orrell. He could see James was crying, and thought it odd that he did not have adult supervision.

They left the road at the reservoir, climbing up the big stone steps, the two boys carrying the child, Jon holding James's legs, Bobby with his arms around James's chest. When they reached the top of the reservoir, long ago a water repository but now a grassy plateau, Jon and Bobby sat on the last step, with James between them.

When a woman who had been walking her dog on the hill manoeuvred around them and onto the steps, James was laughing. As she climbed down, the boys stood and made their way to the far embankment, overlooking a row of houses.

James was punched here, by Jon, as the light began to fade. A woman closing her curtains in one of the houses below looked up to see Jon gripping James by his shoulders, close to his neck, and shaking him briskly, as if trying to quieten him down. A neighbour saw Jon and Bobby holding James's hands; they appeared to be helping him up the incline. She watched as an elderly woman walking her large black dog, regulars on the reservoir, approached them.

The elderly woman was immediately concerned because James was sobbing.

'What's going on?'

'We just found him at the bottom of the hill.'

She saw then that James had two bumps, one on his forehead, and one on top of his head.

'Do you know him?'

'No,' said the boys.

The woman told them that James's injuries needed attention, and they asked her the way to the police station. She directed them to the station at Walton Lane.

The neighbour who had been peering from her window watched as the elderly woman gesticulated, and guessed that the child was lost. She was surprised when the boys seemed to walk off in the opposite direction to the way the woman had indicated, and thought the woman must be uneasy when she turned back to the boys, apparently shouting after them.

The elderly woman was indeed uneasy, though somewhat reassured when she saw and spoke to a friend who was also out strolling that afternoon. This was the woman who earlier had seen James laughing with Jon and Bobby on the steps. The woman told her elderly friend that James had been all right when she saw him. She had imagined the boys must all be brothers.

8

Ser. No. 925BO2V Rec. Tel. by 3642 at 1621 12/02/93 Class 86,91.

Message – we have a 3 yr old male – James Patrick Boulger who has been missing on the New Strand for 30 mins – area searched scanned with cameras – no trace location – mother now at reception New Strand, Washington Parade, Bootle.

Informant – Strand Security 944 2222.

Remarks – announcements have been made over tannoy system without response.

Action–1622 by 3642 BO2V – Resource sent, BM 11.

The B Division command control's computer log chattered in response to the phone call from Peter Beatham, the Strand's security guard.

PC Mandy Waller was working a 2–12 shift, patrolling around Bootle in Bravo Mike One One (BM 11), a Fiesta hatchback Panda car, responding to calls from divisional control. She had been on driving duties for only a month, since passing the driving test.

When the job came through on her radio – missing child at the Strand, please deal – Mandy went first to Marsh Lane to pick up a set of MFH forms. 'Missing child,' she thought. 'Oh, send a woman.'

It galled her that the police sometimes made assumptions about women's work. If they locked somebody up and there was a child involved, Mandy would be called in to look after the child. Mandy had no children of her own, and no maternal instincts to speak of. I don't mind kids, she would say, I just couldn't eat a whole one. Some of the lads with kids of their own were better at those jobs than her, she reckoned, and she'd had frank discussions about it with sergeants in the past: why call me, like, 'cause I'm no better at it than anyone else? Mandy was from South Yorkshire, a small village near Barnsley. Working on Merseyside for nine years had not yet blunted her accent.

Until a year or so ago Mandy had actually lived on the Strand, in one of the low-rise flats near Marks and Spencer. It had been even more popular then than now as a haunt of shoplifters and bag-snatchers. This had been in the days before and during the transformation of the Strand into a fully fledged mall; before the arrival of the security cameras, and while the absence of doors at the entrances made for an easy escape. Mandy had made the occasional off-duty arrest in the walkway outside her own front door. Still, it had been great having M&S as her corner shop.

This year was the Strand's 25th anniversary, though not, as events were now unfolding, much of a year to celebrate. A quarter of a century ago it had been a model of the newly imported American concept of precinct shopping. In a competition to name the centre sponsored by a local newspaper, Little America was narrowly defeated by New Strand, after Strand Road, which crossed Stanley Road at the site of the precinct.

It was opened in 1968, with due ceremony, by the Burgomaster of Mons, the Belgian town with which Bootle was twinned, and Mons gave its name to the New Strand's main square. There were grander plans, in those days, to pedestrianise the neighbouring stretch of Stanley Road and create a major new through route on the other side of the centre, which was Washington

Parade. The New Strand's main entrance, the Hexagon, was therefore built facing Washington Parade. When the grand plans fell through, leaving Stanley Road as the main artery, the Strand was left stranded, somewhat back to front.

The original design was almost entirely concrete, with canopies extending from the shops, leaving wide areas of walkway exposed to the elements of nature. There were no doors and, especially by night, the New Strand was also exposed to drunks and the more unruly elements of human nature.

By the time of the big refurbishment in the late eighties, the psychology of shopping had made great advances. It was one of the duties of the New Strand's manager, Peter Williams, to take the chore out of shopping, and he oversaw a transformation into something approximating the American mall, which is usually pronounced 'maul' by Americans.

The redevelopment was designed to create an ambience of comfort and security which would enhance the shopping experience. The whole place was enclosed by roofing, with the addition of some glass to retain a degree of natural light, and doors were added. Much of the concrete disappeared behind reflective aluminium planking, which gave a bright, warm impression, not unlike chrome; Italian ceramic tiling replaced most of the old flooring, with granite tiles in Mons Square.

To correct the Strand's reversed polarity between Stanley Road and Washington Parade, a series of arches, known as barrell vaults, were created over the Stanley Road entrances.

There were bench seats, pots of flowers and children's rides. A public address system was installed, to relay piped music and the occasional message about a missing child. There were sprinklers, smoke detectors, and closed-circuit television: 20 cameras, though only 16 actually recorded; each one of the 16 cameras supplying a tape with a single still image every two or three seconds. The tape could be decoded to display all 16 images at once on a monitor, or one image, or any combination in between. A private security firm, Guardrite, supplied a small team of men in rubber-soled shoes with walkie-talkies, for additional protection.

The New Strand now became the Strand Shopping Centre, and a logo was adopted, an anchor, to emphasise the nautical theme employed in naming the centre's walkways: Esplanade, Mariners Way and Medway. There were other walkways – Raven Way, Palatine and Hexagon – but these were more obscure nautical references.

Peter Williams organised a Grand Opening Extravaganza for the relaunch in the autumn of 1989. There were personal appearances by Garfield the Cat and Rupert Bear, and live entertainment in Mons Square, and this tradition had been continued, with occasional performances by groups of Morris Dancers or the Bootle Village Pipe Band. The Square was also useful for the occasional community service promotion, and this emphasised the centre's links with the local people. The bulk of the Strand's customers, after all, came to shop there from within a three-mile radius.

The Strand had 114 shops, but the big three were Marks & Spencer, TJ Hughes and Woolworths. It was a sign of the times that there were a growing number of discount stores. As Peter Williams said, you traded at a level that suited the area, and the Strand wasn't Harrods. A few miles up the road in Southport, where the people were posher, you might be able to buy a good-quality ladies fashion suit, but in Bootle there wasn't a lot of call for that.

Peter Williams was an admirer of the new combined shopping and leisure centres like the Metro in Gateshead, with its cinema and bowling alley, its fountains and ponds. There was real theming in Gateshead – Peter particularly liked the Roman Forum – but the Strand could never accommodate something of that nature. It just wasn't big enough to theme. The Metro attracted several million people every year. The Strand was doing all right on 120,000 a week. It was busiest on Saturdays, and at weekday lunchtimes when the local office workers turned out.

Like all centres, the Strand was a popular refuge for the elderly and the young. Older people sat on benches and passed the time of day. Youngsters gathered in groups and, yes, sometimes they were truants, and sometimes they were up to mischief. The Guardrite men kept watch through the cameras, or on patrol, and many of the shops now had their own security, but shop-lifting was prevalent.

The Strand did its best to promote protection and safety. In September of last year, Peter Williams had initiated a campaign targeted at children, warning them of the dangers of strangers. The centre had given away dozens of small items of school equipment, such as rulers and plastic pencil cases, embossed with the slogan, Don't Talk To Strangers.

Mandy Waller pushed the buttons on the Cyfas terminal in her car as she arrived. The code 04 automatically logged her arrival time at the Strand with Divisional Control. 16.37. By this time Denise was sitting in the centre manager's office. As Mandy noted details and description, completing the MFH forms, it became apparent that James had been missing for longer than 30 minutes. It was an hour by now, which was already omin-ously long. Usually, Mandy knew, they were found before the police needed to be called, or clipped round the ear by relieved parents by the time the police arrived.

Mandy radioed through a description, emphasising the time James had been missing. She then went back into the Strand with Denise for another search. They concentrated on places, such as the pet shop, that might have attracted a small child.

Denise, very distressed, could not understand how it had happened so quickly. 'I was only in the shop for a few sec-onds. I turned round and he'd gone.' She was full of guilt and self-blame. If only she hadn't done this . . . she shouldn't have done that. Mandy, who did not regard herself as a natural sort of person for giving comfort, tried hard to be reassuring. The machinery of a police search was being mobilised. Everything that could be done was being done.

One of the Strand's cleaners came up to the office with the news that another child, a four-year-old, had gone missing at around the same time as James. The four-year-old had been found and told his parents that a man in a white coat had tried to entice him into a car.

When James's disappearance was reported on the local radio news bulletins, an anonymous caller told the police that they had seen a man with a ponytail at the Strand earlier that day whom they suspected of being involved in the abduction of children. The ponytail man was known to the police, and a search began to find him.

Another caller thought he had seen James in a car in Southport, 40 minutes up the road. This too was followed up, without success.

The quest to find James gained momentum quickly and methodically. Calls went out to the local media, taxi firms, and bus and train services. Officers began searching on foot and by car, through the Strand and outside, along and around the canal and in the streets immediately surrounding the centre: the walkways, the car parks, the neighbouring shops, the amusement arcades.

Denise suggested that if James had been able to find his way out of the Strand, he would start walking, and just keep on going. But it was reasonable to presume that a two-year-old could not go far unaided.

Perhaps, as is sometimes the case when children disappear, it was a domestic matter? Nicola's Ford Orion, still in its space on the ground floor of the multi-storey car park, was examined, the boot opened and checked. A visit was made to the home address given by Denise. Ralph was still out. He didn't yet know what was happening.

The command control log was busy, recording the requests, the actions, the information, and the negative responses.

1731 by 6796 BO4V – Multi storey car park checked no trace from 7208.
1731 by 3642 BO2V – TB12 widening search – Strand Rd/TA Centre – Irlam Road – Marsh Ln – Merton Rd.

1731 by 6796 BO4V – Service road checked no trace from 720B. Negative at the cafe.

1732 by 6796 BO4V – 6847 checking the Merseybus Cafe/canteen.

1735 by 9173 HO4 – From Insp Owen infd TS33 is making with loud speaker.

1736 by 3642 BO2V – Canal bank Carolina St side checked by 3991 – no trace.

1738 by 6796 BO4V – Building site searched no trace.

1739 by 3642 BO2V – From BS13 – TJ Hughes has been checked by staff/no trace-now locking up . . .

A police motorbike collected a public address system and took it to the Strand so that appeals could be broadcast to passers-by. Specialist search teams from the Operational Support Division were turned out. High-powered Dragon lamps were brought in from neighbouring stations. The Force helicopter, Mike One, went up to illuminate the search on the ground.

There was further news of the ponytail man, though he had still not been found. His presence at the Strand was confirmed and when he had been seen, the log recorded, he had appeared SIM. Strange in manner.

The police were also continuing to try and track down Ralph Bulger, who was somewhere between relatives in Kirkby. Mandy Waller took Denise back to Marsh Lane police station for a cup of tea while they waited for news.

9

When Jon and Bobby came down from the reservoir they turned back on to Breeze Hill and began walking towards the flyover, towards Walton. A woman in a house a few doors away from the reservoir heard a noise on the road outside, a moan that sounded like a child's moan. She looked out and saw the trio on the pavement directly in front of her house. Jon and Bobby were walking past with James between them, each holding one of his hands.

They were seen again as they passed the newsagents on the corner of Imrie Street. A woman heard one of the boys call James. 'Come on.' She thought James, whose hood was up, looked a little bewildered. She went into the shop, and when she came out they had disappeared.

Under the flyover, along the walkways, and out onto County Road, heading for the shops, James is still being held between Jon and Bobby. It's getting dark quickly, now.

There was another woman with another dog, and she was curious. They told her they had found James at the Strand, and she asked why they hadn't taken him to the nearest police station. They told her they were going to Walton Lane Police Station.

'Walton Lane Police Station?'

A younger woman, just outside Gayflowers the florist, overheard this and intervened. She had just been shopping with her daughter, who was tired and nagging her mum to go home so she could watch children's television.

She looked down at James and saw that he was tired, too, and perhaps distressed, but not showing any signs of struggle. He looked up at Bobby.

'What's the matter?' said the younger woman. 'Is there a problem?'

'They've just asked me the way to Walton Lane Police Station,' said the woman with the dog.

'Why do you want a police station?'

'We've found him by the Strand,' said Jon.

'If you found him by the Strand, why didn't you go to the police station by the Strand?'

'That's what I asked,' said the woman with the dog.

'I don't know where it is,' said Jon.

'Well, you've walked a long way from the Strand to Walton Lane Police Station.'

'A man told us to come this way.'

The younger woman thought all this was unusual. She turned to Bobby.

'Why go to Walton Lane Police Station?'

'That's where the man directed us,' Jon replied.

'Where d'you live?'

Bobby opened his mouth to answer, but Jon cut across him.

'The police station's on our way home.'

Bobby let go of James's hand and looked away. The younger woman thought he looked uneasy and nervous.

'Get hold of his hand,' said Jon calmly. Bobby did.

'Walton Lane's in that direction,' said the younger woman, pointing. James looked up, to the woman, and to Jon.

'Are you all right, son?' the woman asked, but James did not respond.

'Which is the way?' said Jon, looking over the road to St Mary's Church. 'Did you say it was over this way?'

The other woman had been talking away to her dog. 'Don't go near him,' she said. 'He doesn't like children.'

'The best way,' said the younger woman, 'is to go across, behind Walton Church.' That was Walton Village.

'No, it's too dark that way,' said the woman with the dog. She told them to go down County Road and left along Church Road West.

The three boys turned to go back down the walkways under the flyover. The younger woman called them to stop, because she didn't think it was safe, young boys down there in the dark. She asked the other woman to watch her daughter and her shopping while she saw the boys across the road. The woman said she couldn't, because her dog didn't like children.

'Which way again, missus?' said Jon.

'The Village,' said the younger woman, pointing to the church.

'Church Road, it's lighter,' said the woman with the dog.

The boys crossed to the central reservation.

'Are you sure you know the way?' shouted the younger woman.

Jon turned round, and pointed down County Road. 'I'll go that way, missus.'

'Our Ken will know,' said Bobby, who did not have a brother called Ken, loudly to Jon.

When they had reached the far side of the road the younger woman was reassured. She turned to walk under the flyover, while the woman with the dog stood watching the boys. 'They're by the bus stop,' she called after the younger woman, who had lost sight of the boys.

It was just after five when Jon and Bobby walked into the County DIY shop on County Road. They had passed Church Road West and gone further down, before crossing back to the other side of County Road. The shop was small and cluttered, like a traditional ironmongers. The sign outside offered 'Glass, Glazing, Patio Doors' and 'Window Frames Fitted'. Jon was still holding James's hand as they went in. The owner was behind the counter, immediately alert. He'd been losing stock to boys this age over recent weeks, so he was keeping an eye on these two.

His attention was caught by James, who seemed slightly distressed. The owner attributed this to the graze on the side of his forehead, which was obviously fresh because it was still moist, and the red mark on his right cheek. Bobby stepped forward and asked if the shop sold some particular item. It might have been something daft like, 'Do you sell fishy knickers?' which was one of Bobby's lines when he was skitting. The shop didn't sell whatever it was he asked for.

'D'you know where there's a sweet shop? We want to buy some sweets for our brother.'

'There's one round the corner, and one over the road.'

They left the DIY shop, and continued back along County Road to the pet shop, 'Animate – Pet and Aquatic Centre', which displays exotic fish in stacks of rectangular tanks, heated and illuminated by brilliant fluorescent tubes. Jon and Bobby were holding James's hands as they entered the shop, and the assistant soon noticed the graze on James's forehead.

They walked over to the fish tanks and Bobby let go of James's hand. They stood looking at the Weather Loach, a sedentary fish which spends most of its time lying motionless at the bottom of the tank.

'It's dead,' said Bobby.

'It's not dead, it's just lying there,' said the assistant.

But Bobby insisted and finally, thinking he was very cheeky, the assistant prodded the Weather Loach to life, to prove her point.

Her colleague came out from the storeroom, and thought it strange that Jon kept hold of James's hand. Small children who came into the shop usually ran around looking at all the animals. The other assistant, who had had enough of Bobby's cheek, told them all to leave.

There was a commotion outside, a few doors down on County Road. The building over the bookies, William Hill's, had caught fire, and passers-by had gathered to watch the flurry of activity. Fire engines, police cars, ambulances. Jon and Bobby stood watching with James for a while, before walking back up towards the flyover, to cross County Road again.

Jon recognised a woman, a friend of his parents, who was standing chatting with a couple of other women outside the bank. The woman knew Jon, too, but she didn't recognise him. She watched as the three boys crossed the road, fearing for their safety. They looked so little against the heavy traffic, two small boys and a toddler. She grabbed her friend's hand, cutting through the conversation. 'Oh, look at them kids with that toddler crossing that road.' It made her so nervous she had to turn away and not look back as the boys ran to the far side.

Her friend thought the boys seemed in a hurry and that it looked out of place, a child entrusted to the care of boys who were themselves so small.

Jon and Bobby turned right by the SOGAT building and into Church Road West. As they walked down they were accosted by two older lads, Stephen, who was 11, and Ibrahim, 12, who were standing outside the newsagents on the other side of the road.

Ibrahim knew Bobby by name and by sight, and had seen him that morning, with Ryan, apparently on their way to school. He knew Jon from the area, though not his name. Stephen, who had left Jon and Bobby's school last July, recognised them both, but did not know Jon by name.

Ibrahim was playing with a pair of handcuffs, which he had bought from the Army & Navy Stores. He and Stephen thought it would be a lark to put the handcuffs on the boys over the road, and give them a fright.

When they approached them they saw that James was upset. Ibrahim saw the bump over his eye, and thought he looked sad. Bobby and Jon held on to James's hands, and did not let go.

'What happened to the lad?'

'He fell over at the top,' said Bobby.

'Where?'

'The top.'

Ibrahim took this to be the top of County Road.

'Look in his hair as well,' said Bobby.

'You all right?' Ibrahim said to James. He turned away and began crying. Ibrahim could see red dots and lines under James's hair.

'Who is he?'

'His brother,' said Bobby, nodding at Jon.

'Where you taking him?'

'Home.'

'If you don't take him home I'll batter you.'

The boys walked on then, having escaped a handcuffing, and turned right into City Road, heading towards the Everton ground, over the broo that bridged the railway line.

As they reached the bridge they were level with a young woman pushing her baby daughter in a pram. She was late on her way to her mum's but noticed the boys, how they were holding James's hands, and thought they were young to be in charge of such a small child. She pointed James out to her daughter.

'Look, Lori, there's a little boy.'

The daughter turned to look, but there was no reaction from Jon or Bobby. The boys crossed the road, and turned down the entry along the side of the railway.

They were only a few yards into the entry when Jon snatched the hood from James's anorak, and threw it into the tree. They walked on, heading for the road at the far end, Walton Lane, with its police station directly opposite.

As they reached the bottom of the entry a motorbike turned into the alleyway immediately in front of them, from one of the side roads. The boys started at the apparition, a red Yamaha XS250 ridden by a man disguised beneath a black one-piece suit and a gleaming white crash helmet. He manoeuvred the bike into the back yard of his home, thinking that the boys had seemed very jumpy.

James was crying again when they got to the far end of the entry. Jon and Bobby loitered there, and James was close to one of them when a man walked past, and heard a moan or a sob from the child. The boy next to James looked straight at the man and said, 'I'm fed up having my little brother, he's always the same.' He turned to the other boy and said, 'I'm not bringing him again.'

As he walked on by, the man guessed that the two boys had been looking after the child since coming out of school at four o'clock. It was nothing unusual. Just another little boy crying with his big brother.

Jon and Bobby walked out of the entry and on to Walton Lane, facing the police station, with the railway bridge on their left. A teenager saw James laughing as she walked towards them. One of the boys was pushing James into the road. James was laughing. When the boys saw the teenager, who was with her father, one of them ran up the alleyway, while the other retrieved James from the road and picked him up, arms around his chest. James was still laughing as the boy carried him into the entry.

When they came back to Walton Lane, one of the boys stood at the edge of the pavement, holding James by the hand. It appeared to a woman who was walking past that they were trying to cross the road. The other boy was hanging back, near the entry. When they saw the woman looking at them the boys turned back into the alleyway with James. The woman was five minutes from home, coming back from seeing a friend in the village. She thought fleetingly about the dangers for a small child, being out in the dark with young lads on such a busy road.

When she arrived home the woman looked at her watch. It was 5.30 p.m.

10

1907 by 6796 BO1V-Cover D/I Mr Fitzsimmons bleeped at request of DS Dolan.

It was his first weekend in charge of the divisional CID. Jim Fitzsimmons had started at nine that morning and was due off at eleven that night. Monday had been his first day as a Detective Inspector, and the duty rota had put him on cover for the weekend.

At seven minutes past seven that evening, when the radio pager on his waistband went off, he was sitting at home in Crosby having a cup of tea and a sandwich before continuing his tour of the stations in the division.

As he left Copy Lane police station, he had decided to pop home on his way up to Southport. There was nothing pressing and, on such a long shift, he liked to get back to see the family, if only briefly, when the opportunity arose.

It should have been a short introduction to his new job. He

was due on a six-week management course in Preston, starting next Monday. There was just time to familiarise himself with the current crime, the new computer system and the CID staff. Tonight was typical of all the tours he would make on his future weekend covers. Going from one station to the next, seeing who was on, if there were any problems, what prisoners they had in, anything out of the ordinary, anything he should know about. Walking talking management, as his old boss Albert Kirby would say.

When the bleeper bleeped, Jim picked up the phone and called in to control. There was a child missing, a two-year-old at the Strand. Okay, nothing terribly unusual about that. He asked the questions. Who was the child, where was he from, how long had he been missing? He was James Bulger, from Kirkby, and he had been missing for over three hours.

This was more alarming, a child missing for so long, and so far from home in an unfamiliar environment. What did they have on the disappearance so far? Jim was told of the ponytail man and the other child, who could not be traced, who claimed to have been enticed by a man in a white coat. A search was under way, and detectives were aggressively pursuing the ponytail man at known addresses and contacts. Okay, good, I'm on my way. Jim set off for Marsh Lane.

Though he had acted up in the senior post often enough in the past, the promotion, from Sergeant to Inspector, had been a long time coming, mainly because he had made a diversionary career move. Four years ago, at the age of 32, Jim Fitzsimmons had entered Liverpool University as an undergraduate – still salaried as a police officer, still carrying his warrant card, but now just another student, albeit a mature one, on campus.

Normally, officers returning to study would have resumed policing duties during the long summer breaks. Jim had chosen to add a Spanish option to his combined Management and Policy Studies degree. It had meant spending his summers in Spain, for the good of the course, naturally.

He had worked hard at the Spanish, but struggled with the grammar. This had brought him a 2:1 BA Honours degree. He had finished on 3 July last year and resumed his career as a Detective Sergeant the day after, working out of headquarters at Canning Place. He had passed for promotion in September, been notified of his new posting in January, and started on Monday.

Going back to work had not been difficult, although he had been so long away from the job. He had not stopped thinking of himself as a police officer, because he didn't think of himself in those terms to begin with. He thought the experience of the degree had changed him in some way he couldn't quite articulate. Something to do with broadening his view of life, probably.

Jim's father had been a docker, and Jim had been the eldest of six children. A large and extended Catholic family from Bootle was no rare thing. A close community, overflowing with children. Jim was the dreamy, dizzy kid with a passion for football and Anfield, and not much talent for playing himself.

His dad bought him a season ticket when he passed his eleven plus. Or rather, Jim was given his dad's own ticket for the stand, and his dad bought a ground ticket for himself, because he couldn't afford two for the stand. Jim went to matches on the back of his dad's Honda.

After a couple of years at a Catholic grammar school, the Salesian College, Jim had begun to develop quickly, finding skill as a sportsman, especially football, and signing schoolboy forms with Liverpool before being taken on as an apprentice professional at sixteen.

His father, who had always smoked heavily, contracted lung cancer, when Jim was thirteen. Jim's father, who was 40, never acknowledged that his illness was terminal. He simply made his eldest son promise that he would never smoke. Jim was in the boys' pen on the Kop when his father died, because he wasn't wanted at the hospital. Jim remembered the loss, but not the grieving. He thought of his father as a strong man.

As the family wage-earner, his apprenticeship to Liverpool

was a godsend. Twenty pounds a week plus twenty pounds keep, which he gave to his mum. He had been signed on by Bill Shankly, and imbued with the great man's philosophy of the game, and of life. He learned to play football the Liverpool way: simple, play it simple, push it and move. That was the word of Shankly. Every successful thing in life is done simply.

At the end of his apprenticeship, Jim was released by Liverpool. He had never made the first team, and accepted that he was not destined for glory as a footballer. He was gutted – but he needed a job.

The father of his then girlfriend – now his wife, Fran – was a police officer. Jim liked his future father-in-law and, on the basis that he couldn't face the thought of going indoors to work, he applied for the police and the fire services. He was accepted by the police, and sent for training in November 1975. His first posting was to Anfield.

He worked at Walton Lane after that, and went into the CID, before being promoted back into uniform as a sergeant. Before long he was back in the CID again, first on special duties at headquarters, which was a euphemism for the Special Branch, then working around the country, even going into Europe for occasional enquiries, with the Regional Crime Squad.

Jim was 36 now, married for some fourteen years, with two boys, Daniel, twelve, and Joe, ten, and a six-year-old daughter, Louise. A family Pools win, a few years ago, had made life more comfortable. The eldest boy was at the Merchant Taylors' school in Crosby; their home a little nicer than it might otherwise have been.

He was a stocky, solidly built man, still playing football for the police and coaching a team of youngsters. Warm and easy-going, he favoured a laid-back style of management in the force. He was known universally to colleagues as Jim or Jimmy Fitz.

In that Shankly way of seeing football as some kind of metaphor for life, Jim saw himself at half-time, and was looking for a good second half. Hence the return to academic study. He continued to believe in simplicity as a policy, and he liked honest players, true people.

As he made Marsh Lane in his Cavalier, Jim had time to reflect on his own wanderlust as a child. He had once disappeared out of the old Woolworths on Stanley Road, while shopping with his mother, and been found 20 minutes later, on the way to Liverpool city centre. There was the time he had hopped on a bus and been found in Allerton. And when the *Hornet* had printed a picture of the Liverpool team, he had walked off and called at every newsagent from Bootle to the south end of the city, trying to buy a copy of the comic. The police had spent two and a half hours looking for him. Hopefully this, or something like it, would be the story with James Bulger.

When he arrived at Marsh Lane Jim was brought up to date by the uniform bosses. Nothing seemed to have been overlooked in the response to James's disappearance, but now, with increasing concern for the vulnerability of such a small child, it would become a CID matter.

Jim phoned round the stations in the division and called in all the available detectives, leaving just one for cover at each location. He began running a manual control, which would be the prelude to a computerised HOLMES major incident enquiry, should that be necessary.

A final and thorough search of the Strand was planned, and the keyholders of every shop were called from their homes to re-open their premises.

Ralph Bulger had also arrived at Marsh Lane by now. He had only heard of James's disappearance when he called at his mother-in-law's home, expecting to meet Denise and James, back from the shops. He went straight round to see Ray, his brother-in-law, because Ray had a car, and could give Ralph a lift into Bootle.

Mandy Waller and another officer were asked to take Ralph up to Kirkby, to search the Bulgers' home. Ralph could not understand the necessity for this – James was hardly likely to have made his own way back – but accepted Mandy's explanation

44

that it was a standard procedure when children went missing.

Ralph had some recent photographs of James on a roll of 110 film, which they brought back to Marsh Lane. Other members of the family were also coming into the station, offering support and help with the search.

The ponytail man finally turned up, at the front desk of the police station, having found out that the police were looking for him. He had been at the Strand that day, but it became apparent that he had not been involved in James's disappearance. He was then the first TIE of the enquiry – he had been traced, interviewed and eliminated.

I I

Afterwards, Jon and Bobby came down from the railway on Walton Lane, just the other side of the bridge from the police station. They clambered down the embankment, following the slope of the supporting wall of the bridge. At the top of the wall they reached out for the lamp-post, and slithered down it to the ground. A drop of some ten feet.

They crossed into the village then and hung around, roaming through the entries. They decided to knock for Gummy Gee, but there was no answer, so they sat on the steps near Gummy's house for a while, until another boy they knew came along and told them Gummy was in. No, they said, we don't think so. But they knocked for him again anyway, and there was still no answer, so they walked back up Gummy's street and into Walton Village, going in and around the entries for a bit, until they came out by the video shop in the Village, and decided to go inside.

Like many of the local children, Bobby was often in the video shop, sometimes chatting to one of the young women who worked there, sometimes propped against the counter watching a film or a cartoon, sometimes being cheeky and getting thrown out. His house was only half a dozen doors along the road and his mum was a member of the shop. Bobby sometimes rented films himself, on his mum's membership.

The two women in the shop worked alternate nights. Dorothy opened on Tuesdays, Thursdays and Sundays, and Joanne took the other nights. Bobby sometimes ran errands for Joanne, in return for money. He often went in to see if she wanted anything from the chip shop. Joanne had noticed that he was usually mucky and untidy, as little boys are when they have been out playing. Tonight she immediately saw Bobby's fingernails were dirty and his face covered in muck. He had what looked like a fresh scratch on his face, which was also caked in dirt. This was not strikingly unusual, and she thought he seemed as normal. She did not know or recognise Jon.

After a couple of minutes she asked them to run a message for her. There was an overdue video at 2 Haggerston Road. They owed £4.75 in fines, and if Jon and Bobby could get the money or the tape, or both, she'd give them 50p each for going.

The boys went out and, not long after, Joanne's workmate Dorothy came in for a chat.

Jon and Bobby walked up Walton Village and turned right into Haggerston Road. Karen at number 2 had rented the video *Rosie and Jim*, a children's drama series featuring two rag dolls that come to life, earlier in the week. She knew it was overdue but her son wouldn't let her take it back.

Karen hadn't long got in from work when there was a knock at the door. Jon and Bobby were on the step.

'The video shop's sent me. You owe £4.75.'

Karen left them standing there and went inside for the money. She came back with three pounds.

'And make sure you give it to them.'

The boys walked back down Walton Village, past the video shop to the Chinese chippie on the corner. Bobby waited outside while Jon went in. Then they both went back to the video shop, and Bobby handed Joanne the three pounds.

Joanne took the money, and separated a pound coin. She had it in her hand, passing it over the counter to Bobby when the door opened and Jon's mother came in. She was angry, shouting at the boys about sagging school, and telling them they were going to the police. She grabbed Jon by the hair and Bobby by the wrist, and dragged them both out of the shop.

Joanne still had the pound coin in her palm.

Jon's mother, Susan Venables, had seen the boys as they walked down Walton Village, and had watched Jon going into the chippie. She had been out looking for Jon, with her eldest son Mark, and had immediately hidden when she saw him – in case he saw her and ran off. Once Jon and Bobby were in the video shop she pounced, knowing there was no escape.

That morning, after Jon had left for school, she had gone shopping with her ex-husband, Neil. They had eventually made their way to her mum's, and in mid-afternoon her mum had given them a lift back, dropping Neil at his home so that he could meet Jon from school, and taking Susan on to her house in Norris Green, ready to meet Mark and Michelle when they arrived back from their school on the bus.

Neil had been outside the school in Bedford Road at half three, waiting with the other parents for the children. One of the dinner ladies had told him that Jon had run out of school at midday. Neil had tried to phone Susan, but she was already on her way back, on the bus with Mark and Michelle.

When Susan arrived at Neil's he told her. 'No Jon.' He said the dinner lady had told him Jon had run off with Bobby Thompson. He said the dinner lady had described Bobby Thompson as 'a fucking little git', and had said that their Jon was a good kid when Bobby wasn't around.

Neil had gone out then, looking for Jon on County Road without success. Returning to the maisonette alone, he had asked Susan if she thought he should go to the police, but she had said they should wait until six thirty in case Jon came home.

At six thirty Susan had set off for the police station, taking their thirteen-year-old, Mark. They had walked through Walton Village, passing Bobby's house. Susan hadn't bothered knocking there, because she knew she wouldn't get any sense out of them.

At the bottom of the village she had remembered the last time Jon sagged with Bobby, and Jon saying that he had gone on to the railway with Bobby, who had a den along the line.

Susan had crossed over by the How and walked up the roadway from Cherry Lane to the fencing along the railway embankment. She had stood there for a few minutes calling out Jon's name along the railway. She had not called Bobby's name.

Then she had walked round the corner, under the railway bridge and into the police station. She told the duty officer, PC Osbourne, that her son was missing, after running out of school that lunchtime with Bobby. She said it had happened before and she had reported it then, too.

PC Osbourne had leafed back through the MFH register, and found the old entry:

Sub Div Ref. No. 05 C2 1999 92. Jon Venables DOB: 13.08.1982. Reported missing from home from 11.00 hours 26.11.1992. He was with Bobby Thompson of 223 Walton Village, Liverpool 4 and both had run of out of school that day. At 17.30 hours that day both Jon Venables and Robert Thompson had been seen outside Kwik Save, County Road by neighbours, and when challenged made vee. Both had been traced at 20.00 hours the same day, in Walton Village, Liverpool 4.

PC Osbourne had then turned to a fresh page in the MFH register, and completed a new entry:

Walton Ln Sub Div Ref. No. 05 C2 29 93. Jon Venables, born 13.08.1982 had gone missing at 12.00 hours 12.02.93. Sex male, height 4'8", birth place Liverpool, with a squint in his right eye, wearing Bedford Rd St Mary's Sch uniform, and that he had run out of school in company with a Robert Thompson. Reported by mother at 19.00 hours 12.02.93. Friends, relatives to be checked as follows: 223 Walton Village, Liverpool.

PC Osbourne had told Susan that he would circulate the details, and that an officer would check at Robert Thompson's address. Susan had told PC Osbourne that she had been looking around County Road and Walton Lane. She had then given PC Osbourne a photograph of Jon, in his school uniform, taken just before Christmas.

Susan and Mark had left the police station, walked back under the railway bridge, and had just got to the corner, facing Walton Village, when Susan had seen Jon and Bobby, and gone into hiding.

Bobby struggled as they left the shop, and collapsed crying on the floor outside, so Susan let him go, and Bobby ran off as she held on to Jon, belting him a few times.

'Where've you been?'

'County Road.'

'All afternoon?'

'Yes.'

When Susan got Jon to the police station she could see in the light that he was very dirty, and that there was something on his sleeve.

'What's that?'

'Paint. Robert threw it at me.'

'Where's it from?'

'He stole it from a shop on County Road.'

Susan saw the paint on his hands and noticed how dirty they were. Usually he was quite clean coming home. She turned to PC Osbourne.

'Look at the state of him.'

She asked PC Osbourne to give Jon a good telling-off.

PC Osbourne asked Jon where he'd been. With a friend. Is that Robert Thompson? Yes. PC Osbourne then shouted at Jon about the police time he had wasted and the paperwork. Jon began to cry but, PC Osbourne noted, there were no tears in his eyes.

PC Osbourne endorsed the back of the MFH report: 'Found by mother, Walton Ln L4 19.15 hours 12.02.1993.' He handed back the photograph of Jon, and Susan Venables left the police station with her son.

Back at Neil's, Susan told Jon about the report she'd seen on the television. A two-year-old boy had been abducted from the Strand shopping centre. Jon was shocked, and asked where the boy's mother had been. Susan told him the mother had been inside a shop, and had only left him for a minute. He asked who it was and Susan said it was a little boy, but it could have been him.

She then gave Jon another good telling-off, and told him to get undressed and into bed. She noticed more paint on his trousers as she threw his clothes into the corner, and was even more angry. Jon kept apologising and when Susan went downstairs she could hear him crying and sobbing for a good half-hour.

He came down and apologised again for worrying his mum. Susan made him a cup of tea to take back to bed, but refused to give him his meal, because he hadn't been home at the right time. Jon went back to bed still crying. Susan thought he sounded broken-hearted – but he'd never seen his mum in such a temper before.

When she looked in later he had quietened down, and asked Susan to close the bedroom door. When she went in again he was asleep.

Neil had popped out to visit some friends who lived nearby. The woman had just come out of hospital, and her daughter arrived not long after Neil. He told them about Jon sagging school. Then there was a knock at the door and Susan came in. She told them about the police station, and finding Jon in the village. She mentioned that he had been shoplifting with Robert Thompson, that he had paint on his coat, and had been on the railway line.

When he wriggled free of the clutches of Susan Venables, Bobby ran home in floods of tears. Mrs Venables had hit him, he said between sobs. His mother, Ann, noticed the scratch on his cheek and the redness around one eye, like the impression left by a smack. Mrs Venables had no right, she said, and decided to go to the police.

Ann already knew Bobby had not been to school. Ryan had told her when he came home at four o'clock. Bobby had met Jon Venables by the school gates and they had gone off together, said Ryan. All this was forgotten in the drama of the moment.

Ann sent Ryan over the road to call out her friend Lesley for support. Lesley met them outside the house and examined Bobby's injuries. She thought the scratch looked more like a cut made by a small fingernail.

'Jon Venables' mum ragged me out of the video shop,' Bobby told her.

They set off for the police station, and stopped at the video shop on the way. Ann asked Joanne if she had seen Mrs Venables hit Bobby. Joanne said no, Bobby had already had that cut on his cheek, but he had been dragged out of the shop. She noticed that Bobby's face looked cleaner now.

Outside the shop, Bobby saw two young girls who, he told his mum, had watched him being attacked by Mrs Venables. They told Ann that Mrs Venables had got Bobby on the floor. This was good enough for Ann, who wanted to report Jon's mother.

As they entered the police station, the local youth liaison officer, Brian Whitby, was also on his way in. He knew Ann and Bobby. 'Hello,' he said, looking at Bobby's face. 'What have you been up to?'

Bobby muttered something incomprehensible. Ann seemed to be angry at him, and Bobby appeared flustered. Brian Whitby asked them to wait for the duty officer, and went into the station.

PC Oughton came out, and Ann went into the story about Bobby being assaulted by a woman called Venables. PC Oughton looked at Bobby's face, and could see only dirt. He told Bobby to go and swill his face in the gents' toilets. Ann led Bobby into the ladies for a wash and presented him back at the counter for inspection.

It didn't look much of a wound to PC Oughton. All he could see was a small piece of broken skin by Bobby's left eye. He told Ann this hardly justified a charge of assault.

Ann went on about Mrs Venables. She's an alcoholic, Ann slandered, lives over by the flyover on Breeze Hill, and is separated from her husband. I know why she's done this, said Ann. Her son's been sagging school with mine, and she thinks Robert's leading her Jon astray.

PC Oughton tried to explain that an assault charge was unlikely. Ann said she had no complaint to make. She only wanted Mrs Venables seen and spoken to. Ann and Bobby then left the police station.

Later, one of Bobby's friends went into the video shop, to collect Bobby's pound for him, from Joanne.

12

The number of alleged sightings of James multiplied as news reports of his disappearance continued. Some were local to Bootle, others were further afield. A woman phoned the police in Cambridge to report seeing a child in a car on the M11. Another thought she had seen James on the platform at Leeds railway station. A builder had seen a suspicious-looking man with a child in a Ford Orion on a building site in Widnes. The man had said he was looking for some twigs, to make a bow and arrow for the boy.

All the reported sightings were logged. Each had to be assessed for its feasibility, and given a place in the hierarchy of priority.

A patrolling officer in Bootle was stopped by a young lad who said he'd heard about the missing child, and thought his neighbour might have seen something. His neighbour was the woman who had been crossing the bridge over the canal that afternoon, and seen James crying on the towpath below. When the officer called in, she told him her story, distressed now at the implications of what she had seen. She had thought he was with the group of children nearby. She hadn't thought there was any reason to interfere.

Jim Fitzsimmons had been joined at Marsh Lane by two senior Superintendents from CID command. It was cold, it was late, and a two-year-old was alone and in jeopardy. They were sure the child the woman had seen was James. It was the first sighting of him. There was no indication of how he had arrived at the canal. He might just have wandered there on his own. Deep down, Jim began to think it probable that James had drowned in the canal.

No option could be dismissed, but there was no reason to suppose that James's disappearance was even a criminal matter. With the elimination of the ponytail man, and the sighting of James by himself at the canal, it was now less likely to involve an abduction than had seemed to be the case earlier in the evening.

There was no chance at this hour, in the dark, of searching the canal itself. Jim requested an underwater team for first thing in the morning. He thought they would find a body.

Denise and Ralph did not know of these developments. Denise was being interviewed, in detail, by a Detective Sergeant, Jim Green, from Southport and his female colleague, DC Janet Jones. The officers are feeling their way through the interview, establishing once and for all that there is nothing amiss with the family, that James's disappearance has no domestic connection.

Denise is quiet and withdrawn, her head bowed. She is looking for reassurance. 'You will find him, won't you? Will he be okay?' It had all happened so quickly. She couldn't understand where James could be.

After the interview Jim Green drove Denise and Ralph round to the Strand so that Denise could show exactly where she'd been when James went missing. Seeing them together for the first time, DS Green wondered if there would be any friction between them; if Ralph would blame Denise in any way for what had happened. But Ralph put his arm around Denise in the back of the car, clearly offering comfort.

The search of the Strand was still going on as they walked through to Tym's the butchers. It was getting on for midnight now, but the police activity continued unabated.

Two more reports came through of alleged sightings of James. One of the women who had been walking their dogs on Breeze Hill reservoir had called Walton Lane police station. She told them that the boy she had seen fitted the description given on the Granada news programme. He had been with two slightly older lads. The boy looked as if he had fallen and grazed his head.

The other caller had been at work in a garage on Berry Street in Bootle when a scruffy, nervous teenager with close-cropped hair came in asking for a light. He had been with another youth and a small child. The child had been carried on one of the boys' shoulders as they walked away. The caller had felt that the child didn't belong with them. Berry Street was behind Stanley Road, towards the docks – the opposite direction from Walton.

The two sightings conflicted with each other. There was no guarantee that either of them was actually of James. They certainly couldn't both be of James. On balance, the latter had to be favourite. The garage was nearer the Strand, and the boys were bigger. How could James have got all that way to the reservoir, and with two boys who were only slightly older than him?

Perhaps, but only perhaps, he was not in the canal, after all?

When Denise and Ralph returned from the Strand, Jim Green and Jim Fitzsimmons tried to persuade them to go home for some rest. It was nearly nine hours since James had disappeared, and the couple were despondent. 'We've lost him. He's gone, hasn't he?' No, don't think that way. There's still time. We can still find him. The officers barely knew what to say.

And Denise and Ralph didn't want to go home. They wanted to stay and wait for news. They were tense and quiet. Denise spoke abruptly to the officers, but gave in to their measured persuasion. Denise and Ralph went home.

The search was losing momentum as the early hours of the morning approached. The Operational Support Division teams had checked 73 of the Strand's 114 premises. Officers were again going over the banks of the canal and the neighbouring streets. One of the senior OSD officers called in to Marsh Lane from the Strand. He'd got men there doing nothing – what else could they do? It was suggested that they start looking at some of the Strand's security video footage. Try the camera overlooking the exit nearest to the canal.

It was after one o'clock, and Jim Fitzsimmons was on his own, upstairs at Marsh Lane. Everyone else had either gone home or was out on inquiries. He was just waiting for statements to come back with two officers he'd sent up to Kirkby.

The phone rang, an OSD sergeant calling in from the Strand. An edge of excitement in his voice. 'I think we've got him. He's on the video, leaving the Strand. Do you want to come and have a look?'

Jim put on his coat, an inexpensive Barbour, and walked downstairs and out of the station. He walked along by the wall of the police car park, past the public car park and across the bus terminal to the Strand's rear entrance, by the cab rank on Washington Parade. It was the bleak backside of Bootle, quiet at the best of times, now deserted and desolate. Acres of empty tarmac, spare lighting, the concrete mass of the multi-storey car park beyond, and the ungainly skyline of the buildings on Stanley Road. It was freezing, and a sharp Atlantic wind was blowing up from the Mersey across the open spaces.

Jim thought of the missing boy, who was not yet much more than a name. He thought the boy would be found tomorrow morning, in the canal.

There was a small huddle of people outside the Strand. Some were relatives of James, but mostly they were local women, Bootle people, poorly dressed against the cold and shivering as they stood, waiting. They were upset, they wanted to help. Anything. Anywhere they could look. God knows how long they had been there.

Moved by their presence, Jim made his way through them and into the Strand. He was shown into the office, and there on a screen, barely identifiable by the blurred, twitching movement of the time-lapse recording, was James, being led away by two boys. It was just possible to see him stumble as he went out through the doors of the Strand.

Jim was upset by these images of James, made real now and no longer just a name, his fate probably determined in these few moments.

Cases involving children were always affecting. He remembered, as a young uniformed bobby, being called to a house just off City Road, and finding a woman there, hysterical and crying. 'Oh, my baby's dead. My baby's dead.' She was upstairs in the bedroom, holding the child in her arms. Jim had taken the baby from her. It was a sudden death. A cot death. He had taken the baby from its mother, and it haunted him still.

Rewind. Forward play. Rewind. Forward play. The officers watched the short sequence for a while, before continuing the process of searching, backtracking through the recording for other sightings of James.

The images needed enhancing. It was almost impossible to discern any distinguishing features about the two boys with James. They looked like young adolescents. Maybe thirteen or fourteen years old.

Jim called the man from the garage on Berry Street, hoping he might recognise James, or the older boys, from the video. It was after two in the morning, and the man was in bed, but he got up and came down to the Strand, and looked at the recording. He watched, and thought. He didn't know, he said. It might be the same boys, and it might not.

Civilian support staff, Alan Williams and Colin Smith from the police photographic unit, were also summoned from their beds to the Strand. The unit had just taken possession of a new image-enhancing computer. They would work through the night to improve the quality of the footage, and produce usable stills that might identify James's apparent abductors.

Everything had changed. It was no longer simply a missing from home. Jim Fitzsimmons remained sure that James was dead, but if he had been abducted, even if he had been left at the canal before he drowned, it was a serious criminal offence.

He walked back from the Strand to Marsh Lane and left a request for the full HOLMES team to be brought out the following morning. And then, some time after three, he drove home.

13

On Saturday morning Jack from next door popped his *Sun* through Neil's letterbox. Susan got up at about quarter past ten, and gave Jon the newspaper to read. She told him there would be reports on television about the missing boy.

Normally Jon just glanced at the paper, the TV pages and the sport. This morning, Susan could see, he seemed very intent as he read the report of the missing boy.

Sure enough, there were the news items about the abduction on television throughout the day. Jon watched them all, including the one that showed the video of the child being taken away.

Jon asked his mum, 'Have they got them boys yet?' He kept saying, 'If I seen them lads, I'd kick their heads in.'

All day, Jon was on his best behaviour. He made his mum a cup of tea, which was a rare event, and told her he was going to start being good for her, because he didn't like to see her being upset. Susan believed she had finally got through to him.

When Neil asked Jon about the paint on his clothes he again

said that Robert had thrown it over him, after stealing the paint from a DIY shop. He told his mum that the shop was Taskers, and she guessed he meant the Fads on County Road. He said Robert had stolen some rolls of wallpaper border as well. The paint had been thrown in an entry by Olney Street, round the back of County Road.

In the afternoon Jon's grandmother came round to pick them up, and they all went shopping on Prescott Road. They went back to his grandmother's for tea, and afterwards they sat watching cable television until it was time to go home, at about seven thirty. They all stayed in for the evening, and Jon went up to bed after ten.

On Sunday Neil went out for the *News of the World*. Jon said, 'Let's have a look at this. Is there any more news on little James? If I seen them lads, I'd kick their heads in.'

Jon cycled down to the village, to St Mary's, where he saw some boys from school who had just finished choir, and were playing football in the churchyard.

Jon was cycling over the graves and one of the boys, who was nicknamed Frog because of his big eyes, told him to get off. Shut it Froggy, said Jon, and he threw some small stones at them and cycled away.

In the afternoon he played outside on his bike for a while, with his brother Mark. When Jon went in his mum told him that the missing boy had been found dead, down by the railway where he and Bobby had been. Susan saw that Jon was gobsmacked. 'His poor mum,' he said. He kept on watching the news after that, to see if the boys had been caught.

Normally, they would have gone back to Susan's house in the evening, ready for the new week at school. But because it was half-term they stayed over, returning on Monday, when Susan took Jon's clothes home in a bag and washed them in the machine.

Early in the week Neil made a couple more visits to the friends he had seen on Friday. They spoke about the murder, and his friend's daughter mentioned that Jon had been sagging that day.

Neil said he had been on County Road and, anyway, the lad in the video was taller than their Jon. By Tuesday the discovery of paint at the murder scene had been reported, and Neil spoke of the coincidence, that Jon should have returned home with shiny blue paint on the sleeve of his coat. More washing for Jon's mum.

Bobby, Ryan and another lad from across the road were in the video shop almost as soon as it opened on Saturday afternoon. They were chatting, and Joanne asked them to come behind the counter and watch a film. In the end they stayed there until it closed, watching some Bugs Bunny cartoons, *1001 Tales* and *Fievel Goes West*. They stopped for a while and Joanne helped Ryan with his homework, doing his sums. Then they started watching *Beauty and the Beast* on ITV, but had to miss the end because the shop was closing at eight. Bobby started getting cheeky, messing around with the shutters as Joanne was closing, until she managed to get rid of him.

Though Bobby did not say much about the abduction of James, he did tell Ryan he had seen the child in the Strand being taken by two boys. His mum noticed he paid particular attention to the reports about the disappearance on television and in the newspapers. She also noticed that one of the boys on the video looked something like her son. That doesn't half look like you, she said, and asked Bobby where he'd been on Friday. He said he had been at the Strand, before going to the library. He told her he'd been with Jon Venables.

When Ann's friend Lesley Henderson came over from her house across the road, Ann asked her what she thought. Lesley said it did look like Bobby, but it also looked like loads of other kids. Ann washed Bobby's jacket, which he had left out by the washing machine for cleaning.

That Sunday, 14 February, Bobby gave Lesley Henderson's daughter Kelly a Valentine's gift of a pink teddy bear with an imitation gold chain inside, which he had bought from the flower shop in the village.

He and Kelly and the other children all played out together that day, and in the afternoon they all ran back to Lesley's with the news that the police had found the body of a man on the track, with no head.

When Bobby's grandmother had died the family had been short of money to buy flowers. Ann had told Bobby that when you wanted to show special love for someone you just bought a single red rose. Bobby had bought a red rose for his grandmother, and placed it on her coffin. On Wednesday he bought a single red rose from the flower shop, and took it across to the embankment, where he placed it on the grass, among all the other floral tributes to James Bulger.

That evening, Ann asked Bobby if he had taken James Bulger. Was it you took that little boy out of the Strand? No. She threatened to take him across to the police station the next morning, thinking that if he had been involved this would frighten him into an admission. He said nothing.

14

Alan Williams called Jim Fitzsimmons at home on Saturday morning, just after eight. He and Colin Smith had been working all night on the videos. He'd got the stills; they weren't very good but they were the best that could be achieved from the original recording.

When Jim Fitzsimmons arrived at Marsh Lane he called his immediate superior, Geoff MacDonald, a Detective Chief Inspector who was then acting up, in lieu of promotion to Superintendent. Geoff MacDonald was at home. We've got a bit of a job on. There's a missing child; have you heard about it? No. Well, there's a child gone missing; it's unusual. If you get yourself ready and come down, I'll brief you.

Other Superintendents were already at work at Marsh Lane, the HOLMES team was assembling, and uniformed and plain clothes officers were being drawn in from all the Merseyside divisions to assist with the inquiry. The underwater team had begun dragging the canal, and the OSD had organised sector searches of the Bootle area, working outwards from Stanley Road.

When Denise and Ralph Bulger arrived they had to be told of the discovery that James had been abducted. Geoff MacDonald and Jim Fitzsimmons spoke to them in the old television room along the CID corridor. They told them what the video showed, and tried to be positive about the implications. At least James had not been alone. He's been taken by two bigger people. Perhaps it's just a lark; maybe James is squatting somewhere with them. Denise and Ralph were at least a little reassured. They asked to see the photographs of the two boys.

Jim Fitzsimmons produced the pictures, and the couple studied them while he briefly left the room.

As he returned, Denise pointed out of the window, to the low building by the waste ground across Washington Parade. Look, over there, that's the two boys. Jim looked, but could see no one. They were there a minute ago, said Denise, they must have gone behind that building. It looked just like them. Jim Fitzsimmons walked out of the station and across the road, and behind the building he found two boys, with a young girl, smoking. He asked the boys where they had been yesterday afternoon. They had been at the Strand. He took them back for questioning.

Of course, they were not James's abductors. It seemed to Jim Fitzsimmons that this was a nightmarish moment: the yearning expectation of Denise and Ralph, and an inquiry getting under way to find two boys, based on indistinct images on a video that might just about match every other young male on Merseyside.

It was hard to get a fix on the ages of the two boys on the video. The tape was replayed endlessly. Attempts were made to compare their heights with objects or people around them on the footage. By general agreement, they were around 13 or 14 years of age. A little older, quite possibly; a little younger, maybe. Most, though not all, of the witnesses who came forward with alleged sightings of the boys concurred.

Mandy Waller should have been on another 2–12 shift that day, but she came in early, around 11, and took over from the Crosby policewoman who had been sitting with Denise. Ralph spent much of the day out searching with other members of the family. They came and went from the television room, offering snippets of news and any reassurance they could muster. Mandy kept an eye on developments along the CID corridor, and endeavoured to be a filter for information emerging from the depressingly unproductive inquiries. It was a day of tea and sandwiches, and increasing despair.

When the trawl of the canal had been completed, and no body found, Mandy Waller, who had believed James would be found there, tried to make it sound positive, a good sign. For Jim Fitzsimmons, Geoff MacDonald and the other inquiry officers it only added to the uncertainties. Could a body have been carried elsewhere by the current? If so, in which direction? If he wasn't in the canal, then where was he? Was the sighting on Berry Street good? Was James nearby, or was he one of the rising number of far-flung sightings? There had to be a chance that he was still alive, and the officers clung to this possibility, though rationally it was a remote hope.

Amid the speculation and the brainstorming lay the more methodical process of examining all the incoming information, selecting priorities, and initiating inquiries. Names of potential suspects were coming in; detectives were being dispatched to check them out.

On the Saturday evening, officers finally visited the elderly woman who had been walking her dog on the reservoir. Her description of the two boys was limited – she could only say that they were ten or eleven years old and spoke with local accents. She remembered James as two or three years old, with blond hair and a round face. She remembered a dark anorak with orange-coloured lining, light-coloured trousers and white shoes. She was shown a photograph of James and thought it similar to the toddler she had seen. She said she had been on the reservoir just after quarter past four, less than an hour after James had been abducted.

It was by no means conclusive, but when the statement was read, back at Marsh Lane, it was decided that this was a sighting of James, even if the woman had apparently underestimated the ages of the two boys with him.

This suggested a fresh direction for the search, away from Bootle and into Walton, and opened up a whole new area for speculation. There were cemeteries, more stretches of canal, hospital grounds, old railway lines, open spaces, city farms . . .

Jim Fitzsimmons found Saturday a difficult and frustrating day, plagued by slow progress and uncertainty. They needed something, anything, to move forward. A direct line to the Pope.

Before clocking off at one o'clock in the morning he and Geoff MacDonald again spoke to Denise and Ralph, again persuading them that it was time to go home, again trying to sound reassuring. If James had been in the canal we would have found him by now. He must be in the custody of someone, things are positive. Denise said, 'Do you think we've got a chance?' Jim could see and feel her desperation. Holding on to the slightest hope. Yes, they could still find him, he could still be alive.

Albert Kirby was off that weekend, at home, and had been following the events that were unfolding in Bootle from news reports and the occasional phone call from officers of his team who had become involved in the inquiry.

He had been at work on Friday, at his desk in Canning Place, where he was the Detective Superintendent in charge of the Serious Crime Squad. He had heard of James's disappearance that afternoon, and hoped the boy would be found. As time went on he began to wonder whether it might warrant his involvement. He had run through the options in his head – a relative, perhaps, had taken James; he was hiding somewhere; or being held against his will – but in his heart, as time went on, he knew those options were evaporating.

He had decided on Saturday that if James was not found by tea time he would go in on Sunday, either to help or to take over the inquiry.

Like a doctor on call, Albert always kept his black leather briefcase at home, packed and ready to go to work. It contained pens, writing pads, a pager, a mobile phone, and the latest in the series of red, A4-sized, spiralbound notebooks in which Albert chronicled his work. He often took a prepared lunch in with him as well, in a small Tupperware container.

Albert was a meticulous and controlled man. He had never smoked and had been teetotal for the past ten years, since giving up the occasional pint while in training to run the London marathon. People had once been nasty about it, passing comments on his abstinence. Albert had concluded that they were responding to their own weaknesses and nowadays, when he sat with a Kaliber or a Barbican, everyone just accepted it.

He still ran, two or three times a week, in the streets around Blundellsands, at the north end of the city, near his home. If he was troubled by work he could run the problem out in half an hour. The coast, the sea, the fresh air and the occasional burst of sunshine made him feel tremendous, after a day at his desk. His heartbeat, when he was relaxed, would register at 36.

Both his parents had died of problems related to high blood pressure when he was still a boy. They had married as first cousins, from a family in Widnes, and been living in Liverpool, where his father was a seaman, when Albert was born. They had moved to Barrow-in-Furness when the father had become a harbour master, and he had died there, on Albert's fourth birthday.

When his mother died five years later, Albert had been taken in by an aunt who sent him to boarding school. He had been fortunate to be cared for so well. The school had been full of boys who were either orphaned or had only one parent.

Albert did not associate the loss of his own parents with his attention to fitness and well-being, but he had found that, at boarding school, he had developed resources, such as the ability to identify other people's strengths and weaknesses, which had served him well throughout his police career.

As a young man he had been envious of contemporaries from conventional family units, especially those with a good father-and-son relationship. He had been pleased to be able to replicate that in his own marriage. A son, Ian, was now 21 and studying at St Andrew's University – conveniently for Albert, who had recently taken up golf.

His wife, Susan, had been a police officer when they met and married, but after the birth of Ian she had developed a chronic and disabling rheumatoid arthritis. She had endured seven or eight major operations for joint replacements, including her wrists and shoulders.

Albert was distressed by his wife's suffering and his inability to ease it for her. He hated the irony of their extremes: Susan in so much pain, Albert so fit and healthy. He had the greatest admiration for her continuing cheeriness in the face of such agony.

The church, and the support of the friends they found there, helped. They had both been raised as Catholics but had begun attending the local Church of England when they moved to their current home. Roy, the vicar, knew and accepted the origins of their faith, and had become a good friend. The values of Christianity, of course, were universal. Quite frankly, Albert thought, it didn't matter a toss what religion you were. He would quote Dave Allen from the television: 'May your God go with you.'

Albert worked with men who were very strong practising Christians, and did not believe it was unusual among police officers. Going back a few years, it might have been frowned upon as a mark of weakness, but not now – not in this day and age.

He was not obligated to go to work that Sunday but, Albert

being Albert, it was the kind of thing he'd do. It was about responsibility and commitment, even devotion to the job. Albert knew when he had to go to work, and his wife, Susan, understood this, after nearly 25 years of marriage.

Albert was lucky in that respect. Susan had at least learned to live with the unpredictability and the disruption. It was a 24-hours-a-day, seven-days-a-week job, after all. He knew the pressures on CID officers and had seen the damage that it inflicted on their relationships. The failed marriage was by no means rare, and Albert thought there was a hard truth in the joky notice he had seen on the desk of one of his detectives: 'You only get one chance in the CID – but you can have more than one wife.'

Unusually, Albert had been a detective for nearly all his years in the police service. He had been a cadet at sixteen, and a serving policeman at nineteen, in Liverpool city centre. That was in 1964, and within two years he had been moved to plain clothes work . . . vice squad . . . CID . . . and, with one brief interlude as a uniformed inspector, he had remained in plain clothes ever since.

As a manager, Albert saw himself as merely the leader of a team. He always said he didn't detect the offences; it was the officers on the ground who were responsible for getting the job done. He simply believed that, in life, people worked better with leadership and direction. He had been brought up in that creed, and had always responded to it as a youngster; he didn't see any reason why the adult world should be different. Applying those trusted principles, he could get results.

He knew that people accused him of being rude, of being arrogant and abrupt. But that was how he was. It was his style; in management and in life, he was always the same. He liked to think people knew where they stood with him. He would say what he thought, and if he bollocked the arse out of somebody one minute for some misdemeanour, once he'd said his piece it was done and over with. He didn't hold grudges.

His colleagues said of him that Albert was not a man to cross. He could be fierce, with his chilly, deep-set eyes and tightly drawn lips. Titty-lip, he was sometimes called. To most people he was not Albert, he was Mr Kirby. But he was not without humour and warmth, not above the banter and the storytelling, and, above all, he was a good detective and a positive manager.

Albert went out with his briefcase first thing on Sunday morning, down to Marsh Lane, ready now to assume the mantle of Senior Investigating Officer. He spent the morning catching up with what had happened so far and, with other officers, began planning the next steps in the inquiry. They wanted to further enhance the video footage, maximising public awareness of James's disappearance and jogging memories of seeing the boys, perhaps even prompting an identification. The media would be used, posters distributed, and special attention given to the Strand, where a vacant shop site had been made available as a temporary police station.

The search for James, in all likelihood the search for a body, was expanding, spreading across Walton without forgetting Bootle. There were no certainties, only an unwieldy set of possibilities.

By lunchtime, Albert felt that he was up to date. He would have a midafternoon briefing with Geoff MacDonald and Jim Fitzsimmons. In the lull, Jim slipped out and drove over to Walton Hospital where his mother, an inveterate and incurable smoker, was being treated after a mild heart attack. She was a warhorse, Jim's mother, the survivor of a brain operation for a tumour a few years earlier, and determinedly smoking through a continuing heart problem. He was worried for her but felt instinctively that she would survive her current illness.

At the hospital, he sat with his mum for a few minutes, his mind not quite letting go of James. 'I've got to be off now.' He said goodbye to her and walked out of the hospital. On the spur of the moment, he decided to carry out his own search of the barren land behind the hospital buildings. He rummaged around for 20 minutes, finding nothing, and drove back to Marsh Lane for the briefing with Geoff MacDonald and Albert Kirby.

15

In the early hours of Sunday morning, not long before five, a British Rail train driver was picked up from Orrell Park by the staff bus and taken to Formby station to start work. The loco there had been used overnight to bring materials from Tuebrook sidings for some engineering work.

The driver waited while a crane was detached from the engine and the engine was run around on to the up line. When the guards and the conductors were aboard he set off, at about seven o'clock, leaving the Liverpool–Southport line at Bootle junction and crossing to the Bootle branch line. The other men were in and out of the driver's cab. The driver made sure he kept to the speed limit of 20 miles per hour.

The branch line to Edge Hill had been a freight-only route for many years. The line had been built in the 1860s, and in 1870 a station had opened at Walton Lane bridge. The station was originally called Walton for Aintree, and later renamed Walton & Anfield. It was quiet, just two small buildings with chimneys facing each other across the tracks, awnings above the doors. On winter nights after matches at Goodison Park, lamp-posts that ran the length of the platforms would illuminate supporters returning to meet their football specials after the game.

During the Second World War, all the US servicemen arriving in Britain by sea had been transported down this line, and though passenger services had long since ceased to use it, the track was still on an MoD list somewhere as a key transportation link in time of war.

The station was closed in 1948 and the buildings demolished. The raised brick of the platforms, overgrown with bushes and rough grass, remained, and were just shielded by the foliage from Walton Lane Police Station, whose yard backed on to the embankment.

Rarely, nowadays, would more than a dozen trains a day go through, mostly to and from the docks of Gladstone and Seaforth. Some collected and delivered containerised goods for or from Southern and Northern Ireland; others transported open carriages of Colombian or Polish coal to Fiddler's Ferry, the power station in Warrington.

Sometimes, as on this Sunday morning, British Rail ran its own engineering services. For most hours of the day the ralla was quiet, and it had been a shortcut and a playground for successive generations of local children, despite increasingly determined attempts to fence off the line and deny them entry. Successive generations of the ralla's adult neighbours had found the noisy presence of playful kids an irritation.

If the line had any criminal use, other than trespass and being a good place to sit and smoke dope, it was as a vantage point for assessing the burglary potential of neighbouring houses. It was possible to gain access to properties at certain places, and the line was useful as a getaway route.

The driver of the early-morning train kept watch ahead as the engine trundled out of the cutting at Walton, heading towards Edge Hill, still travelling no faster than 20 miles per hour. He was on the up line, on the far side from the police station as he crossed the bridge, his seat in the cab also on the far side. He noticed something lying on the ground near the other track and leaned forward to get a better view.

The object looked like a dummy or a doll. Kids were always putting things like that across the tracks.

When the train arrived at Edge Hill the driver was told to take the engine to Arpley sidings in Warrington to pick up a couple of wagons. He went to the sidings and shunted the wagons, and then drove back to Edge Hill. The driver was relieved there by a colleague, but stayed aboard the engine for the journey back to Formby, on the down line. He stood at the rear of the driver's cab as they came through Walton, and did not think to look at the track again as they passed the old station there.

Yet the sighting of the object on the track played on his mind. Something about it was not quite right. He had seen and remembered the press coverage of the lad going missing. Later, that evening, when he called the Transport Police to tell them, he realised exactly what it was he had seen.

On Sunday afternoon Beckett's mum dropped him by the Rileys. Osty came to the door when Beckett knocked, and said they weren't ready yet. They were just having a sandwich for lunch, and Osty wanted to try and get some money off his mum.

Beckett waited outside, by the Rileys' garden wall, until Osty and his brother Pitts came out. They were always together, Osty and Pitts, like a stamp stuck on an envelope, as another boy said of them. They all decided to call for Georgie, who lives by the Sportie on Walton Hall Avenue.

As they walked along they met Stee, who had been doing weights at the Sportie. He said he'd just knocked for Georgie, and there was no answer, but he walked with them anyway, and when they called at Georgie's there was still no one in.

They went looking for Kelly and Emma, who always hang around by the newsagents, and found them there with three lads. Osty went in and bought a packet of ten Embassy filters, so that they could sit off on the rocks in the cemetery later and have a ciggie.

When Kelly and Emma and the other three lads went off they sat on the ledge by the newsagents for a bit, and then Osty and Pitts said let's go and get our hats back from the police station. The hats had been in the police station for ages, since a kid had got his bike robbed. The kid said the lads who'd done it were wearing hats, and the police had taken the two hats for identification: Osty's leather hat with the flaps and the fur lining, and Pitts's Puma baseball cap.

They walked round to the police station on Walton Lane,

and the man at the desk told them to come back on Monday. So they went back down Walton Lane to Queen's Drive, where they met Stee's brother Lee, and he joined them for a while.

The five of them knocked at Chris's house by the Ebenezer Chapel and, when there was no answer there, they carried on to Leon's in the Village, and sat on his front for a while, talking to Leon.

Lee left them then, and they called back at Georgie's house again, and he wasn't in. As they were walking away, Joanne came out of her house nearby. Osty and Pitts had been round at Joanne's with Mick the night before. Now she said a watch had gone missing and she wanted it back.

Osty had been saying he wanted to go to his nan's because he might be given some money, but they thought Mick might know something about the watch, so they walked over towards Chepstow Road, talking to Natalie and Jenny for a while as they crossed over the broo. Mick's sister came to the door and said he was out. They thought Mick might be at his girlfriend Amanda's house.

When they got to Amanda's she told them Mick wasn't there, and she didn't know where he was. They stood talking with Amanda on her front, until Amanda's mum came out and told them to move.

They went back to Mick's, and left a message that they were going to the park. Then they walked down towards the new Kwikkie on County Road, near where their nan lived. Sack me nan's, said Osty, so they went down the entry by the pizza parlour, and down another entry, to the railings by the ralla.

Pitts said that footballs sometimes got kicked from the school on the other side of the ralla onto the line, so they climbed over and dropped down on to the embankment. A train went past, carrying big white stones in open carriages.

A woman came out of her house and told them to get down off the railway. They ignored her and carried on until Pitts found a football. It was only a plastic flyaway thing but they kicked it along the line for a while, and as they got by Church Road, just before the bridge near the police station, they saw a lad with his mum and dad on the road below, so Osty picked the ball up and kicked it to the boy so that he could have the ball. They thought about making a den on the ralla, in the bushes along the embankment.

As they crossed the bridge they heard dogs barking in the kennels at the back of the police station. They went down the pathway, to try and see the dogs. Sometimes they had Pit Bulls and that in there, but today there was only a couple of little mutts. They came back up the path onto the ralla, by the old platforms and Beckett said, eeh, look at that, a dead cat or something. They all looked. It was like a bundle wrapped up in a coat. There were halfies piled around it. Beckett touched it lightly with his foot, but there was no movement. Then he looked back across the track and shouted, look, there's its legs.

Pitts said it looked like doll's legs. Beckett was frightened and wanted to run away. Pitts went close to the legs. He said they weren't doll's. There was a little pair of trainers nearby. Someone said it was like a baby. Stee said, I think it is a baby, and he ran, shouting and panic-stricken, up the line, towards the police station. They were all frightened now, and ran after Stee. They dropped down from the embankment at the back of the police station, and ran round to the front desk.

Beckett was ahead as they went into the police station, shouting and screaming, and ringing the bell at the inquiry desk. PC Osbourne came through from the office behind the one-way glass and asked what was wrong. The boys looked very excited and agitated. There's a baby on the railway line cut in half, they shouted, just round the back on the railway. Stay there, said PC Osbourne and went back into the inquiry office to collect his radio. He called to two other officers, there's a baby on the line, and ran round to the front of the police station, followed by his colleagues. The boys called, it's round the back of the police station.

The officers ran through the yard, to climb up on the kennels, on to the embankment. They told the boys to stay behind, but the boys followed them up anyway. They watched PC Osbourne recoil as he saw the body. At 15.13 he radioed an urgent message to C Division control. He asked that supervision and CID be informed, and he asked for British Rail to be told to close the line.

16

By Sunday, Denise and Mandy Waller were running out of things to say to each other. They just sat there in the television room, with Nichola Bailey. Mandy had found it increasingly difficult to offer words of reassurance. 'We're not going to find him, are we?' Denise would say. 'Of course we are,' Mandy would reply, knowing it sounded simplistic. Knowing, against all hope, that he would not be alive.

You could only drink so many cups of tea. It was getting claustrophobic in the room. There was nothing to be said and nothing to be done. They were beginning to get on each other's nerves.

Ralph was out, driving around, searching with other members of the family. 'Why don't we go out?' Mandy said to Denise and Nichola, thinking the change would do them all some good, and break up the day. She took a radio with her, and told the control room that they were going for a drive.

They didn't get far, just in and around Bootle. The radio was on, and then it was speaking to Mandy. 'Can you come straight in.' It was Noel, the control operator, who was Welsh with a thick accent. Later, Mandy discovered that he then said, 'and can you turn your radio off.' She had heard him, but did not understand what he was saying. Fortunately, she automatically turned the radio off, anyway.

73

Denise had also heard the first half of the message. She wanted to know what was happening. Mandy said she didn't know, but she thought to herself that a body had been found. They turned back for Marsh Lane.

Albert Kirby, Jim Fitzsimmons and Geoff MacDonald were sitting in Geoff MacDonald's office, reviewing the inquiry, working out where to go next. An officer knocked and walked in. 'Sir, we've a report of a body, back of Walton Lane.' As the officer gave them the details, the three men were putting on their coats and making their way to the car park, to drive to the scene.

When Mandy Waller arrived back at Marsh Lane an Inspector was waiting in the car park. They didn't want Denise to hear the news casually; they wanted to protect her until confirmation had been made. The Inspector walked ahead from the car park to the back entrance of the station, with Denise and Nichola. Mandy was just behind them.

As the group went in, Mandy saw the bosses coming out of the door. 'What's wrong? What's wrong?' Denise was panicked by the sight of the three senior officers. 'It's all right,' said Jim Fitzsimmons, 'Don't worry.' What else could he say? They walked past Denise, and Geoff MacDonald broke away to speak to Mandy. 'They've found a body on the railway line. We think it's James.'

Mandy knew then, but could say nothing. She could see that Denise was putting two and two together. Denise kept asking what was happening, but would not ask directly if they had found James. 'We'll just have to wait,' Mandy said.

Geoff MacDonald drove the couple of miles to the railway line. He turned off Cherry Lane into the cul-de-sac by the How. A cordon was already set up, the railing pulled back to give access to the line. Jim Fitzsimmons, hoping it wasn't James, but knowing it would be, tried to create a convincing scenario in his head. James had wandered up on to the line, and been knocked down by a train. He made his mind up this was what had happened. But he didn't believe it.

They clambered up the bank, while an officer who had met them described the barest details of the scene. They could see in an instant that it was James, even though his head was hidden by his clothing. The anorak, the scarf, the tracksuit bottoms, all too familiar, by now.

No one spoke for a few moments. There was only silence and stillness. Then Geoff MacDonald said, 'I'll do it.' There was no discussion about this, no weighing up of which of the three senior officers should perform the duty. Jim Fitzsimmons and Albert Kirby would not say, 'That's very brave of you, Geoff,' because that's not how it works. Though both of them thought it.

Geoff MacDonald turned, to go back to his car, to drive to Marsh Lane and tell Denise that they had found James's body.

It was a long and difficult half-hour in the television room, Denise wanting to know what was going on, Mandy wondering how long it would be before word came through. Eventually, unable to bear the waiting any longer, Mandy went down the corridor to try and get some news.

As Mandy walked back to the television room, Geoff MacDonald was just ahead of her, going in the door. He had expected to find Mandy inside, and he would have called her out, before they went in together, when Mandy would have told Denise.

As it was, Geoff MacDonald told Denise himself, and Mandy was just behind him, coming into the room, as he spoke. 'Yes, I'm sorry, we've found James.' Denise screamed. It seemed to Mandy that she collapsed internally. They all cried. Mandy went to fetch some toilet roll, because there were no tissues available.

Ralph was still out, and could not be contacted. The police feared that he would arrive back and hear the news from one of the numerous men and women of the media who were camped outside the station. But they had followed the story to the railway line, and Ralph had heard nothing when he walked into the front entrance of Marsh Lane. He was met and told by Geoff MacDonald. Ralph's distress manifested itself as anger.

He punched and kicked a screen that was standing nearby.

Later, after Denise had been taken home, Ralph paced up and down, throwing out questions, demanding to know what had happened, how James had died. There were no answers, then, but there was already speculation.

Albert Kirby had taken his red, spiral-bound notebook to the scene. He did not start a new notebook for each inquiry, but simply turned to the next clean page. He was about a third of the way through the latest book, and kept the old ones, God knows how many, in his desk at work. He called them his ongoing bible of investigations.

The last page before the Bulger inquiry had been notes for a management structure he was developing. The first page of the Bulger inquiry was his introductory notes, in small, precise handwriting, and on the second page he made his sketch of the scene at the railway line.

He noted the position of the lower half of the body, between the track and the embankment, on the side nearest the police station, and the position of the upper half, seven sleepers further down towards Edge Hill, between the same tracks.

Nothing was moved, everything left as it was. Preserving the scene, keeping it sterile. The pathologist was on his way and, until he arrived, there could be no way of knowing how James had died.

As he studied and thought and made notes, Albert did not allow himself any emotional response to the sight of the body. He dreaded to think how many he had seen over the years. He must have been involved with 35, even 40 murders since his days as a junior detective. He remembered three in one week as a DI, and he had come to realise that they always seemed to go in runs, and always in the winter months, from October through to the early part of the year. Never in the nice weather and long daylight hours of summer when you were out searching scenes.

It was not something he could ever get used to, the scene of a killing. It was always different, by way of the age and gender of the victim and the circumstances of their death, and it was always hard.

He had learned that the emotional impact always came later. It had to be suppressed at the time because it would only interfere with the work. He was duty-bound to be professional. It was his duty to find out how, and why, somebody had died, and who was responsible for that death. There was no room for emotion. He had to put himself on automatic pilot.

This was true for Jim Fitzsimmons, too. There was no conscious process of repressing feelings. It was simply about doing the job. Looking at what evidence could be gathered at the scene, making sure everything was done properly. It was odd, like seeing the scene from a distance, but that was the way it was.

The light would fade fast, and they had to work quickly. Jim was up and down the embankment, between the police station and the scene, clambering over the kennels, briefing people and leading them on to the line. He tore the jacket of his suit on some bushes.

SOCO officers came in to oversee the searches and the recovery of forensic evidence. They photographed and made a video record of the scene. A search log was opened, and OSD teams formed cordons to make line searches along the track. The upper half of the body was covered with a forensic tent, and the fire brigade used salvage sheets, stakes and rope to create a cover for the area around the lower half of the body.

A press photographer got up on to the line and was spotted trying to take pictures of the body before the covers had been erected. He was the target of some anger from the officers.

It appeared that the body had been lying at a right angle across the track nearest to the police station, the upper half inside the track. It appeared to have been covered in bricks, and had probably been dislodged when a train had severed the body at the waist, dragging the lower half, which was naked, some fifteen feet, seven sleepers, down the line.

The clothing which had been removed was scattered around the upper half of the body. Grey tracksuit bottoms, lightly stained with blood and paint, a pair of white training shoes with the left shoelace undone, and the right shoelace still tied, and a pair of white socks with blue stripes and light bloodstaining. A pair of underpants, heavily stained with blood, was found, placed under one of the bricks. There was a heavy strip of steel lying against the bricks. It was a fishplate, which is some two feet long, and is used to attach railway track to sleepers. It weighed over 10 kilograms (22 pounds) and was stained with blood.

The white scarf, also bloodstained, was lying on the side furthest from the police station, between the track and embankment. One bobble had been separated from the scarf, and this was found in the middle of the other track, back towards the bridge.

Three Tandy Evergreen AA-sized 1.5v batteries were scattered near the scarf, two of them stained with blood, and a fourth was still in the cellophane packet which was also lying there. The sleepers and the ballast around the scarf were bloodstained, and there was blood spattering on the neighbouring wall of the old station platform. A trail of blood led across the tracks to the upper half of the body. There were two bricks stained with blood near the scarf, and others around the body. There was an S-shaped Pandrol securing clip with blood staining, and some blond hairs adhering to it. The clip would normally be used with the fishplate in the construction of track. British Rail kept emergency supplies of fishplates and clips at intervals along its railways.

A tin of Humbrol Azure Blue paint was found on the track, on the other side of the bridge, and there were stains of blue paint in the area by the tin. A box of Quality Street was found further down the line, together with some sweets.

The doctor, arriving in advance of the pathologist to complete the formality of certifying death, could not touch the body and, not seeing the head inside the clothing, thought the head was missing from the body.

With the arrival of the Home Office pathologist, Alan Williams, at five o'clock, the clothing could be moved, and it became evident that the body had sustained multiple head injuries. There was a great deal of blood, and blue paint had stained the left side of James's face, ear and neck, and his anorak.

Later, in the evening, two men from the Co-op Funeral Service came in a van to collect James's body and deliver it to the mortuary for identification and the post mortem. They drove into the car park at Cherry Lane and reversed the van up to the fence at the bottom of the embankment. They picked up the child's body bag, which Alan Williams had placed by the fence, and lifted it into the back of the van.

They took the body to the mortuary at Broadgreen Hospital, where it was identified by Ralph's brother, Ray Bulger, at nine o'clock. Geoff MacDonald and Jim Green both attended the post mortem, which Alan Williams began at 10.45 and completed at 1.30 the following morning. It was the first post mortem Jim Green had ever attended as a police officer.

There was a lull now, for the senior officers, awaiting the pm report in the morning. The search for James, for a body, was over, and they would now be looking for the perpetrators of a violent death, surely a murder. All efforts would now be focused on those two teenagers in the video.

Back at Marsh Lane the atmosphere was as solemn and as quiet as it had been up there on the railway line. Everyone had hoped James would be found alive, but expected to find a body. No one had expected such violence. Details were still scarce, but word was getting round.

Jim Fitzsimmons answered the phone to Geoff MacDonald's wife. She hadn't spoken to him, but she'd heard the body had been found. She had been going to go to bed, but thought now she would stay up, because she knew her husband got upset. Jim Fitzsimmons said it would be better if she waited up for him. He'd had a difficult task to perform. Officers did not tend to go around asking each other how they felt, but Jim knew how Geoff MacDonald would be feeling.

So did Albert Kirkby. First there had been the breaking of the news to the family, and then the post mortem. Albert could think of no one who found post mortems easy. It was the smell as much as anything, the antiseptic, the chemicals, the stink that seeped into your suit and clung to you afterwards. Albert always tried to keep a discreet distance, hanging back, talking to the pathologist.

This time he had been spared the post mortem, but he would go home now and be unlikely to sleep soundly. It was always the same in the difficult stages of an investigation. You worked late, your mind running at full pitch, then you'd go home, unable to switch off. Albert would lie in bed in the dark, knowing at least that he was resting, trying to steer his thoughts in sweeter directions, like hitting a golf ball squarely down a fairway.

He would not talk to his wife about the day's events. He rarely did. If he had to bring his troubles home, he would try hard not to shed them there. Susan, his wife, had told him off for this over the years, but it made no difference. When Susan sensed he was preoccupied and quiet she would tactfully suggest he went for a run, though it was a little late to go running tonight.

For Jim Fitzsimmons Sunday night was the welcome opportunity of an early finish. Or relatively early, it already being eleven o'clock. He left the office and went down to his Cavalier in the car park. Sitting in the car, alone suddenly, and no longer busy, he felt upset. It just came over him and he began crying. He drove home, distressed and puzzled, unable to understand his reaction. What's it to do with me?

He had been fine at the railway, not bothered at all by what he had seen there. Yet, over the last couple of days, it was as if he had come to know James, and feel for him. Now, on the first and last night of the inquiry when he was home before midnight, he walked in getting more and more upset. His wife, Fran, had waited up, and Jim sat and talked to her while he downed a can or two of beer. He sat up until gone two in the end, but it seemed to help. In the morning he felt better.

A reporter from ITN took Osty, Pitts and Stee to the park, to film an interview with them, about their discovery of the body. Osty and Pitts were wearing big weatherproofed jackets, one green, the other purple, with hoods and high collars that almost covered their mouths. Stee, who was taller and wearing a black bomber jacket, stood between them.

As the tape rolled, Pitts said, we'll be TV stars. They called to the other children gathering around them. Go away.

Reporter. OK, so do you want to tell me how you came to find the body?
Stee. 'Cos we were walking along the railway and, erm . . .
Pitts. (*smiling*) We was having a ciggie on the railway.
Reporter. You was having what?
Pitts. We was having a ciggie on the railway.

Off camera, children are gathering around, laughing. Osty says, pack it in, laughing, all youse go away.

Stee. He dropped his money, him, at the, erm, bridge, right, didn't you, and like he couldn't find it, like that, and then we all went back 'cos we were in front of him. He says, I've lost me money, so we all walked and had a look for his money and, erm, what happened then? And then, like, I found it, didn't I.
Pitts. (*laughing*) He says, I find everything, me.
Reporter. Yeah, when, er, what, er, when did you first see the body?
Stee. About, like, and then we 'eard dogs barking away the compounds . . .
Pitts. In the police station.
Stee . . . so we went down, and we walked past it and never noticed it in the beginning, right, then we went down to have a look at the dogs, came back up, like that, and I jus' seen it there, just in a like a coat, like an 'orse, with the organs all coming out.
Osty. All the organs coming out, like big fat worms.
Stee. So like and then I said, 'ere, look at that, doesn't that look like a baby.

They all laugh, except the reporter, and Stee falls away, cracking up.

Stee. Can we start it again?

Reporter. Yeah, we'll start it again. Just tell me how you came to discover the body.

Stee. Right, we were walking along the railway and, er, like, we, erm (*laughing*), and he dropped something, and he said, oiyo, come back 'ere, I've lost me money. This was by the bridge, so we walked back, I said, and he was throwing all the bricks and all of that off the railway, like that, and someone went, you're never gonna find this, and I went, here are, there it is, like that, and then, er . . .

Pitts. He says, I find everything, me, and then he walked up and then he found the baby.

Stee. Like we had a look at the dogs and then found the baby.

Pitts. Yeah, we walked past him, right past him we walked. They were about there, and we walked round past him.

Reporter. So you walked past the child at first?

Pitts. Yeah, we would've walked past it, only he says come and have a look at the dogs in the compound, there might be big dogs and that.

Reporter. What did the body look like?

Stee. Terrible. We couldn't see the face. We couldn't see the face.

Pitts. Wrapped up in a little, like a coat.

Reporter. OK, start again, tell me what the body was like when you found it.

Pitts. Wrapped up in a coat, with all housebricks all round it and bars on it.

Stee. And all organs hanging out from the waist.

Pitts. Like just there, not pouring out, just all in a big, big like hill.

Stee. And then he turned round, no, and then he went, it's a cat. It's a cat wrapped up. Then we seen its legs.

Pitts. No, we said, no, it was you that said, well I said, it's a dead cat, and you went no it's not it's sausages.

Reporter. Tell me, sensibly now, tell me what did you think it was when you first saw it.

Stee. A baby. I did. Honestly. Didn't I say . . .

Osty. Socks and shoes.

Stee. Shoes, yeah. 'Cos I said, it's a baby, 'cos I seen the legs.

Pitts. Then you see doll's legs, and they all ran, and I said no, it's not, and I walked back over and it had no pants on or nuttin', and all dirt round its feet, so then I jus' went, it's a baby.

Stee. And then we all ran towards the bridge, got down and went to Walton Lane.

Reporter. What did you do once you'd found it? Who did you tell?

Stee. The police. The police. Walton Lane, 'cos it was only the back.

Osty. Next to it.

Reporter. So tell me sensibly, were you surprised that you found something like this on the railway line?

Stee. Yeah, very, like, 'cos you don't really find dead bodies on the railway, do you. When we seen it we jus' ran to the police station.

The reporter pauses for a moment or two. Children begin to gather round, encircling the boys, in front of the camera. They creep into the view of the camera in twos and threes. Eventually there are nearly 20 of them, all gathered around Osty, Pitts and Stee, jostling, pushing and laughing. One girl, in a red sweatshirt, has her headphones on, attached to a Walkman. In the fields beyond, a man is walking a dog.

Reporter. So what did, er, what did you think when you found it? (*Pitts looks around him.*)

Reporter. Don't worry about the people behind you. Be sensible. It's not funny.

Stee. He thought it was a dead cat wrapped up.

Pitts. Doll's legs.

Reporter. Tell me, this one on the right here, tell me, what did you think when you first saw the body?

Osty. Don't know. All of us jus' seen it and ran away.

Reporter. Were you surprised that you found it?

Osty. No.

Reporter. So tell me, just once again, and as sensibly as you can, forgetting everyone around you, tell right from the beginning what happened, tell me really from the beginning what happened.

Stee. We were walking along the railway . . . from the beginning?

The reporter nods.

Stee. We were walking along the railway from our mates, then he dropped his money, and I found it. Then I said, erm, come on, let's have a look for it, 'cos he was on the floor already, throwing the bricks and that up, and I said there it is, like that, picked it up, and I says, I find everything. Walked a bit further on and we 'eard dogs barking, didn't we?

Osty. So we went in and had a look.

Stee. Went in and had a look at the dogs and that.

Pitts. Just as we came out, as we went in we must have run through the middle of the body and the legs and everything, 'cos we all ran in to see the dogs, and as we came out, walkin,' you could jus' see it there on the floor, right there as you looked. (*To the children around him*) Go away.

Reporter. Sensibly as you can, when did you first see the body?

Stee. When I jus' came out from the dogs. Looking at the dogs, that, I just seen it then.

Pitts. Like, you jus', as you're walking like that, there's a drop off a little wall. We looked down it, and jus' there.

Reporter. OK, thanks very much lads. Cheers. Can we just get a shot of you looking at your friend there? Don't laugh. Don't laugh, it's serious. Look as if he's talking. Don't laugh. Fine. Good lads. And the same with you looking up at your mate there. Good lad.

The interview lasted for eight minutes, but only a couple of lines were broadcast.

Monday morning, eight o'clock, and all the officers who are taking a senior role in the Bulger inquiry are gathered in the officers' dining room, upstairs at Marsh Lane, for a management briefing. The room has several tables pushed together to create a square, central table, around which the bosses are seated. It is not unlike a military Mess.

There will be two such briefings every day from now on, the second at eight o'clock each evening, followed by briefings for the whole inquiry team, at nine o'clock in the bar along the corridor.

Albert Kirby is now formally installed as the senior investigating officer, with Geoff MacDonald as his deputy. Albert will take sole responsibility for everything that happens. He carries the formatted Management Policy Book, in which he documents every, decision that is made, maintaining a complete record of the inquiry.

Geoff MacDonald has talked Albert Kirby and Jim Fitzsimmons through the post mortem, and Albert has decided to withhold the description of the injuries that James Bulger suffered from the Bulger family, from the press, the public, and the entire inquiry team, including most of the managers. The only detail that is officially released is that the body had been severed by a train.

Albert knows the family will have to be told eventually, but to do it now, he reasons, will be the straw that breaks the camel's back for them. Also, public feeling is already inflamed, and the disclosure of such horrendous information will only further incite emotion. The inquiry team has enough to handle already.

But the decision cannot prevent, and perhaps encourages, the rapid spread of rumour, which extrapolates from the known facts into lurid fantasy. The stories are always different, but none of them are true. Denise Bulger was out shoplifting when James was taken, and had to delay reporting James missing because she was getting rid of goods she had stolen. James was kept in a house and tortured before being left at the railway. He was abducted by boys for a paedophile ring. He was tied to a tree and beaten. He was strangled and set on fire. The genitals, the fingers, the head had been removed.

These tales will often begin, 'Someone who knows a police officer told me . . .'

The post mortem had shown that James had died from severe head injuries. There were multiple fractures of the skull, caused by a series of blows with heavy blunt objects. Death had occurred some time after the injuries were inflicted, but before the train had severed the body.

There were wounds all over the face and head; more than 20 separate bruises, scratches, abrasions and lacerations. A patterned bruise on the right cheek suggested a blow from a shoe. The lower lip had been partly pulled away from the jaw, perhaps by a blow or a kick.

There were bruises, and some cuts, around the body, on the shoulders, chest, arms and legs. There was no conclusive evidence of any sexual assault, but there was a small area of haemorrhaging in the pelvis, near the rectum, and the foreskin appeared 'abnormal'; it seemed to have been partly pulled back. There were linear abrasions across the buttocks, but these might have been caused by the body being dragged.

Brick dust and fragments were found on the body and in the clothing. There were no other injuries.

The managers in the dining room concentrated on the means which would lead to the identification of the two boys, and the gathering and examination of forensic evidence at the scene which would support a prosecution. There would be house to house inquiries, posters, the collection of last Friday's truancy lists from local secondary schools, and a continual round of press conferences, fronted by Albert, to feed the media and maintain public interest. Someone, somewhere must recognise those boys.

To support the forensic efforts Albert decided that every suspect would be asked to give intimate samples. Blood, fingerprints, hair, nail-clipping and a photograph. Every suspect would be entered on HOLMES as a PDF. Personal Description File: surname, forenames, birthplace, birth date, age, sex, school, height, build, hair colour, hair type, eyes, complexion, facial hair, glasses, jewellery, accent, scars and marks.

This process of trawling, the painstaking method, was the reality of detective work. It always amused Jim Fitzsimmons watching that fella on the television, the one they'd been doing the wind-up on in the ads. John Thaw, yeah, Inspector Morse. He always sat there on his own and worked everything out. If only it was that easy. You couldn't do it alone. You needed a system and the interaction of a team. And, these days, you needed a computer.

HOLMES, the Home Office Large Major Enquiry System, had evolved out of the inquest into the large, major disasters of the Yorkshire Ripper investigation more than a decade ago. Human error and the inadequacies of old-fashioned policing had allowed Peter Sutcliffe to extend his series of killings long after he should have been identified as the Yorkshire Ripper.

A Home Office research unit had developed the HOLMES system as a programme which would allow all the information coming in to the incident room on a major inquiry to be stored and indexed on computers, with a complete facility for cross-referencing. In theory, no detail could be lost, ignored or its potential significance overlooked, as had happened with Sutcliffe.

The HOLMES procedure was that all information would go to receivers for assessment, before being passed on to the indexers to be entered into the computer. If an action had been generated it would go to the allocators who assigned officers to the inquiry. The officers brought the result of the inquiry back to the receiver.

To Albert Kirby, after 26 years in the CID, there was nothing to beat HOLMES. As a management tool it was absolutely first class. Priceless. What it had saved in time and efficiency was tremendous. As the SIO he could never be expected to know everything that was happening at any one time. With the safe-guards of HOLMES he could at least know that nothing would be missed.

Merseyside's processer was at headquarters, where the equipment was kept in storage. Each of the Service's seven divisions had one station which had been wired for the installation of the Bull hardware. There were no spare rooms kept ready for major incidents at the stations. The equipment came in, and the usual occupants of the rooms went out.

At Marsh Lane it was the Parade Room which became the epicentre of the Bulger inquiry, where the HOLMES terminals were installed. Nearby were rooms G/48 and G/49, normally used by sergeants and constables, now given over to receivers and allocators. Along the corridor was G/46, the Inspectors' Locker Room, where shelving was built to take all the case exhibits.

The phones were ringing off their hooks, and boys' names were accumulating in the Parade Room. Local police officers considered the troubled and troublesome youth of their neighbourhoods, and offered up the names of any who they thought might have been involved. Friends, neighbours, relatives – mothers and fathers, brothers and sisters – phoned in with their own suspicions. Some names came up over and over again. It was surprising that so many boys could be thought capable of such a crime.

Osty and Pitts, the two brothers who had found James, had a special notoriety, not helped by the unhappy coincidence that they had discovered the body. They were favourite TIEs. They were traced, without difficulty since they were already in the police station on the Sunday, interviewed at some length, and eliminated. Their Friday had meandered in similar fashion to their Sunday afternoon. But they had not been near the Strand.

There was a Bootle boy in care who was brought to Marsh Lane on Monday. His card was marked – literally, for card filing is the system used by Merseyside Police's youth liaison officers to keep tabs on youngsters who come to their notice – with a series of allegations of previous offences. A sexual assault, a couple of physical assaults – he was said to have broken a teacher's arm – and carrying an offensive weapon, an eight-inch knife. He was also suspected of having tied a baby to the back bumper of a taxi. He was known to have been the victim of a male rape in Anfield Cemetery.

He might have been prosecuted for any or all of his offences, had he not been below the age of criminal responsibility at the time they were committed. He was now just ten years old.

There was no other boy whose alleged record more suited the killing. Albert Kirby said that if he wanted to fly by the seat of his pants, he'd say that this was the one. Case closed. But Albert did not fly by the seat of his pants. He preferred to keep his options open.

One of the officers assigned to interview the boy walked into the detention room where he was being held.

'And you can fuck off.'

The officer, Phil Roberts, a detective sergeant with considerable experience of interviewing young people, looked behind him in mock puzzlement. There was no one behind him.

'Who're you talking to?'

Phil Roberts thought this boy was totally uncontrollable, but he was able to prove his innocence. He had been nicking a bike at the time of James Bulger's abduction.

In any case, this particular boy's age had counted against him as a suspect. He might have resembled one of the two figures in the video, but he was just too young to be convincing.

The caretaker at AMEC Building, the office by the roundabout on the corner of Hawthorne and Oxford Roads, had seen all the publicity about the killing of James Bulger when he went into work on Monday.

The firm's premises were protected by a three-camera video surveillance system which ran 24 hours a day. Camera One was positioned on the front of the building, by Oxford Road. It looked down on the firm's car park and was always trained on the manager's car, wherever it might be parked.

When the caretaker got to work he thought it might be worth having a look at the recording Camera One had made on Friday afternoon. Sure enough, there were three girls, walking up the road towards AMEC, and two boys ahead of the girls, swinging a small child between them as they walked.

The caretaker called the police, and on Monday afternoon a detective called to collect the tape from him.

Albert Kirby, Geoff MacDonald and Jim Fitzsimmons sat and watched the recording. The quality was poor, poorer even than the material from the Strand, but there was no doubt it was the same three boys. As they walked past the AMEC office, they were directly alongside a low wall. It was possible to measure

89

the boys off against the wall. It looked relatively high, above their waists.

On Tuesday morning, after looking at the video again, the three men took the tape round to Hargreaves, a local supplier of professional video equipment, to see if they could enhance the quality of the tape. Despite all their high-tech hardware, Hargreaves could do little to improve the recording. The officers decided then to drive up to AMEC and see the location for themselves.

They parked, and walked over to the flower bed. Albert Kirby stood by the wall and put his hand against his leg, level with the top layer of brick. His hand was at the top of his calf, just below his knee. He had expected it to be quite a bit higher. He sat down on the wall.

'Christ, these are small kids.'

It was apparent, for the first time, that the two boys could be much younger than they had thought possible. They had been misled by the Strand video.

That afternoon, at five past four, a policewoman at Marsh Lane took a call from a man who said that the picture of the lad was the twin of his son and he didn't know what to do. His son looked like the dark-haired one. Other people had even said it was him, but the boy wouldn't talk about it. He just went up to his room. The man didn't want to come to Marsh Lane because there were too many cameras. He said he was calling from a friend's house, and would call back in half an hour. He'd rather not say his name.

The policewoman, in a state of some excitement, went rushing to Geoff MacDonald's office, and Geoff MacDonald went to share the news with Jim Fitzsimmons.

By the time the man phoned back, nearly an hour later, the policewoman had a tape recorder attached to her phone. He again said he thought his son was responsible. He said he had been passing the Strand on a bus on Friday, and seen his son there when he should have been at school. The man said that his wife and mother-in-law also knew, and were trying to protect the boy by washing his jacket, to destroy evidence. On the Friday evening he had come home to find his son trying to wash his own jacket, and now it was at the mother-in-law's home. The man gave his Christian name and again agreed to call back.

He phoned for the third and final time at twenty past five, and this time the call was being traced. The man said he would bring his son in, he just wanted it sorting. His wife didn't know he was doing this, and she would stand by the son. He had no idea who the other lad might be, but his son was in the Strand a lot. He had been given a game for Christmas that needed batteries, and the father didn't have the money for batteries. His son was thirteen. He wasn't at school on Friday, though his mother would say he was. The man finally agreed it would be better for the police to go to his son, and gave the home address: Snowdrop Street in Kirkdale. The call was traced to an address in Bootle.

There seemed to be no time to lose, and no reason to wait. Jim Fitzsimmons called together a team of detectives, and they all left Marsh Lane twenty minutes later, in a fleet of three unmarked Serious Crime Squad cars.

At Snowdrop Street one car went round to the street at the back of the house, another parked some way down the road, and Jim Fitzsimmons parked 20 yards from the front door. It was tea time, and the street was quiet.

Knowing there were two other children in the house, Jim Fitzsimmons went to the door with two male detectives and a policewoman. The mother led them in and stood there as he told her son he was being arrested on suspicion of involvement in the killing of James Bulger. The boy became upset, screaming, so Jim Fitzsimmons put his arm around the boy as he led him to the car. The mother went too, and they drove to St Anne Street station in the city centre, leaving the policewoman and other officers in the house, awaiting the arrival of an OSD search team.

There was a knock on the front door of the house, not long after Jim Fitzsimmons had left. An officer opened the door to find himself illuminated by an arc light and facing a television crew.

'Are you a police officer? Have you just arrested somebody here for the murder of James Bulger?'

By now, other people in the street were alert to the fact that something was going on. A crowd began to gather. The crowd grew and grew, and turned ever more unruly. The media gathered and watched, as the crowd's anger fermented. More police were turned out to control the crowd, and there were arrests for public order offences. It made an unhappy spectacle on the evening news.

The police brought in a van to protect the departure of the remaining people in the house. The father was collected from Bootle, and also taken to St Anne Street station. He caught up with his son while the doctor was taking the boys intimate samples. Go on, the father said to his son, tell 'em you've done it. I know you're responsible.

The father was adamant, and so was the mother. The mother was adamant that her son was not, and could not have been involved in the killing of James Bulger. She offered an innocent explanation for the washing of the jacket, and went with officers to her mother's home to collect it.

As statements were taken from the boy, the father and the mother, Jim realised that all was not as it should be. It felt wrong. It seemed that the father, for whatever reason, had mistakenly convinced himself of his son's guilt.

The boy was held overnight. Jim Fitzsimmons went home at three in the morning, and was back on at seven thirty. The truth emerged that morning. The boy had sagged school, and the father had seen his son as he passed the Strand on the bus. But this had been on the Thursday, not the Friday. When confronted with this, the father conceded that he might have got his days mixed up. The boy was released.

Later, after the family had been forced to leave their home, there was criticism of the police, the suggestion that their heavy-handed treatment had caused the family suffering. Jim couldn't help taking this criticism personally. He believed it was misplaced, but still he was angry and hurt.

By Wednesday evening, the inquiry had seen 55 TIEs and, though there were lingering suspicions over one or two names, the police did not feel any closer to finding the boys. It seemed inconceivable that no one had put them in, and yet, despite all the footwork, the press conferences, the re-runs of the video footage on television, the thousands of phone calls, sometimes 200 an hour or more, their identities remained a mystery.

There was disappointment after the drama of Snowdrop Street, and frustration at the criticism being made. There was also political concern within the Merseyside Police that the criticism could undermine public confidence and support. The pressure for a result was enormous, there was intense national and international scrutiny of the investigation, and the last thing the service needed was the erosion of its image by the growing perception that it was overzealous or bungling.

The senior officers did not have much time, or inclination, to watch TV and read the newspapers. It was like working in a vacuum. But they could hardly fail to notice the ever-swelling ranks of photographers, camera crews and reporters on duty outside Marsh Lane, swarming all over the story. They were in Albert's face three times a day at the press conferences.

He was also getting letters from people he'd never met and people he'd locked up years ago who were not in regular correspondence. They had seen Albert on the news. He was a figurehead for the inquiry, and a listening post for their views on the degraded state of society, the breakdown of the family. Albert was not entirely out of sympathy with these opinions. He was touched, really quite emotional, that people had seen fit to communicate with him.

Then, on Wednesday afternoon, and again on Thursday morning, he went out, surveying the scene at the railway, examining the likely walk the boys had taken. People kept approaching him, offering help and encouragement, and their best wishes. They all recognised Albert. He felt the encroaching burden of responsibility, the sense that he was public property.

Still, Albert would not be daunted. He knew the boys would be found. If no teachers, friends, relatives had identified them, then it was unlikely that the boys were being shielded by parents. Albert wondered if he was dealing with a freak incident in which two boys had come from outside the area. He wondered if adult paedophiles had been involved, after all.

All the evidence now suggested that the boys who had abducted James had been responsible for his death. Albert had taken the counsel of Paul Britton, a consultant psychologist he had worked with in the past, who was developing the theory and practice of offender profiling. Britton concluded that the boys would live near the location of the killing. It made sense, but there were no certainties.

Albert was going down to London on Thursday afternoon, to appear on BBC1's *Crimewatch* that evening. Perhaps that would do the trick.

Jim Fitzsimmons was pretty much on his own, at about ten thirty on Wednesday night, when a uniformed lad came through to his office with a tear-off sheet from a message pad. A woman had just called in to say that her mother's friend had a son, Jon Venables, who had been sagging school on Friday with another boy, Robert Thompson. The friend's son had come home late with paint on his jacket. The woman had seen the video, and thought there was a similarity between the figure in the light jacket and the friend's son. She had given her name and address but did not want to be contacted again. She didn't want to get involved.

Normally, the message would have gone into the system, been passed to a receiver, on to HOLMES, and out for an action. At this late hour, the system could be bypassed. Jim was sitting there reviewing a couple of TIEs rejected earlier in the week; he was brooding a little on the Snowdrop Street saga.

He went down to the HOLMES room, and found a couple of DIs from the Serious Crime Squad there. They tossed the information back and forth for a while. Jim was wary of a repeat of Snowdrop Street. On the face of it, though, the information looked good. In the end he decided to go for it.

Against the woman's wishes, someone was sent out to take a statement from her. Jim asked for local intelligence records to be checked to see if they had anything on the two names. He went through to the bar to see what detectives were still around to take on the arrests, first thing in the morning.

Among others, Phil Roberts, the detective sergeant, was there having a couple of pints. Roberts had interviewed the Snowdrop Street lad, which had left him in need of a drink.

'Listen,' said Jim Fitzsimmons, 'will you deal with this job tomorrow morning?'

'Yeah, okay.'

'Good. Just hold it there, while we make some more arrangements.' Jim asked all the detectives in the bar to wait.

Another arrest. Another boy. Phil Roberts wondered if Jimmy Fitz had it in for him. He had been off the fags for a couple of weeks. It was costing him a fortune in nicotine patches. How much longer could he hold out?

There were no local intelligence records for the two boys, but Thompson had an elder brother with some minor offences. There was a photograph of the brother, and it was possible to see a likeness with the video image of the boy in the dark clothing.

When the statement from the woman came back she had given the name of Bedford Road School. The headmistress was called at home, and added one or two details, confirming that the two boys were ten years old. Venables had two addresses, his mother's in Norris Green, and his father's in Walton. Jim found the duty night detective and asked him to get some search warrants sworn out. There would be plenty of time tomorrow for more extensive background inquiries.

Shortly before one o'clock, Jim called the detectives from the bar and, having gathered all the available officers together, led the way into the canteen, which had shut down for the night. They turned the lights on and sat around one of the canteen's circular tables, about a dozen men, all somewhat jaded at this late hour. There was no excitement. It was no big break. Just two more boys to be pulled in.

Two teams were appointed, and two team leaders: Phil Roberts for the Thompson arrest, and Mark Dale for Venables. Dale was a detective constable, but he'd been acting up to sergeant and was about to be promoted. With the memory of Snowdrop Street all too vivid, and the anxiety that it was about to be repeated, Jim thought it would be wiser if the officers came on in the morning at stations away from Marsh Lane – the Thompson team at Walton Lane and the Venables team at Lower Lane. The boys would be held and interviewed at those stations. That and the early start, he hoped, would keep the arrests secret from the press.

Jim decided not to go out on the arrests himself. He would need to brief the management team in the morning. He wanted to hear immediately afterwards, though, how the arrests had gone, and whether or not the officers thought Thompson and Venables were likely candidates.

17

At seven thirty on Thursday morning, Ann Thompson was woken by her son Bobby. 'Mum, there's four men on the doorstep, you'd better get up.' Ann answered the front door to find Phil Roberts and three other detectives on the steps. Two more were round the back of the house, down an entry. Phil Roberts produced the search warrant, and explained why they were there.

Ann Thompson was flustered and anxious, but she invited them in, and they followed her down the hall into the front room, past baby Ben, Bobby's 18-month-old brother, in his pram.

Ryan was in the front room, and went to fetch Bobby, who came in and sat down on the edge of the settee. Phil Roberts, who was over six feet tall, got down on his knees in front of Bobby and told him he was being arrested on suspicion of being involved in the murder of James Bulger. They had reason to believe he was responsible. Bobby started to cry. 'I didn't kill him,' he said. His mum began crying too. She was very distressed.

While Bobby went off to get changed, Phil Roberts spoke to Ryan, who told him that Bobby had said he'd seen James Bulger with two boys at the Strand. Phil Roberts thought this was probably fanciful. A figment of Ryan's, or Bobby's, imagination.

Ann Thompson's friend, Lesley Henderson, was called in from across the road to mind the house and look after Ben and Ryan, because Ann was going to Walton Lane police station with Bobby.

An OSD search team would be going into the house later, but the detectives were particularly keen to find Bobby's shoes and his school uniform. They collected a pair of shoes, a pair of trainers, some black trousers, a white shirt, a grey jumper and Bobby's black jacket. There was another bag of shoes upstairs, with Bobby's brogies inside. The bag was forgotten in the rush, and someone had to go back for it, later. When the brogues were examined, it appeared, even to the naked eye, that they were spattered with blood.

When they arrived at Jon's father's maisonette, at ten to eight, Mark Dale and his five colleagues had no idea if Jon would be there or over at his mother's in Norris Green.

Neil Venables invited them in. He had Michelle and Mark staying with him, but Jon was with his mum. Two detectives stayed to meet the OSD team and supervise the search, and the other four drove to Susan's house, the old family home in

Scarsdale Road on the Norris Green estate.

Mark Dale produced his second search warrant and Susan Venables ushered them into the hallway. 'I knew you'd be here,' she said. 'I told him you'd want to see him for sagging school on Friday.'

See whom? Mark Dale enquired. 'Our Jon.'

Jon Venables came down the stairs then, and they all went into the living room. Susan turned to Jon.

'There you are, sagging, I told you they'd be here.'

She turned back to Mark Dale.

'He came home on Friday, coat full of paint.'

Back to Jon.

'Paint, sagging, I told you they'd be here.'

Mark Dale asked Susan to show him the coat. They all went back into the hall, to the well under the stairs. Jon took his mustard anorak from one of the coat pegs, and threw it down at the officers' feet. George Scott, one of Dale's colleagues, picked it up. He and Mark Dale could see the blue paint on the sleeve. Susan said it was Jon's.

They went back into the living room, and Mark Dale told Jon he was being arrested on suspicion of the abduction and murder of James Bulger. Jon grabbed hold of his mother, crying and yelling.

'I don't want to go to prison, mum. I didn't kill the baby.'

'Don't be silly, Jon, you won't go to prison. They're just doing their job.'

It seemed as if Susan Venables could not or would not grasp the seriousness of Jon's arrest. Mark Dale and George Scott took her into the kitchen, to speak to her and explain the meaning of the caution that Jon had been given.

Jon was still crying. The other officers tried to calm him down with chat about school. 'It's that Robert Thompson,' said Jon. 'He always gets me into trouble.'

As Mark Dale and George Scott returned, Jon asked, 'Are you going to speak to Robert Thompson?'

'Why, do you think we should?'

'Yes.' Jon went upstairs to get washed and dressed, still very upset.

When Jon left, Mark Dale and George Scott stayed behind with Susan Venables, to oversee the OSD search. They asked Susan what Jon had been wearing on Friday, and she produced a pair of black trousers from the pile of clean washing in the corner of the living room. The wash had not removed a blue paint stain from the trouser leg.

Jon was driven to Lower Lane police station. The officers in the car told Jon he could have breakfast at the station, and asked him what he'd like. He wanted Rice Krispies. 'Is someone with Robert Thompson now?' Jon wanted to know. 'Which police station will he be going to?'

When they arrived at Lower Lane, Jon was signed in at the bridewell, the cell area, and installed in the juvenile detention room with a mug of tea and a plate of toast from the canteen. The detention room was small and bare, not unlike a cell, with plain painted walls bearing the graffiti of previous occupants. There was a high window with reinforced glass, and one piece of furniture – a long, wooden bench, firmly embedded into the wall. Jon sat on the bench and ate his breakfast.

Jim Fitzsimmons phoned round at the first opportunity, keen to know how the arrests had gone, even keener to canvass opinion on the two boys. It was not overly encouraging.

'What d'you think?' Jim asked Phil Roberts.

'I haven't got a clue,' said Phil Roberts, who knew how excitable the bosses could be, and wasn't about to commit himself. A ten-year-old boy, responsible for that killing? Phil Roberts found it hard to believe, though he wouldn't dismiss the possibility.

Reaching Dave Tanner, one of the officers who had delivered Jon to Lower Lane, Jim found no greater enthusiasm. They had a coat, which resembled the coat in the video. It had blue paint on the sleeve. But they could see little if any resemblance between Jon and the boy in the video.

When he arrived at Marsh Lane for the morning briefing, to bring the management team up to date with overnight developments, Jim was not exactly jumping up and down. Two more boys in, and nothing more than a few fragments of circumstantial evidence to link them to James Bulger's killing. They would simply have to wait to see what came out of the interviews. Meanwhile, a great deal of preparatory work had to be completed and a dilemma was building for Albert Kirby. To go, or not to go, to *Crimewatch*.

Earlier in the week, a policewoman on duty at the Strand had been approached by a counter hand from the Bradford & Bingley Building Society. He had seen all the publicity surrounding the abduction, and thought the two boys had been in the Society's branch, across Stanley Road from the Strand, that Friday afternoon. He handed over two video tapes from the branch's own surveillance system. The boys ought to be on the tapes.

The tapes had been delivered to Marsh Lane, and stored on the shelves of room G/46, the Inspectors' Locker Room, along with all the other case exhibits. On Wednesday, late afternoon, a detective constable retrieved the tapes and played them through. He could see two boys, fooling around and touching, as they did so, the walls, the fittings, the windows.

The detective called in a couple of forensic officers from SOCO, and showed them the videos. Then they all went round to the Building Society, where the forensic officers dusted with their white powder and, using tape, lifted nine good finger and palm prints from the inside and the outside of the front display window. The prints were taken to the Fingerprint Bureau at headquarters, where they were given serial numbers before being stored. 1048/93E was an impression of a small, left thumb, and 1048/93F was an impression of a small, left middle finger.

It was late morning on Thursday by the time the arresting officers got around to fingerprinting Bobby and Jon. The police surgeon was on her way to the two stations, to take the intimate samples, but the surgeon was not required for fingerprints.

While his hands were being inked with the roller, Jon asked, 'Do you leave these on whatever you touch? Will Robert Thompson be getting his done too?'

The completed prints were driven down to the Bureau at headquarters, and there compared with the prints from the Bradford & Bingley Building Society. There was no similarity for Bobby's, but the Senior Fingerprint Officer had no doubt that Jon's left thumb and left middle finger were an identical match with 1048/93E and 1048/93F. This, at least, put Jon in Stanley Road by the Strand, last Friday afternoon.

When the police surgeon arrived at Walton Lane, just after midday, Bobby gave up his intimate samples: blood, a nail clipping from each hand, a plucked hair from the head, and a combed hair. The surgeon also had to examine the two boys and make sure they were in a fit state to be detained and interviewed. Bobby, she noted, was well nourished, with no visible injuries. She found mud on his hands, and on his left ear.

Throughout the examination Bobby's mum was sitting just outside, weeping quietly.

Bobby was returned to Walton Lane's detention room which, though possibly decorated with more graffiti, was otherwise indistinguishable from its counterpart at Lower Lane. After a while, Bobby began crying and banging on the door. The custody sergeant went to see what was up.

'Why am I here? I wanna go home.'

'Come on lad, you know why you're here.'

'I didn't kill him. I saw him once with his mum.'

The custody sergeant told Bobby he was under caution and would be wise not to say anything more. He did his best to placate him, and locked the door.

At Lower Lane, the police surgeon found a slim, healthy boy with a graze on his right knee. She took Jon's intimate samples and, as she did so, Jon asked, 'If you touch someone's skin does it leave a fingerprint? If you drag someone really hard do you leave your nails in his skin?'

18

The news filtered back to Marsh Lane. Blue paint stains on clothes, possible blood stains on shoes, bizarre comments from the boys . . . Jim Fitzsimmons began to think it looked good. He had to caution himself. Snowdrop Street had looked good, too.

Here at the heart of the inquiry, the mood was becoming electric. Tired people, depleted of energy, with little more than adrenalin to keep them going, wondered if this was the last stretch. They were anxious to get the interviews started, but didn't want to trip up in the rush. There were so many things to consider.

The station was awash with senior officers. The Chief Constable, Jim Sharpies, had come down from headquarters with Pauline Clare, the Assistant Chief Constable in charge of Crime, and George Bundred, the chair of the Merseyside Police Authority. They weren't there to take over, they just wanted to offer some encouragement, and to see for themselves what was happening.

The interview teams had to be selected. They had to be briefed. The interviews could be video recorded, but the only video suites were at outlying stations. Was it better to move the boys and risk unsettling them, or forget the video, and go with conventional sound recording?

There was also the new Downstream Monitoring equipment. A twin cassette recorder, not unlike those fixed in the interview rooms, but portable, and with an additional unit which could be placed in an adjoining room with a speaker or headphones, to enable other officers to eavesdrop on the interviews. It also meant a Pallen typist could transcribe the interviews as they went along. Merseyside had Downstream Monitoring, but it only had one set. It could only be used if the interviews were staggered, one after the other, running the machine back and forth between the two stations where the boys were being held. Also, the machine was already in use elsewhere, and they would have to wait until it became available.

Albert Kirby was keeping an eye and an ear on these discussions, and preparing his own brief for *Crimewatch*. He still wasn't sure whether to go. He was due on the four thirty flight from Manchester. He didn't want to be away overnight. George Bundred stepped in and said the police authority would pick up the bill for the helicopter Mike One to meet Albert outside London after the programme and fly him home. This helped, but it didn't remove the central dilemma.

It was Jim Sharpies who finally resolved the issue.

'Are you happy', he said to Albert Kirby, 'that these are the right two boys?'

The answer had to be, and was, 'No sir, I can't say I'm happy it's them.'

'Well, go for it then.'

And Albert went, blazing down the outside lane of the M62 in a marked police car, round the M56 to the airport, where he just made the flight.

At Heathrow, he was met by the *Crimewatch* researcher, who sat with him in the back of the car, going over notes as they drove through West London to Television Centre. Albert was impressed by the meticulous attention to detail. But the travel and the tension were taking their toll. He was beginning to feel decidedly manky.

Throughout the day, OSD search teams had been back and forth from the three addresses, rummaging for anything that might be significant. They bagged and labelled numerous extra pieces of clothing, and various pairs of shoes and trainers.

At Bobby's home they found a bamboo cane, a copper cylinder

with protruding prongs, two studded leather bracelets, a belt, a Sainsbury's carrier bag full of cassettes, and a Manchester United tracksuit top. At Jon's father's maisonette an officer found a child's drawing lying in the bottom of a wardrobe. It depicted a scene in the film *Halloween*. From his mother's home they took Jon's *Thunderbirds* computer game and his sketch pad.

As the OSD searches were finishing, the arresting officers gathered at Marsh Lane for a last briefing before the start of the interviews. Video recording was out, and they could wait no longer for the Downstream Monitoring. In any case, it would be too cumbersome, staggering the interviews for the benefit of the extra equipment.

Jim Fitzsimmons would dearly have liked to have been one of the interviewers. All detectives think they are good at interviewing and Jim was no exception, but he knew it wasn't his job this time. He would stay at Marsh Lane to act as the coordinator. It would take the pressure off the two teams, and he could feed information from one to the other.

Phil Roberts remained team leader for Bobby's interviews. He would be accompanied by Bob Jacobs, and there would be two back-up officers in the station for support. Mark Dale would go in with George Scott, and they too would have a back-up team.

There was no question of telling them how to conduct the interviews. They were all trained and experienced, and they knew what was required. But the ages of the boys could not be ignored, and neither could the fact that it seemed as if the whole world was watching. To fuck up now would be catastrophic.

Interviews were about getting to the truth. Sometimes this meant putting people under pressure, pushing them that bit further. You might provoke anger or tears, if that would get an honest response. It was about judgement, and instinctively suiting the approach to the moment.

There could be none of that now. No pushing, no pressure, no ploughing on through a child's distress. That would be wrong. It could be disastrous. The boys' lawyers would be there; let them decide. Watch for tiredness, hunger, and keep checking with the lawyers: are they happy to carry on?

Okay, good luck, keep me informed, let's go.

19

Roberts. This interview is being tape recorded. I am Detective Sergeant Roberts . . .

Nicotine was seeping into Phil Roberta's system through the patch on his arm. It wasn't much nicotine. If he could bottom this lad quickly, maybe he could still hold out.

Roberts . . . the other officer present is . . .
Jacobs. Detective Constable Jacobs.

Bob Jacobs was from the Serious Crime Squad. It was the first time he and Phil Roberts had interviewed together.

PACE – the Police And Criminal Evidence Act – demanded that interviews be recorded. Each interview could last no longer than three quarters of an hour, determined by the length of the one-sided, 45-minute tapes. The recorder was a twin-deck machine, requiring two tapes recording the interview simultaneously. The tapes came individually packaged, to be unwrapped in the room. At the end, one would be retained for police use, the other sealed with a wrap-around sticky label and signed by an interviewing officer and the suspect's lawyer. A buzzer sounded when the machine began recording, and sounded again a few seconds before the tapes finished.

Roberts. Now, what's your full name?
Bobby. Robert Thompson.
Roberts. And what's your date of birth, Robert?
Bobby. Twenty-third, I think, of the eighth.

Roberts. Yeah, is it August?

Bobby. Eighty-two.

Roberts. Say yes. You nodded your head there.

Bobby. Yes. (*The voice is slight, timid and unbroken.*)

Roberts. Okay. Right, the date is the eighteenth of February, 1993, the time on my watch is now 17.57 hours. That means it's three minutes to six, all right. Also present in this room is your mother, if you could introduce yourself . . .

Ann. Ann Thompson.

Roberts . . . and your legal representative . . .

Lee. Jason Lee from Paul Rooney and Company.

Lee is a smart young clerk from Rooney's, a city firm of solicitors. He works out of the branch office on Stanley Road in Bootle, a writ's throw from the Strand, and has been called out because he's worked for the Thompson family before. He got out of bed to answer the phone, first thing this morning, and went down to Walton Lane. He's playing it by ear, waiting to see what unfolds.

Roberts. Right, this interview is being conducted in an interview room at Walton Lane Police Station . . .

The interview room, just off the bridewell area at the back of the station, is barely big enough for the five people it now contains. There is one small, reinforced window. The tape recorder is fixed to the wall, with the microphone suspended from a hook just to the right. Beneath the recorder is a formica-topped table around which the group are seated. Bob Jacobs is nearest the mike, next to Phil Roberts, who sits sideways on, close up to, and facing Bobby, to establish an intimacy between them. Bobby's feet touch the ground, but only just. Phil Roberts will notice that he seems to shuffle them back and forth when he is being evasive. Ann is next to Bobby, and then Jason Lee, leaning on the table, making notes.

Roberts. Now, at the conclusion of this interview I will give you a notice, right, which will explain what's going to happen to the tapes after, do you understand? Right, now I want you to listen to this. You are not obliged to say anything unless you wish to do so, right, but whatever you do say may be given in evidence – do you understand? Right, that means what you say here, you don't have to say anything, right, but it's entirely up to you. You say yes, don't nod your head. Say yes.

Bobby. Yes.

Roberts. Do you understand?

Jacobs. Just that you understand . . .

Roberts. Are you all right? Do you understand what I mean? Erm, and that, er, if you do say something it may go to court, may be given in evidence. Do you understand all that?

That was the caution. It has to be repeated at the start of every interview. The officers and the lawyer have to be satisfied that Bobby knows what it means.

Jacobs. So you understand what . . .

Roberts. You're shaking your head again there, Robert.

Bobby. Yeah.

Roberts. What do they call you? Robert or Bobby?

Bobby. All of them.

Jacobs. Bobby, isn't it?

Roberts. All of them. Bobby's a more friendly name, do you agree? You did it again.

Bobby. Yeah.

Roberts. All right, then.

Jacobs. But, yeah, what we'll be doing is asking you some questions, and you don't have to answer them if you don't want to, right. But, if you do answer them, then they can be brought to court at a later stage. Do you understand that Bobby, yes?

Roberts. You nodded your head again.

Bobby. Yeah.

Roberts. Mrs Thompson, are you all right?

Ann. I've got a headache.

Roberts. Pardon?

Ann. I've got a terrible headache.

Roberts. You've got a terrible headache. Are you all right to, are we all right to continue with the interview? Yes? You're nodding your head now.

Ann. Yeah.

Roberts. Righto, okay. Right Bobby, I came round to your house this morning, didn't I?

Bobby. Yeah.

Roberts. And what did I say to you?

Bobby. I'm arresting you.

Roberts. Correct. What for?

Bobby. James.

Roberts. James, what about James?

Bobby. That you said on suspicion of murdering him.

Jacobs. That's right.

Roberts. That's well remembered, very well remembered. That's good. I'm going to tell you something else now, which is more or less the same. I'm also arresting you, right, for abducting James, okay?

Bobby. What does abducting mean?

Roberts. On suspicion of abducting, meaning taking away from.

Bobby. I never took him.

Phil Roberts cautions Bobby for the abduction of James Bulger. He doesn't have to say anything, but if he does say something . . .

Bobby says yes, he understands this, and Roberts begins questioning him about last Friday, about how his day began. Bobby describes calling for Gummy Gee, meeting Jon on County Road, and going to the Strand. When they begin talking over the route Bobby and Jon took to the Strand there is some confusion as the two officers fail to recognise Bobby's references to local places.

Bobby says that, once at the Strand, he and Jon ran round, going through shops, though he can't remember which shops they went through, and then went to the library. When the officers wonder how long this took, and whether he was hungry, Bobby remembers going to McDonalds. Asked if he ate at all that day, after breakfast, Bobby jumps forward to the evening when they ran the message for the girl in the video shop, and Jon's mum came and battered him. That was at about six o'clock.

Roberts says he's struggling with the time. Bobby wants to know what he means, struggling. Roberts says he's trying to find out what time it is.

They talk about the library, and Bobby says they were in the kids' corner. Then Roberts asks if Bobby knows about James. Bobby says he took flowers over yesterday. Roberts says did Bobby see James at the Strand. Bobby says, yeah. In the morning. On the Friday. When he and Jon were going up the escalators. He was with his mum and he was wearing a blue coat. He can't remember the colour of James's hair. He thinks it was black or something.

Roberts moves the time frame forward to the video shop, asking about Susan Venables and why she had gone after Bobby and Jon. There has been no change of tone, but Roberts's heart is pumping at Bobby's mention of seeing James and his mother. Surely, this means . . . no, keep cool, tunnel vision, don't show any reaction.

They talk for a while about the clothes that the two boys were wearing that day. Descriptions of jackets and shoes. And can you remember anything else that James was wearing? Just the coat. He had never seen him before, and never saw him again, except in the paper.

Bobby is asked if he understands the difference between truth and lies, and says he does. What team does he support? Everton. If they said Everton won ten nil last Saturday, what would that be? A lie. If they said there were five people in the room, what would that be? The truth.

Bobby agrees that he knows the difference between right and wrong. He agrees it's wrong that James should have been killed.

He didn't take special notice of James in the Strand, he was just looking round. Roberts thinks that looking over the escalator it would be hard to look over and see. Over the sea? Over the escalators. You said the sea then. No, escalators.

They go back and forth, over this sighting of James and his mother. Where they were standing, where Bobby and Jon were standing. How Bobby looked at James and his mother. Then Bobby describes leaving the Strand, going to the library, and going back towards home. It was getting dark then. They didn't call at any other shops.

The buzzer goes. End of interview. 18.40 hours. Phil Roberts comes out of the interview room. Give me a packet of fags, now.

At Lower Lane, the first interview with Jon Venables begins five minutes after Bobby's has started, just after six o'clock. The procedure is identical, and though the interview room is slightly larger, it is otherwise the same as Walton Lane's. It could be the exact same formica-topped table, in the corner, below the window. The tape recorder, the mike on a hook, Jon, his mother Susan, their solicitor Lawrence Lee – nearly 40, balding slightly, office out of town, on the West Derby Road – and the interviewing officers, Mark Dale and George Scott.

Jon is very intimidated. His voice little more than a nervous squeak.

Scott. Do you understand what the truth is, Jon?
Jon. Yeah.
Scott. Go on, you tell us what you think the truth is.
Jon. Something that's true what you done.
Scott. And so if you were telling lies what would you be doing?
Jon. I don't know.
Scott. Explain what you think by what telling lies means.
Dale. Is telling lies wrong?
Jon. Yeah.
Dale. Okay, that's important isn't it?
Jon. Yeah.
Dale. So if I said Jon Venables had a green face and pink hair that would be a lie?
Jon. Yeah.
Dale. Okay, so you understand what a lie is, don't you?
Jon. Yeah.
Dale. And you understand what the truth is, don't you?
Jon. Yeah.
Dale. It's the opposite, okay. Now we've never met before this morning, have we?
Jon. No.

Dale. So I don't know anything about you, do I?
Jon. No.
Dale. So I'm going to have to ask you some questions about yourself.
Jon. All right.

Jon describes his two homes, his brother and sister. He says he's happy at school, but sometimes the lads bully him, especially one lad. But that lad bullies everybody. Jon lists his friends, including Robert Thompson, and says he doesn't go near him at school, because Robert causes trouble. They're in the same class, but don't sit together. Robert calls people names. He likes skitting. He doesn't have many friends because he's too naughty. He only plays with girls now because he can't play with anyone else.

Jon had been fighting Robert when they first met and became friends, before Jon knew he sagged off and that. Jon only sees Robert out of school when Jon's staying at his dad's. At Norris Green he plays out on his bike with other children. He usually has to go in quite early, but with Robert he comes in dead late, because Robert says they can do good things, like going on the railway. Robert stays out all night sometimes, going down the entries, lighting fires to keep warm, walking on the railway. He said he walked all the way to London once, but Jon doesn't believe him.

Dale. Would you say that he was your good friend?
Jon. No.
Dale. Why not?
Jon. Oh, I know, 'cos he gets me into trouble and that.
Dale. Don't you think you get yourself into trouble?
Jon. Yeah.
Dale. Really?
Jon. Yeah.
Dale. So that's not fair on Robert, is it?
Jon. No.
Dale. 'Cos you're blaming him a little bit, aren't you?
Jon. Sometimes I tell him to do things and he does.
Dale. So you're as bad as him really, aren't you, in that respect?
Jon. No, when I say to him sag, he doesn't. He said, 'cos you won't,

you'll get a bad education

Dale. Who said that?

Jon. Me, and he says, all right then, and the teachers kidded him up. He said, she said if you stay a whole week at school I'll give you a prize at the end of the week, and she never.

Jon says he is not Robert's best friend any more, but he was once, when Robert gave him things, like toy trolls.

Dale. Well, what are they?

Jon. You know, the things that have the, their hair sticks up, you know them little thingies, them little you know them troll things where their hair sticks up in different colours.

Dale. Are they a doll, though? Are they like a little doll?

Jon. Yeah.

Lee. Gonks.

Dale. Oh, like they used to call gonks years ago?

Jon. Yeah.

Dale. Right.

Jon. It shows you their bum and that.

Dale. Do they? That's a bit rude, isn't it?

Jon. Yeah.

Dale. I hope you don't look?

Jon. No.

He didn't know at first that Robert was robbing them. Jon threw them away, but you were supposed to collect them.

Dale. Robert collects them?

Jon. Yeah. He's much of a girl.

Dale. Mmm.

Jon. He's much of a girl, he sucks dummies.

Dale. You think he's a girl, do you?

Jon. And sucks his thumb.

Dale. Well, that's not so bad, sucking your thumb. I mean, you shouldn't do it, but . . .

Jon. No, he does it all the time.

Sometimes they played out together with Robert's mates, and sometimes they went off on their own, down the entries, walking on the walls, and climbing over into people's gardens. He knew it was naughty, but it was fun. He had only gone pinching with Robert once, and that was last Friday.

They talk then about robbing from shops and being on County Road. Jon says Robert sags off nearly every day, and once he had gone to the Strand with Ryan, and lost him, and the teacher had to go and and collect Ryan. Jon never sags without Robert, except one time, at his old school. Normally, with Robert, he runs out of school at playtime. Except last Friday, when they didn't go to school first. Sagging is something to do. They can't usually go out at playtime because they're naughty in class. Also, he's slow at his work, and has to stay in at breaks and finish it. He does like school, though.

As the tape finishes, Mark Dale says he'll put another tape in, and talk to Jon about the three times he's bunked off since he's been in the third year.

In the quarter of an hour between interviews, Jon has a Mars Bar and a tin of Coke, and the second tape starts running at seven o'clock. Dale begins to talk Jon through his sagging experiences.

In September he had been in the park with Robert when they were found by a boy and a girl who knew Robert. They said they were taking him home, and Robert began crying because he didn't want to go. So the boy and girl picked him up and carried him. Jon went back to his dad's, but his dad was out, so he went to wait with friends.

They had been going to rob some milk out of the dairy that day, but a man saw them and shouted. They just wandered around Walton.

The next time, they had run out of school at the first break. It was the idea of both of them to sag, but it was Jon's idea first. He didn't go home for 12 hours, until half ten at night. They went to County Road and robbed, calling people names out the shops and that, stealing crisps and drinks from Kwik Save.

Robert poured a tin of Roses down inside his coat. Jon ate about ten and felt sick.

They went into the wallpaper shop and Robert stole some borders. Robert said he was going to throw the borders, and Jon said that was a silly thing to do. Dale wonders if he really said that, or actually said it would be a laugh. Jon laughs. Dale says, you thought it was a laugh, didn't you? Mmm, a bit, says Jon. You blame Robert all the time, don't you? It's me sometimes.

> *Dale.* Do you think it's exciting being with Robert, really?
> *Jon.* Yeah, a bit.
> *Dale.* Be honest, be honest with me.
> *Jon.* Yeah.
> *Dale.* Is it, do you do things with him you wouldn't normally do with your other friends?
> *Jon.* Yeah, I wouldn't do anything with me other friends.
> *Dale.* Why?
> *Jon.* Because they're good.
> *Dale.* Are they?
> *Jon.* Yeah.
> *Dale.* Would you do these things on your own?
> *Jon.* No.
> *Dale.* Why?
> *Jon.* I'm too scared.

They go back to the day, and Jon tells how they had called for Michael Gee later, after the shops closed, and were in Walton Village messing around in the chippy, climbing the back gardens behind his dad's old flat, going down the entries, knocking on doors and running away, playing in the bin yards. Robert had once asked Jon if he liked breaking in houses, but Jon had said no.

Finally, that night, Jon's mum had found him and chased him in Walton Village. He stopped because he didn't want to run away.

There had been another time, not long after that, when his mum found him, at two o'clock in the afternoon on County

Road. He had not bunked off again, until last Friday, when they didn't even go into school in the morning.

It had been Robert's idea to sag. Jon had wanted to go to school, because he wanted to take the gerbils home, but Robert had said they could get the *Where's Wally?* books. What are they? There's big pictures of different people, you've got to find this one person, you know, like somewhere in the picture. Lawrence Lee wants to know what the books are called. Jon says *Where's Wally?* Lawrence Lee says *Where Is Wally?* Yeah. Ah, right.

Robert said to Jon, you better come with me, or I'm setting these lads on to you. Is that the truth? Yeah. Susan says, God's honest truth? Yeah, you think I'm telling lies don't you? Dale says he doesn't know, he just hopes Jon is telling the truth; sometimes it's hard to tell.

Jon says he Robert and Ryan had sagged together, and Ryan didn't go in until six that evening. They went to Walton Park. The weather was greyish, a bit warmish and coldish. They went to the old unused railway. Not the one that's alive, the one that's dead. They went along the railway for a bit, and then to Long Lane and the MFI, going in the kitchens, playing around, hiding in the showers and that.

Dale and Scott are uncertain of the locations, and Susan Venables tries to explain them. She says she knows her areas. Jon says they played on the big swing by the Littlewoods on Walton Hall Avenue, then walked through the park to the Aldi on County Road, cutting through the streets by the Argos, going up the road to the chemists, messing about in the lifts in the big block of flats.

They went down Scotland Road and across to the Liverpool football ground. Robert said they should look at the names on the Hillsboro' things, and asked Jon if he wanted to get the flowers. Jon said no, they're people's memories. So they looked at the names, and then went up to the cemetery, where Robert showed Jon his family's graves, and Jon showed Robert his nan's and grandad's.

They saw the fire in the betting shop on County Road, and then they went into the Village to the video shop. Susan, who has been helping out with locations, says aren't you forgetting something? Jon says, oh yeah, they went to Fads and stole that paint, and Robert threw it over him, down the entry by Olney Street. When Robert threw the paint Jon said his mum was going to kill him, and Ryan was laughing. Then they went to the Village and Ryan said he was going in, and Robert and Jon went to the video shop.

Jon tells the story of going to collect the money for the video, and being caught in the shop by his mum and taken to the police station. The policeman had said if he did it again he'd go in a home. Then his mum took him home, and Jon went to bed.

The buzzer goes, the second interview finishes. It is just before a quarter to eight. Dale and Scott, of course, know that Jon was at the Strand on Friday. But there's no rush. Plenty of time to get to that. Jon has become comfortable, and more confident, with the relaxed, unchallenging questions.

Bobby's second interview begins shortly after eight o'clock. He's been in the detention room, having a cup of tea and a cheese sandwich from the canteen. Jim Fitzsimmons has been liaising with the two interviewing teams, passing on to Phil Roberts the news that Jon has been everywhere on Friday, except the Strand.

Roberts asks Bobby about his interests. Bobby says he supports Everton, but doesn't go to matches. What's his hobby then? Skipping school, says Bobby laughing. Bob Jacobs says that's not a hobby that's a profession, when you do it as well as Bobby does.

When he was at the house this morning, says Roberts, he noticed the trolls. Yes, Bobby has been collecting them for a few months. Was he in a shop at the Strand last Friday, looking at trolls? No. Well, the officers believe he was. Bobby asks what shop. A shop in the Strand that sells trolls. There's quite a lot of them says Bobby, but yes, he was looking at trolls in a shop. Then why did he say no? Because he thought they meant a troll shop, a shop that just sold trolls.

Roberts says Jon has been talking to other officers. Bobby wants to know if he's here at Walton Lane. No, he's at Lower Lane, and he's saying he wasn't at the Strand. But we were, says Bobby. Why is he scared of saying he was, then? Because his mum or his dad will come down and get him. No, that's not the reason, it's because something happened, didn't it? Like the baby got took, says Bobby. Yes. Not by me. Bobby says he wasn't with Jon all the time. Did Jon grab the baby? Bobby doesn't know, perhaps Jon made the baby follow them, and then got him lost somewhere. Is that what happened? Bobby doesn't know, he didn't look back.

The officers now speak of the video footage, and explain that they've been able to pick out James with two boys. Bobby says it's not him because he wouldn't take James. Roberts says there's a boy with a similar jacket. Bobby says many jackets get sold the same as his. But there's also a boy with a jacket like Jon's, walking next to James. Yeah, well he's not walking along with me.

Bobby will not admit that he or Jon have been with James. The officers leave the subject, and begin to talk again about what Bobby did on Friday. Bobby admits that he sometimes steals food from the shelves of shops. Not trolls. Just food. Pepperami.

The officers tell Bobby they're not bothered about anything he's stolen. It doesn't matter to them if he's taken 20 trolls. And they know a lot of lads go to the Strand and steal. They're not bothered about that, they just want to know the truth about Friday.

Bobby again says, I never took the baby. Everyone by theirs says it looks like him and Jon on the video. It looks like Jon that's taken the baby.

Roberts tells Bobby about speaking to Ryan this morning, Ryan telling him how Bobby had said that he'd seen two boys with James. Bobby says he never said that. Roberts says he wouldn't tell lies. Bobby says no, but Ryan is.

They talk about Ryan for a while, about the time Bobby lost

him at the Strand. Then Roberts says they have a description of two boys from the shop that sells trolls, which matches the two boys on the video, and matches Jon and Bobby. He says he thinks Bobby saw more of James, because he wouldn't remember the blue coat from a brief glance. They go to and fro over this, with no concession from Bobby.

> *Roberts.* We believe that you left with baby James and with Jon.
> *Bobby.* Who says?
> *Roberts.* We say, now.
> *Bobby.* No. I never left with him.
> *Roberts.* Well, tell me what happened, then.
> *Bobby.* It shows in the paper that Jon had hold of his hand.

Roberts isn't asking about what it says in the paper, or what Bobby's friends say. It's not trying to make Bobby feel bad, it's not to bring up nasty memories or anything. It's just the truth, that's all. Bobby says he never touched him. He begins crying. I never touched him.

That's why you've noticed the anorak, says Roberts, because Jon had hold of James's hand, isn't that right? Yes. Bobby says Jon grabbed the baby's hand and just walked round the Strand. Then he let him go loose. He let him go when they were by the church, by the Smiley. Bobby says he told Jon to take him back. He begins crying again. He's getting all the blame. He's going to get all the blame for murdering him, but they left him by the church.

Roberts asks if James could talk. Bobby says Jon asked him his name and where he lived. Bobby imitates a baby's cry. He went, I want me mum, and started crying. Jon said he was going to find her. James didn't say his name or where he lived.

The officers try to challenge Bobby's assertion that they left James at the church. Roberts says they have a statement from a woman who saw three boys on the reservoir. Bobby doesn't know anything about that. There's lots of people with the same coats as him and Jon.

The buzzer goes. Bobby asks if he'll be able to go home tonight. We don't know yet, we don't know yet. Okay.

Bobby isn't going home, and neither is Jon. The two interviewing teams are talking to Jim Fitzsimmons, swapping information, wondering how best to proceed. Should they do another interview, or will the boys be too tired? Ideally, let's get another one in tonight, but leave the choice to the lawyers.

They decide to close the two police stations, which means no other prisoners will be accommodated in the cells. The boys' families and their legal representatives will have the run of the bridewell. Duty social workers are called in. Bedding collected from local care homes. Police stations are never closed, but this is different, and it looks like being a long haul.

Even now, there can be no certainty that these two boys killed James Bulger. Forensic will show if James's blood appears on the boys' shoes and clothing. But, essentially, it's all down to the interviews. They need admissions, just like the old saying: no cough, no job.

After some discussion, everybody is happy with one more interview. Bobby goes again just after nine thirty, a few minutes before the start of *Crimewatch* on BBC 1.

Straight off, Bobby says you'll find out in the end it was him that took the baby. You know I'm not lying, you'll get his face up on the video. I never had hold of his hand.

Again, he says that they left James by the church. Phil Roberts describes in detail the statement given by the woman on the reservoir. He says he believes it's Bobby and Jon with James. Bobby insists they left him at the church. They never went up on the hill.

Phil Roberts reminds Bobby that he's said he understands the difference between truth and lies. He told a lie before, and then said it was Jon, holding James's hand. Bobby knows, but he never had hold of his hand.

The woman on the reservoir spoke of an injury on James's head, says Roberts. Bobby says that was on his head when he saw him. A bump or what? No, it was like a graze. Like a stone had been thrown at him and it had just grazed him. Bobby points to his forehead.

Roberts says the woman on the reservoir was worried about the injury, and thought James should go to the hospital. Bobby says they never went up on the hill. The woman might be lying.

Roberts and Jacobs press, and press, but Bobby will not concede to the reservoir. He fences with the officers. He says they could be lying, too. Finally, his mother intervenes.

Ann. Do you want to sort all this tonight?
Bobby. Where?
Ann. Do you want to sort all this out tonight?
Bobby. Yeah.
Ann. Tell the truth.
Bobby. I am.
Roberts. Bobby, I know, I know when you're about to tell us the truth because you fill up with your eyes, do you understand what I mean? And I can say that, it was like before, you know, when you told us eventually about the, meeting him in the Strand, right, you filled up before again. I think you were going to tell us that you were on top of that hill.
Bobby. We were.

That's better, isn't it? Just tell the truth. Roberts wants to know what happened there. When James fell. Bobby says the graze was already on his head. He was crying for his mum. He said he wants his mum, and they said they were going to try and find her. Then when the lady with the dog had gone they left James on the hill.

Now that's not right, is it? It is. It's not. That is the truth. Now would Bobby have left baby Ben, his brother, on the hill, if he was two? No, 'cos he's my brother. And would he have left a similar boy? He's not though, he's not any relation to us. Mum, is Jon getting asked this?

Jacobs says Jon might tell them the whole truth from the start. That's all they're after. Bobby says Jon won't tell them he took the baby out of the Strand. Why not? Because he knows that he'll get into trouble by his dad.

Jon asked the woman on the hill where the police station was, but they weren't going to take him to the police station. Well, they were, but Bobby wasn't going to carry him, because Elizabeth lived round there and she'd spread it to everyone. Spread what? That they found a little boy in the Strand while they were sagging.

Roberts thinks they were going to take James to the police station. They were, says Bobby. Roberts thinks they led him from the hill and went towards the police station. I never killed him, says Bobby. Now, Bobby, I haven't got as far as that. But you're trying to say that, though. You're trying to say that we got nearer the police station. Roberts asks why that is. Bobby says because that's where he was found, isn't it? Where did you leave him then? On the reservoir place, on the hill.

Jacobs changes the theme, to paint. Did Bobby get any paint that day? Why would I want paint? Bobby doesn't know if Jon got paint on his clothes. Ask Jon. The interview is only 25 minutes old, but Bobby is tired. They're all tired. As they close the interview, Bobby wants to know if he's allowed home.

Bobby is returned to the detention room, and at ten to eleven a uniformed Inspector goes through the formality of a custody review, explaining why Bobby must be further detained.

'Why do I have to stay here?' Bobby asks. 'Jon's the one that took the baby.'

When Jon's third interview begins, at twenty to ten, Mark Dale asks Jon if he really did go to all the places he mentioned visiting on the Friday. Jon again starts to invent elaborate detail, and George Scott breaks in, saying he thinks Jon should know that Robert's at Walton Lane police station, and has told a different story of what happened on Friday.

Jon says Robert's probably told lies, and when Dale asks what lies he thinks Robert's been telling, Jon starts to cry, his voice full of fear as he says, I don't know, you think I've killed the kid. His mum says they don't think that, and tells him not to be getting upset. Lawrence Lee tells Jon not to get upset. Nobody's saying that, says Lee. His mum explains that they just want to know where he's been. If he's been robbing all day he should tell them. Jon whimpers. He didn't go to Bootle Strand. Ssh, says his mum. They want to know where you've been.

Susan says that Jon had told her before this interview that Robert was going to tell all kinds of lies. Jon had told her he was going to tell the policemen about this when he came in for the interview.

Jon, still crying, says Robert took him to places that he didn't know. Susan explains for Jon that he's frightened, because he doesn't know the places and Robert does. She had asked him if it was Bootle Strand, and he had said no. Jon is still crying, and Dale asks Lawrence Lee if he's happy for the interview to continue. Lee says he's monitoring it very closely.

The officers ask Jon again about the places he visited, and introduce the Strand. Jon says he doesn't know where the Strand is, but he's been there with his mum. He can't describe it. He hasn't been there many times. Susan explains that she doesn't shop there. She goes to St John's in the city normally.

Dale asks if Jon was at the Strand on Friday. No. Was he with Ryan? No. Then why did he say he was with Ryan? He doesn't know, Robert told him to say it. Say what? Susan asks. That we were with Ryan. Susan says, but you were with Ryan in the morning. I know, says Jon, till half three. Dale asks if Jon is sure about this, because Ryan says he was in school. Jon says Ryan is lying. Susan tells Jon to be honest and asks, was Ryan with you? No. Robert said tell that Ryan was with us so that we can get him into trouble with us. But I never went to Bootle Strand.

The officers change the subject, and talk for a while about the clothes Jon and Bobby were wearing. Then Jon concedes that he has told two lies, about being with Ryan and being in the Everton area. He is reminded of the importance of telling the truth.

> *Dale.* You see, Robert says that he was with you, and that you were indeed in Bootle New Strand together.
> *Jon.* We wasn't.

Dale. Robert says you were.

Jon. Yeah, we was, but we never saw any kids there. We never robbed any kids.

Dale. So you were in Bootle New Strand.

Susan. (*shouting*) Was you in Bootle Strand?

Jon. Yeah, but we never got a kid mum, we never, we never, we never got a kid. (*He is crying, sobbing, getting up and out of his chair, distraught.*)

Dale. Mrs Venables, would you, I must ask you not to get angry with him.

Jon. But we never got a kid mum, we never. We saw those two lads together we did, we never got a kid mum, mum we never got a kid, you think we did, we never, mum we never.

The four adults in the room try to calm Jon. Lawrence Lee says it's not a criminal offence to go to Bootle New Strand. Scott says they're not saying he's taken any children. They just want him to tell the truth. Susan warns him. He'd better carry on telling the truth. Jon continues to cry.

Dale tries to proceed, along a more innocuous line of questioning. Talking about the shops Jon and Robert went to, and what they did there – which, Jon says, was robbing. He begins crying again. His mum tries to hush him.

Jon. If you knew that I went to Bootle Strand.

Susan. I would have strangled you, yeah.

Jon. And wouldn't have you thought I'd killed a kid. I never, because . . .

Susan. Well, I wouldn't think that.

Lee. We don't think that.

Jon. Because, because, if you thought I went and I sagged off and you think that I killed him . . .

Susan. I wouldn't think you'd done that at all.

Jon. Because, because, I would've told, because I thought you'd think I done it.

Susan. If I would've known this all now, Jon, I would've had you down the police station right away, instead of them banging on my front door and making a show of me in the street . . .

Jon. But I . . .

Susan . . . humiliation.
Jon . . . I thought you'd think that I killed him.

Jon sobs, and sobs. Lawrence Lee and the officers agree that it's time to end the interview and let Jon calm down. Susan says she wants this over and done, because she's livid now. George Scott says she should try not to get angry with Jon. Susan says she's not going to. She just wishes he would've told her in the beginning, and saved a lot of time on her part.

Interview over, one minute past ten.

There would be no more interviews tonight, but the two teams of officers were expected back at Marsh Lane for a debriefing. A lot of people were waiting to hear what was happening.

The bosses were gathered in Geoff MacDonald's office, where he and Jim Fitzsimmons were now encircled by Chief Superintendents, Superintendents, and sundry other managers. They had dozens of questions, and Phil Roberts could barely speak. He was bushed. He let Bob Jacobs do the talking. It was like that in the interviews too, even though they had never worked together before. A look from Roberts and Jacobs would step in. A sign from Jacobs and Roberts would take over. That was how it should be.

They were all exhausted. Jim Fitzsimmons had been pulled to one side earlier by one of the Superintendents, and told to get some rest. He looked as though he needed it. Today should have been his duty rest day. No one was taking their days off. There was anxiety and concern all round that they should close the case as quickly as possible. After the briefing, Phil Roberts went up to the bar, to see the *Crimewatch* update, but mostly to have a cigarette and a pint before trying to get some sleep.

Albert Kirby had been phoning in to Marsh Lane from the BBC at odd intervals throughout the afternoon. He wanted to hear how the interviews were going, naturally, but he had to be discreet about it. He didn't want the *Crimewatch* team catching on before the arrests had been made public. He used the

Vodaphone from his briefcase. Conversation was guarded. Any developments? Okay, good, speak to you later.

Mike One was waiting for him at the McAlpine's headquarters in Hayes, not too far from Heathrow. Albert sped there from Shepherds Bush after the programme. He had never been in a bloody helicopter in his life. He had been feeling rough earlier, so much so that he had taken a stiffening drink to cope with being on live television. He certainly wasn't feeling any better now.

The co-pilot, a police sergeant, strapped Albert in, and showed him what to do. If you feel bad, sir, there's the bag. Shit, thought Albert, it's going to be a hard night this.

They set off for Birmingham, where the helicopter was scheduled to refuel. The first half of the journey was harmless. At Birmingham they landed safely and sat on the tarmac waiting for a fuel tanker to appear, and when it did there was a problem. Something to do with credit clearance for fuel. The tanker couldn't oblige. They waited a little longer, and longer still. Sitting there dwarfed by 747s and assorted aeroplanes, half two in the morning, and the wind's blowing up. Albert wasn't very happy.

Finally, the fuel problem was resolved, and they took off, into what now seemed to Albert like a hurricane-force gale. Wedging himself into the corner of his seat, he thought he might die. He hoped he'd die having led a successful investigation into the killing of James Bulger.

He survived the flight and arrived home at half four, vowing that wild horses would not drag him back into a helicopter.

20

Jim Fitzsimmons was unaware of Albert Kirby's late-night adventure when he arrived at Albert's home at seven thirty on

Friday morning to pick him up for work, as they had arranged yesterday afternoon. Albert had only been home for three hours, and he was still in bed.

Susan Kirby admitted Jim to the house and sent him upstairs, where he sat at the foot of the senior investigating officer's bed, drinking a cup of tea.

'What do you think?' Albert asked.

'Yeah,' said Jim.

They were talking about the two boys, of course.

'Are you sure?'

'No, I'm not sure.'

Jim left Albert to get ready and make his own way to Marsh Lane, and went in ahead of him for the morning briefing. He decided they should make some changes to the interviewing teams.

It seemed to be a problem that Phil Roberts and Bob Jacobs were not familiar with the area, and Jim wanted somebody in there who knew the locations they hoped Bobby would mention as he described the route taken with James. Jim knew the area well and thought again about taking the interview himself. But no, that would be wrong. The best alternative was John Forrest from the back-up team, who also knew Walton.

With Jon's interviews, Jim felt that a woman officer might be an advantage. Michelle Bennett, on Mark Dale's back-up team, had experience of interviewing children, particularly in sensitive child abuse cases, and she might bring something extra to what was clearly a very difficult process.

By nine o'clock Albert had arrived and the senior officers and the interview teams sat down in a corner of the bar to discuss the changes. Albert was feeling terrible, and looked it. He didn't know how he was going to survive the day, but suspected that adrenalin would see him through.

Phil Roberts and Bob Jacobs were not keen to alter their team. They were working well together, and had made good progress over a relatively short period of time. They'd got hold of a map which they would use with Bobby in the interviews, and this would overcome their lack of local knowledge. Jim Fitzsimmons relented. Let's see how it goes then, and keep John Forrest on stand-by.

Michelle Bennett wasn't happy going in cold. She felt unprepared, but if she could read up the notes on yesterday's interviews during the morning, she'd be ready to take over.

What they really needed was the Downstream Monitoring equipment, so that Michelle Bennett could listen in and get a proper feel for the interviews. Unfortunately, the facility was still in use elsewhere. Jim Fitzsimmons was annoyed, but there was nothing he could do about it.

Albert now briefed the teams on the injuries that James had suffered. Officially it was the first time they had been told, though in practice they were already familiar with many of the details. Albert also had some tips from his offender profiler, Paul Britton, who suggested, among other things, that the boys would be highly unlikely to admit any sexual assault of James, whether it had taken place or not.

Susan Venables had stayed the night with Jon in the juvenile detention room at Lower Lane, and in the morning they had a cooked breakfast and a change of clothes, brought in by Jon's father.

The fourth interview begins not long after eleven o'clock, with Jon agreeing that he had told a lie before, about not being at the Strand, then admitting that he had been there, messing around, but had not seen any kids. He had seen kids, waiting outside shops but he never saw any kids with two boys or nothing because he wouldn't go near any kids.

The officers steer Jon through a description of his activities at the Strand, and Jon gives a selectively truthful account of the roaming in and out of shops and the robbing. He didn't go into a card shop to look at trolls. He enjoyed looking at the Thunderbirds figures in Woolworths. Jon likes Thunderbirds and his favourite character is Lady Penelope, because she's rich. Dale asks if Jon is going to get himself a rich girlfriend. Susan says she hopes so.

Jon remembers being in Tandy twice, and says there was nothing to pinch in the shop. He is not asked about the theft of a packet of batteries. He mentions being in a sports shop, and says he's hoping to be given a Liverpool kit for his birthday. His mum says they'll have to wait and see how he behaves. Jon says he wants a Blackburn Rovers shirt now.

He and Bobby were at a charity stall, tapping the old woman on the back and running away. How would you like it if you were splattered on your back, she says, and runs round after them with a walking stick.

How about the toyshop, Toymaster, did he go in there? No, the woman chased them out because they weren't with their parents.

Jon thinks it was about half three when they left Stanley Road and started making their way up to Walton. They went along County Road and into Fads where they nicked a tin of blue paint and some borders. Round the corner, on Olney Street, Robert tried to open the tin, and as he was banging it the lid opened quick and the paint went all over Jon.

Dale says Jon's jumped forward suddenly, and he wants to go back to half three at the Strand. Jon says he didn't know the time exactly but Robert said they should leave because it was getting dark. Then he says they were looking at the big clock at the front and it said four o'clock.

The interview ends, after 44 minutes, just as Jon begins to describe the route he and Bobby took on their walk back to Walton.

Ann Thompson had not wanted to leave baby Ben and Ryan overnight, and had felt it would not be safe, staying in the Village. Social Services had put them up at the Gladstone Hotel in the city centre, while Bobby stayed at the police station, under the watchful eye of the custody officer and a duty social worker.

On Friday morning Ann was back at Walton Lane in time for Bobby's 24-hour custody review, which Phil Roberts attended, before going on to Marsh Lane.

Bobby's fourth interview began at 11.35. He had already told the officers he had something new to say. He and Jon had sagged off, and Ryan had gone to school.

Bobby. Then we went to the Strand and we picked little James up . . .

Roberts. Yeah.

Bobby . . . and took him out of the Strand.

Roberts. Yeah.

Bobby. Well he, Jon did.

Roberts. Right.

Bobby. Then we took him down and left him on the How.

Roberts. On the How?

Bobby. By the railway.

Roberts. By the railway, all right. Now you went past the reservoir, yeah?

Bobby. Pardon?

Roberts. Did you go past the reservoir?

Bobby. Yeah, we went up on the reservoir, yeah.

They begin to go over the route that Jon, James and Bobby took from the reservoir to the railway, and the map is produced. Bobby says that they saw two women with dogs on the reservoir and, after Jon had asked one of them where the police station was, they had walked down Bedford Road to County Road, and then down Church Road West. They had not gone into any shops on County Road. From Church Road they had crossed over to the How, and left James there. Bobby and Jon had then gone to the video shop.

After some detailed discussion of the whereabouts of the How, Bob Jacobs asks Bobby why they left James there. Bobby says if they had taken him to the police station they would have had to go in. There was a taxi there, and the fella would've took the baby. James wasn't crying, he was just looking round. He just had a graze on his eye.

They talk for a while about the video shop, and what happened with Jon's mother. Then Phil Roberts says, okay, now who had the tin of paint? We never had a tin of paint. We know you had the tin of paint. We never.

Bob Jacobs explains how the police can find paint that's been splashed on clothing. Jon had paint on his jacket. Bobby doesn't know about that, he never saw it. Well, it was there, so where did it come from? Bobby says he doesn't know but his mum's painting the house. It's not house paint. Baby James had paint on him, didn't he? Bobby doesn't know. Have a think about it. Bobby begins crying. Yeah, well, youse are trying to say I killed him. He slumps in his chair. His mum tells him to sit up.

We want the truth, says Roberts. They know he can tell lies. We never killed him, Bobby cries. Well, the police know he was on the railway line. He wasn't. They had all this yesterday, and now they want the whole truth. It's about time for the truth.

Ann is getting upset now, and Bobby is still crying.

I left him at, on the end. I don't think you did, I don't think you did. I did. Bobby, we didn't want to upset you, we don't want to upset your mum, now if you don't . . . Yeah but youse are trying to say that we killed him. We have found things on your clothes, right Bobby, and we know you're telling lies, you see. But I never killed him. Well, tell me what happened, the paint, tell me all about the paint. I never got no paint. Well, somebody got the paint, did Jon get the paint? I don't know, he might've picked it up from a shop. It must've been a small one, 'cos I never seen him with a big tin of paint.

Again, Roberts and Jacobs press Bobby to admit that James was not left at the How, and that they had a tin of paint. Bobby resists them, and continues to cry . . . crying, the officers observe, without tears.

He stops when the subject changes, and Jacobs begins asking

if James, Jon or Bobby were bleeding, or had blood on them. James wasn't bleeding when they left him, and Jon would have said if he was bleeding. Bobby says he might have got blood on him after Jon's mum dragged him out of the video shop.

Did you see anybody who had blood on him? Who? Did you see anybody who had blood on him? No. No, and James was okay? What? And James was all right? No, he's dead. When you last saw him, was he all right at the time? Yeah.

The officers decide it's time for a break. Would Bobby like a cup of tea or some dinner or something? He's just had one. Well, they're going to give him a break. He's told them a little bit more about the story, but they need to go further into it.

Bobby begins crying again. Yeah, well, why can't I go home with my mum? Because we haven't asked all the questions we need to and we haven't had all the right answers. Well, when they're all right can I go with my mum? Bobby, we need to speak to you a little bit more, we want to know. We want to know. Well, I don't want to sleep here again.

Phil Roberts says it's up to Bobby to tell the truth. He says he is. Roberts says they know he's not telling the truth about the paint. Ann says she told him before, just tell the truth.

Bobby. We did have paint. It was a little enamel wasn't it?
Jacobs. Yes it was.
Bobby. Jon took it.
Jacobs. Where from?
Bobby. I think it was Toymaster.
Jacobs. When was that?
Bobby. Friday.
Jacobs. No, but at what stage, Toymaster in the Strand was it?
Bobby. Yeah.
Jacobs. What colour was it?
Bobby. I didn't know, it was in a little silver tin with a white label on.
Jacobs. Was it. Now, did he take that before you took baby James?
Bobby. Yeah.
Jacobs. Where did he put it?

131

Bobby. In his pocket.

Jacobs. Okay. Now, did he open it at that stage or when did he open it? When did he open the tin?

Bobby. When we were walking along the road.

Jacobs. Which road?

Bobby. Bedford.

Jacobs. Bedford Road. Okay, now you still don't have to tell us anything unless you wish to do so, anything that you say can be given in evidence, you understand that do you? We still want to know what happened with that paint, all right? Now what happened with it?

Bobby. He threw it in baby James's eye. That eye, I think it was. (*Bobby points to his left eye.*)

Jacobs. Where was that?

Bobby. On the railway.

Bobby says he doesn't know what happened then. He ran away from Jon. What did James do? He sat on the floor. He was crying. Why did Bobby run away? Because Jon had splashed stuff in James's eye. Why did Jon throw it at him? Bobby doesn't know. What did Bobby think about it? Were they having a joke or what? No, Bobby was crying himself, because he threw it in his face, he could have blinded him.

When Bobby ran off, Jon ran after him. James was crying but, no, he was not injured in any other way. Bobby is sure he wasn't bleeding.

The officers produce the map and Bobby shows them where he, Jon and James got over the railings on to the railway line. It was by the entry on the far side of City Road, the bit with the tiny railings. They had walked back up the entry between City Road and Walton Lane to get there. Phil Roberts marks an X on the map.

Bobby explains how they walked along the embankment, Jon holding James's hand. He thinks Jon threw the hood from James's anorak into the tree, after they had walked under the City Road bridge, the broo. Another X on the map. Bobby doesn't know why Jon threw the hood. He just ragged it off him and threw it.

They walked on and, just by the bridge, Jon threw the paint. James was looking down and he went like that and it hit him in the eye. Bobby gestures in demonstration of Jon's throw, an upward movement with his arm. Bobby told Jon to throw the tin down, and he threw it on to the bridge.

The buzzer goes. Bob Jacobs says they'd like to carry on speaking straight away. It takes four minutes to change the tapes and start the fifth interview.

Before Bobby ran off, had anyone hit baby James? Jon might have hit him in sly. What makes Bobby say that? Because Jon is sly. Okay, when was that? No, I only said he might of, in sly. You didn't see him? No, but, 'cos he is sly. If baby James had been hit, he would have started crying, wouldn't he? James was already crying. Was he? 'Cos he wanted his mum. He wasn't crying all the way along, he just started crying when Jon threw the paint in his eye.

Jacobs goes back to the theft of the paint. Did Jon take anything else that day? Pepperami. He ate it before they were with James. Did either of them take some batteries? No. Are you sure about that? Yeah. Phil Roberts says he wants to point something out. Bobby went all red in the face there. He went a bit red in the face as if he knew something about it. Yeah, well, I'm hot. Bobby begins crying. Yeah, but, I never took no batteries. I'm terrible, says Phil Roberts.

Bobby is asked again about the batteries, and, still crying, says that Jon might've took them. Where from? I don't know. You do know, this is what you said last time, but you told us where the paint came from, didn't you? Yeah, well, I don't know where batteries . . . why do we want batteries? That's what Phil Roberts wants to know. Why did they want paint? Ask Jon, I didn't. I didn't want paint.

The officers can make no further progress with the batteries, and decide to end the interview, which has lasted for eight minutes.

*

Jim Fitzsimmons still thought Michelle Bennett should be in the team interviewing Jon, and Michelle Bennett still felt she wasn't ready. At least the Downstream Monitoring equipment had finally got to Lower Lane. Michelle Bennett and her colleague Dave Tanner set themselves up in the small medical room next to the juvenile detention room, and eavesdropped on Jon's fifth interview through the extension speaker. It was twenty past twelve on Friday afternoon.

Mark Dale and George Scott picked up the theme of the previous interview, taking Jon through his walk back to Walton with Bobby. He said they had gone to Hillside School (which was almost opposite the reservoir) and played in the long jump sandpit. They both jumped, and Jon won because Bobby doesn't know how to jump. Mark Dale says there must have been sand in his toes when he got home. No, says Jon, he took his shoes off.

They went to County Road then, and Bobby stole the paint and the borders from Fads. Jon goes into great detail about what they did with the paint and the borders, and is supplied with a sheet of paper on which to draw the size of the tin of paint. He says it was bigger than the little tin that was found at the railway. It was Crown paint, and it was thrown round the back of the chip shop by Olney Street.

The officers allow Jon to continue with this for a while, and George Scott says Jon's given them a good story for that day. Now does Jon remember last night when he told them the story of where he'd been and they found out it was a lie because Robert had said they'd been at the Strand. Yeah, Jon remembers.

Scott says, well, Robert's told a different story about being at the Strand. What does Jon think he said. Jon doesn't know. What does Jon think he might have said about what they did at the Strand. Robbed. Something different . . . not just robbed. Jon doesn't know. He doesn't know what else. Scott says Robert said that the two of them were in the Strand and saw the little boy.

Jon is immediately anxious. We never, we never. Susan says is that the God's honest truth? God's honest truth, I'm telling you, we never, he was too scared, he was probably too scared.

Robert said that you took him by the hand and led him out of the Strand shops. We never. No, not we, Robert is saying that you took him by the hand. I never. Not Robert, you did it. I never. Well, why would Robert say that about you? He's a liar.

Jon is beside himself with distress, out of his chair, going to his mother, who tries to pacify him. It's all right, come on, all right, all right love, you tell them the truth and you never, did you. Lawrence Lee is asked to monitor the situation. Jon is crying uncontrollably. I never took him by the hand, I never even touched the baby. All right, I believe you, says Susan.

George Scott then tells Jon that the fingerprints he had taken yesterday match the fingerprints at the Bradford & Bingley. Jon says, yeah, he did go in there. He thought before they meant the Halifax. Jon describes what they did in the building society and says they then went to the Strand. He's crying again. I never touched a baby. I know, says Susan.

They tell Jon not to get upset. They're only asking about the building society. Scott says the man in there remembers seeing them again outside, and that they asked for money. Is that right. Tell the truth, says Susan, did you ask for money? Jon says it wasn't him, it was Robert. I never took the baby, mum.

Lawrence Lee asks Jon if he's all right to carry on. Yeah. If he wants to stop at any time just say so. Scott says he must tell the truth, because he keeps telling them stories. I never got the boy.

Scott. Well, well, if you never got the boy tell us what happened, was it Robert? You're nodding your head.
Jon. Yeah, he left him in, he left him in the road.
Scott. Right, well, let's go back to, into the Strand.
Jon. No, I never touched a boy, mum, I never.
Susan. Okay.
Scott. All right.
Jon. I haven't touched a boy.
(*Jon becomes hysterical and cannot be consoled. It is a terrible distress.*)
Dale. Hold on, come here son, all right, come on.
Susan. Oh God, no.

Dale. Settle yourself down.

Jon. I never touched him.

Dale. Sit down, go to your mum.

Susan. All right, all right, you're going to get me crying now, look.

Jon. I never, mum.

Susan. I know you wouldn't, you wouldn't do that to a boy would you?

Jon. Robert's getting me into trouble.

Jon continues to sob, and Susan says that he had been warned, about Robert. George Scott says he's going to have to tell them what happened, and he's not going to have to cry. He's going to have to be a big boy. Don't be telling lies.

I never touched a boy. Well, tell us what happened then, but remember don't be telling lies now, 'cos we keep finding you out, don't we. Well, I never touched, I never. Are you all right to carry on? Lawrence Lee asks. No, I never touched him. Susan says, calm down first. I can't. I never touched him.

Scott. All right, well, you tell us what happened then.

Jon. We just went home, and I went, I left Robert on his own till he came back to Walton Village.

Susan. Tell me the truth now Jon, please.

Jon. I never killed him mum, mum, we took him and left him at the canal mum, that's all.

Scott. You left him at the canal by the Strand?

Jon. Yeah.

Well, where did you find the boy in the Strand? I don't know, he was just walking around on his own. Is this little James is it? No, he had brown hair. He had brown hair? This other lad. So which other lad's that? I don't know, this, really, there was only one lad. How old did he look? Two, I don't know. About two? I never killed him, mum. I believe you.

Jon begins sobbing again, and gets out of his chair, knocking over a can of drink on the table. Lee again asks if he wants to carry on, and Jon says, yeah, but I never killed him. Dale says they don't have to ask him anything, he can just sit there and be quiet and get himself back together. Jon says, I left him in the Strand. Susan says, you left him in the Strand? Yes. Who with? Nobody. Whereabouts in the Strand? In, just, no we left him in TJ Hughes, this boy with brown hair, and his mum got him. Oh, says Susan. Is that James? Jon asks.

Well, no, says Dale.

The officers ask Jon about the boy, and he says they found him in TJ Hughes. Robert probably thinks he was James. Scott says, well, let's get this straight, you left him at the canal, and then we've left him at TJ Hughes. Jon says, that was made up, at the canal. Susan says perhaps that's because of the news.

Jon says they were with this boy trying to find his mum, and were walking with him until his mum got him. They discuss where Jon and Robert took the boy, and Jon says his mum got him when they were by the carts by TJ Hughes. Jon says he spoke to the mum, and fumbles for the words he said to her. I'm trying to get you to, I'm just trying to, I said to her I was trying to get him to get to go, I was . . . Susan helps him out, saying, I was looking for you so he could get to you. Yeah.

Then Jon says he came out of the Strand on his own, without Robert. Hang on, says Scott, we've got two stories here. Susan says, don't get yourself confused, think, and Jon begins crying again, I never killed him, mum. No one's saying that, says Susan, and Lawrence Lee says it too. Jon cries and cries. Wailing. Susan says, he's frightened. Jon says, you're going to put me in jail.

They decide to stop the interview. I wouldn't hurt a baby, says Jon. I mean, I know you wouldn't hurt a baby either, says Susan.

Michelle Bennett calls Jim Fitzsimmons as soon as the interview is finished. After listening, she and Dave Tanner feel that Jon is frightened of telling the truth, because he doesn't want to upset his mother. They think that if they can talk to Susan they might be able to resolve the problem. Jim says they should go ahead. They take Susan to one side for a quiet chat.

21

Phil Roberts had only started again yesterday, but his cigarette intake was soaring rapidly. Already it looked like being a two-pack day. They were hard work, these interviews.

Like Michelle Bennett, Phil Roberts had interviewed in several child abuse cases. Kids were much more difficult to deal with than adults. Their imagination was brilliant and they were the best liars in the world. You only had to think back to your own childhood, to the things you'd got away with.

Roberts thought Bobby was a crafty little lad, but his shuffling feet were a giveaway, and the false crying, the crying without tears, was transparent.

From the beginning, Roberts had tried to develop a rapport with Bobby. Close up in the chair, bent forward, trying to provoke a smile with the odd light remark, touching Bobby on the knee occasionally . . . it was totally false but it created the right mood.

There was no room now to think about James Bulger, or react in horror to Bobby's disclosures. That, you could never do. What was required now was tunnel vision, thinking down a straight line, to the truth of what had happened.

It was now two fifteen, and Bobby's sixth interview began with his suggestion that Jon might have taken the batteries for his Game Gear. He might have taken them and they fell out of his pocket. What, on the railway line? Wherever you found them. Well, the batteries were scattered, they weren't found together. It was unlikely that they had fallen from Jon's pocket.

Phil Roberts says that, just like the paint, he thinks Bobby knows more about the batteries. Bobby fences. Okay, then I'll say that he took them. No, no, they don't want that. They want the truth.

Bobby repeats his story that he ran off from the railway after the paint was thrown. He will not be budged from this. The officers say that if baby James was bleeding and his blood is found on Jon or Bobby's clothes then it means they were there when baby James was bleeding. Bobby asks how they know it's baby James's blood. Jacobs says they know what baby James's blood is because they've got the body. Where? Well, it doesn't matter where, Bobby. It's probably been to the hospital first. What for? To take blood out of his arm like they've done to yours. They've taken him to try and get him alive again? No, says Ann. Bobby says, yeah, well, I was told he got chopped in half. Well, he couldn't come alive again, could he, if he's got chopped in half?

Bobby says the blood might have been his because he was bleeding from a cut. He demonstrates how he scratched the cut on his face. Jacobs says he couldn't do that with his shoe, and the blood's been found on his shoe. Bobby begins crying. I never murdered him. Youse are just trying to say that I murdered him. What happened that afternoon? Come on, Bobby.

We left him there. Why aren't you doing it to Jon? Jon has got the same. Ask Jon, I never touched him. We will be asking Jon. How can you be asking Jon if you're here?

Jacobs goes through the sequence of events Bobby has described to them. Jon held his hand, Jon took him from the Strand, Jon took him up to the reservoir, threw the hood into the tree, threw the paint. Now, says Jacobs, they don't know, it might be Jon that's done all this stuff. Yeah, well, why would I want to hurt a little boy? Well, we don't know.

Bobby is crying again. He says Jon might have kicked James in sly. How? He doesn't know. They go back over the story again, pointing out that Bobby had at first denied things and then admitted them. Roberts says he was right about those things, and he's right about this as well. Yeah, well, I never killed him. Who did then? Well, not me.

Bobby is sobbing now. They ask if he wants to stop.

Ann. It will be all over in a few minutes if you just tell them the truth.

Bobby. Jon threw a brick in his face.

Ann. Why?

Bobby. I don't know.

Roberts. Right, try and stop. Right let's, we've got, we're getting there aren't we. We're getting to the truth now.

Bobby. Yeah, well, I'm going to end up getting all the blame 'cos I've got blood on me.

Bobby repeats that Jon threw the brick. James just fell on the floor. Then Bobby left the railway, he got down the lamp-post at the edge by the big white house. They got down the lamp-post. He is asked again, and repeats the story. Roberts says something else happened. Bobby says Jon was on the railway and he was down the lamp-post. Ann asks what the baby was doing. Bobby says he was on the floor crying. Awake or asleep? What do you mean? Was he like asleep, or . . . He was awake.

Roberts asks Bobby why he didn't try to stop Jon. Bobby did. He tried to pull Jon back, but he just threw it. He was standing right in front of James, with Bobby just behind him. When the brick hit James his face started bleeding. He wasn't screaming, he was crying. He fell onto the floor and blood was just pouring everywhere. Bobby demonstrates how James fell to his knees, and fell face forward. He was fully clothed.

Ann has begun crying, and Phil Roberts suggests a break from the interview. He says Bobby hasn't told them the full truth, he's blaming everything on Jon. I'm not. You are. 'Cos I took things to eat. We're not bothered about stealing Bobby, we never have been. You know that. We want the whole truth.

They press Bobby, who insists that he has told the truth. He never touched the baby. He went down the lamp-post.

Bobby begins crying. I never touched him. I never touched him. That's all I seen. No it isn't. It is. We already know about things that happened and it doesn't explain a lot of things. And were you there like, and seen me? No. Well, that's what youse are trying to say.

The officers try to explain the basics of post-mortem examinations to Bobby. A clever man, a pathologist, looks at every part of the body and can see where it's been hurt. Bobby says why would I take flowers over to the baby if I killed him. I know the truth, says Roberts. So do I, says Bobby, I was there, you weren't. He begins crying again. Yeah, well, it's all our family, it's always our family that gets the blame. Your family might have been blamed in the past . . . but on this occasion we're right though, aren't we? No, 'cos I never touched him.

Jacobs. Well, tell us what happened, then.
Bobby. He threw another brick.
Jacobs. And where did that hit him?
Bobby. (*pointing to his body*) On there.
Jacobs. On the chest?
Bobby. On the belly.
Jacobs. What kind of brick was that?
Bobby. A half one.
Jacobs. And what happened then?
Bobby. And then he hit him again.
Jacobs. What with?
Bobby. There was like a big metal thing that had holes in.
Jacobs. A big metal thing with holes in, where was that?
Bobby. When it hit him?
Jacobs. No, where was it, where did he pick it up from?
Bobby. Off the . . . you know, where the railway track's like that.
Jacobs. Yeah.
Bobby. In the middle of them.

Where did he hit him with that? In the head. Now which part of the head? Up there. On the top of the head, what did that do to him, to James? Knocked him out. Did it? What happened then? And then he hit him again.

The buzzer sounds.

What with? A stick, and then he threw that. A stick? And you threw that? No, he threw it. Where did he throw it? You know, the nettles. Yeah. By where he's found. Yeah. He threw them into there. Where, where did he hit him with the stick? In the face. In the face, whereabout in the face? I don't know where, he just went like that and hit him. The tape finishes, the interview ends.

They change the tape in two minutes, go through the caution again, and continue. Ann is crying. It's three o'clock.

Bobby says the stick was a little branch off a tree, lying on the floor. James was knocked out. He wasn't moving. His eyes were open. Might he have been dead? Bobby doesn't know. They went then, and left him there. He thinks James was lying on his back, over the railway track.

The batteries? Jon might've took them for his Game Gear. Did he have some batteries with him? Who? Jon. Yeah, he took them out and threw them. He threw one at James's face and threw the others away.

The officers go over the sequence of events again. Bobby describes how Jon threw the metal bar on to the top of James's head. And then they went. They went to the video shop. Bobby tried to see if the baby was still alive, and he wouldn't move. He was trying to see if he could still breathe. I've got me ear against his belly and he wasn't breathing.

Roberts. And you didn't say anything to Jon?
Bobby. Who?
Roberts. You.
Bobby. No, only in the video shop I did.
Roberts. What did you say to him in the . . .
Bobby. I asked him, is he coming up, to do the message.
Roberts. Is that when you spoke to him?
Bobby. Yeah.
Jacobs. Why did, why did he do all this, why did Jon do all this?
Bobby. I don't know. That is what I don't know.
Roberts. You say you didn't do anything at all?
Bobby. I only pinched.

They again say they're not bothered about Bobby stealing.

He says it's on the tape, it'll get brought up another day. No, it doesn't matter.

Phil Roberts says he doesn't think Jon's done everything. Bobby says yeah, well, I never. Roberts thinks Bobby hit him. Well, that's what you think. Roberts says there's only one person here that knows the whole truth. No, I've just said all the truth, says Bobby.

They finish the seventh interview at ten past three.

Ann is in shock now, disturbed and terrified by what is happening. She says she cannot sit in on any further interviews. She barely knows what's going on around her. Later that day, she is in the bridewell when a uniformed officer passes through. Ann hears him whistling the death march. It might be a deliberate wind-up, it might not. She mentions it to Jason Lee, who mentions it to the interviewing team. The whistler does not reappear.

Bobby seems more concerned about his mum's welfare than anything else. He asks the policeman, excuse me, can you get me mum a glass of water so she can have a Beecham's Powder? Excuse me, can me mum have a cup of coffee? Can you get me mum a doctor 'cause she's not well? There was talk of getting a psychiatrist to see Ann. She said it wasn't her that needed a shrink, it was Bobby and Jon. She just couldn't take it all in.

Later, when she regained her senses, she asked Bobby, why the fuckin' hell didn't you do something, why didn't you go and tell someone? How could you stand there and . . .? Bobby said, but I tried to get him off, he just kept hittin' him and hittin' him and hittin' him and I couldn't do nuttin' about it.

Ann said, well how could you take a bloody flower over? Bobby said, 'cause then baby James knows I tried to help him up there and I'm thinking of him now.

Bobby asks his mum, if you die before me dad, will you come back and haunt him? Too friggin' right I will, said Ann, I'll bleedin' haunt him every day. Bobby said, yeah, but that's because he's hurt you, but if he hadn't've hurt you and you died, you wouldn't come back and haunt him then, would you? Ann said, well, no, I'd have no cause to, would I? She thought it was a funny question for Bobby to ask.

In the Lower Lane interview room, Michelle Bennett and Dave Tanner told Susan that, after listening to Jon's last interview they both felt that he wanted to talk about the incident, but was inhibited by the way she consoled him. He didn't want to upset her. Susan realised that because she didn't think Jon was involved, she might have been making it more difficult for him to talk.

The officers said she would have to be strong, and reassure Jon that his parents loved him and that he could say anything to them. If Jon did know anything about the killing of James Bulger he might be able to talk if he felt safe and secure that his parents would always love him.

Susan spoke to Neil for a while and, at three o'clock, they went to see Jon in the detention room. As they went in, they called Dave Tanner to join them, and he stood by the door.

Jon's mother and father sat either side of him on the bench. They put their arms around him, and said they would always be there for him. They loved him very much, and wanted him to tell the truth, no matter what it was. They weren't going to tell him off. They would understand.

Jon became upset and was crying. He climbed into his mother's lap, and she cradled him like a baby, hugging him close. Through his tears he said that he wanted to tell. 'I did kill him,' Jon said.

They were all very distressed. After a while Jon turned to Dave Tanner. 'What about his mum, will you tell her I'm sorry?'

Jon said he had been going to give himself up and, as Mark Dale came in, he added, 'Can I tell you about Robert trying to get another lad away?'

The officers waited a while before returning to the interviews.

144

Susan said she could not go back in, and Neil said he would replace her. Dave Tanner called Jim Fitzsimmons at Marsh Lane to tell him what had happened.

Jim put the phone down and turned to Geoff MacDonald across the desk. 'He's coughed it. Yeah. He's having it.' They went up the corridor to tell Albert Kirby. Jon's admission was the breakthrough they had been waiting for. No cough, no job.

Later, Jim spoke to Michelle Bennett. If Susan was not going to be in on the interviews, he did not want an all male environment. Now he wanted Michelle to go in. She said that, from listening, Mark Dale and George Scott had built up a good relationship with Jon, and it would be wrong to break the bond. But Jim is sure he's right. He doesn't want all men. He just doesn't want it, but they're telling him it would be wrong to break up the partnership. Okay, he says, leave it as it is. Stick with it. Decisive bastard aren't I, thinks Jim.

Jon's sixth interview begins at four o'clock, with Mark Dale saying that he knows it took a lot of doing, Jon making his admission, and he knows Jon was upset, as they all were. He asks Jon to tell them exactly what he did that day, from the beginning.

Jon describes going to the Strand with Robert, and says that Robert got three tins of paint from Toymaster, by putting them under his sleeve. Then this other kid came up, and Robert says let's get this kid lost. They walked him through TJ Hughes, Robert going, come on mate, and then his mum came up behind them and got him. Why did Robert want the little boy to follow him? I know, he said let's get him lost outside so when he goes into the road he'll get knocked over. What did Jon say to that? I said it's a very bad thing to do, isn't it.

They found James outside the butchers. They both saw him, and it was Jon's idea to walk towards him, but it was Robert's idea to kill him. Jon said to Robert is that boy lost or something? Robert walked up to him, and they were walking round, and Jon took his hand. They were looking for his mum for a bit, then they got fed up and went outside to the canal. The boy couldn't talk at all, he was just going I want my mummy, all the time.

Robert said, lets throw him in the water. Jon said if you wanna, like. He was only going to throw him in the shallow thingy. Robert was persuading him saying kneel down and let's look at the water and all that, but he wouldn't. Robert picked him up and threw him on the floor, and that's where he got the bump on his head.

Neil goes to take a sip of the drink Jon has with him in the interview. That's mine, says Jon. Well, let your dad have a drink, says Dale, I think he might just need one.

Jon describes how Robert picked James up, under his arms, lifted him up to about head or chest height, 'cos he was heavy, Robert said, and slammed him down on the floor. He landed on his head. Was he crying then? Yeah. I should imagine he would be.

They ran away from him, but came back, and he was already walking up. Jon doesn't know why they went back. Just to walk around with him.

Jon goes through the walk they took, remembering the three girls laughing, to the reservoir where the woman spotted them. James was all right then. They were taking him to Walton Village. Why? I don't know, we didn't know what to do until we were walking through, I took his hood off and threw it up in the tree. Hang on. Jon's jumping the gun a bit there.

They cut through from Bedford Road to County Road, and along Church Road West. They didn't talk to anyone by the Breeze Hill flyover. They didn't go that way. They climbed on a wall by the entry to get on to the railway.

Jon's getting upset now. He can't tell them anything else. Why? 'Cos that's the worst bit. Okay, right, now let me tell you, I know that's the worst bit but you know what you did and you know if you try hard you'll be able to tell us. What you need is to have a little rest, think about it, and just tell us what happened.

Jon. We took him on the railway and started throwing bricks at him.

Dale. Who did?

Jon. Robert, he just said, he said, just stand there and we'll get you a plaster or something.

Dale. Why did he throw bricks at him?

Jon. I don't know.

Dale. What else did he do, apart from throwing bricks?

Jon. Threw the big pole at him.

Lee. What's that?

Dale. Threw a big pole at him, is that what you said?

Jon. That knocked him out.

Dale. What was the pole made of?

Jon. Steel.

Dale. Like a bar?

Jon. Yeah, off the track

Dale. Where did the stick, where did the stones and bar hit him?

Jon. In the head.

Dale. And you say the bar knocked him out?

Jon. Yeah, on to the railway track.

Dale. And then, and what happened then?

Jon. He was just lying there.

Dale. Okay, keep going.

That's what happened. We just ran to Walton Village into the video shop and she, then she told us I'll give you a pound if you do this and we did and that's when my mum caught me and we went to the police station. I went home then.

When they left him, James was lying on the track, bleeding all over, from his face.

Is it finished now? 'Cos I can't speak any more. Do you want a little break, do you want to have a little drink? No, I've said all that's, I've said it now. Okay, if you don't want to say any more. No, I don't. No. You don't have to.

Scott says can he just ask something about the paint. Jon says the second one went on him and the third one on the train track. And all those things that happened to James, they were all done by Robert? Some from me. Tell me what you did? Just threw two bricks at him, that's all I done 'cos I wouldn't throw anything big at him. How big were the bricks you threw? Only teeny, little stones. Where did they hit him? On the arms, I wouldn't hit him in the head.

The stones that Robert threw were like a building brick. Jon didn't want to throw anything at him. Why did he throw those stones at James? I only threw three or five, they were only dead little ones though, the white ones. He doesn't know what harm they did and he doesn't think he did anything else.

Jon thinks it was quite a long time after the stones that James was hit with the iron bar. He thinks it was only one hit. Jon was saying stop it, stop it, like that. He said, let's go now.

> *Dale.* I shouldn't really have to ask you this, but what do you think of those things?
> *Jon.* They're terrible. I was thinking about it, all the time.

Lawrence Lee says as soon as you want this stopping, Neil, you say so. Okay, terminate it, says Neil.

Later that evening, the two boys had to make their first appearance in court, so that the police could request a further detention. They were taken to South Sefton Magistrates Court in Bootle, just around the corner from the Strand. Albert Kirby made the application, which was granted. Lawrence Lee stood to thank the police for their delicate handling of the case.

Seeing the boys for the first time, Albert Kirby and Jim Fitzsimmons were astounded by their size. They had been told the boys were short, of course, but had not expected them to be this small. The two officers watched the two children and wondered.

In the court Bobby and Jon did not once look at each other. Afterwards, they were led to the secure car park at the back of the court to be driven to their respective police stations. Jon was already inside his unmarked car, and Bobby was just walking past. They turned and caught each other's eye. They both smirked. A look which some of the officers who saw it interpreted as an evil smile.

22

On Saturday morning, Bobby had a newly appointed appropriate adult to replace his mother in the interviews. The social worker had arrived at the station the night before, carrying a football comic, a *Quizkids* magazine, some sweets and a card game, *Spot Pairs*, to keep Bobby occupied. Together, he and Bobby had watched a children's video on a portable television in the interview room.

They were back in there at midday on Saturday, for Bobby's eighth interview. Bobby had an admission to make. He had touched the baby, trying to get him off the railway track. He had lifted him by the belly, with his arms around his chest, but he put him back because he was going to get full of blood. He was sure James had all his clothes on then.

Phil Roberts tells Bobby they've been talking to the officers interviewing Jon, and he doesn't think Bobby's told them everything. Bobby says he has.

They go over the way that Bobby and Jon came down from the railway line, and then they show Bobby a fluffy toy lamb, brand new, which has been found at the reservoir, and which the investigating team thinks may have been used to lure James from the Strand. Bobby says he's never seen it before, and he doesn't know if Jon had it. Why would we want a teddy?

Right, says Phil Roberts, we're going to go through now, again, what happened to James on the railway. He wants to know the truth, because a little more has happened, a lot more, in fact, than Bobby has said. But I've told you, says Bobby. No, there's been a little more than that. You just said there was a lot more. Right, there's a lot more, yes.

Roberts says he doesn't think James had all his clothes on.

He did, says Bobby. He didn't, you know. Well, why would I want to take his clothes off? That's what I want to know, Bobby. I never even touched him. Well you did, you've already told us that you picked him up. I know, I never hit him. You've never told us any other way that you've touched him, or done anything. Because youse stopped the interview.

They go over what Bobby had said in the previous interviews. Bobby picks up Bob Jacobs for mentioning Jonathan. His name's Jon. It was after Jon had finished hitting James that he threw a battery at him. It was also after Bobby had put his ear to James's chest, to see if he was still breathing. The battery hit James in the face. Why did he do that? I don't know, ask him. Well? I can't read his mind.

Jacobs says he doesn't believe Bobby had been standing idly by, and Bobby says he was trying to pull Jon back. Jacobs doesn't believe that. Bobby says that's what you don't believe.

They tell Bobby that Jon has admitted throwing stones and things like that, but is also blaming Bobby for a lot of things. They want to know the truth, especially to do with clothes. Bobby doesn't even know what they're talking about.

Again, they go over the sequence of events. Bobby says that after Jon had thrown the paint over James, Bobby told Jon to throw the paint away. He asked Jon why he'd thrown the paint. Jon said because he felt like it. Bobby told Jon he was going, 'cos he kept on hitting him.

The first thing Jon did was throw a brick in James's face while he was sitting on the wall. James fell on the floor, on his back, and Jon threw a brick on his belly, then he picked up the metal bar and hit him over the head. James had a big cut on his forehead. Jon had thrown the bar at him after James got up again. Bobby demonstrates Jon's throw, making an exclamation of Jon's effort, pffff. He doesn't mean Jon brought the bar right back to throw it, he's just showing he threw it at him. James fell down again, facing up, and then he wouldn't move. Bobby was seeing if he was breathing, and told Jon he wasn't breathing, and then

Jon started hitting him with a twig, which was about as thick as a centimetre on one of the little school rulers. He hit him about three times in the face, on the eyes, Bobby thinks, then threw the twig into the nettles. Then Jon threw the batteries at James's face. He threw one, and then threw the other ones on the floor. Bobby asked Jon why he did it, but Jon just ignored him. He had a smirk on his mouth, like the way he was in the car yesterday. Bobby was crying, trying to pull him back. Then, when Bobby tried to pick James up, Jon said what are you doing, and Bobby said, picking him up. He was doing that so he wouldn't get chopped in half, to put him on the side, at least. He put him down because he didn't want to get full of blood. He doesn't like blood. It stains, and his mother would have to pay. So he put James back down. He wasn't going to put James somewhere else, because blood was already there, and then they'd think he and Jon had dropped him all over the place. That they'd killed him and then put him in one place and then put him in another and put him in another.

Can we put that heater, that fan on? Can't you open the door? No, we can't do that, son.

Bobby never touched James, except for getting him under the fence, seeing if he was breathing and trying to pick him up. Roberts says he's put all the blame on Jon. He doesn't believe Bobby. Bobby says you don't know for cer . . . exact. He knows he's never hit him, so he's got nothing to bother about.

The officers press Bobby, who fences, and finally starts to cry. Is that what you're trying to say, I'm telling lies and Jon's telling . . . swearing on the Holy Bible that he's telling the truth. Well you can go and ask our teacher who's the worst out of me and Jon and she'll tell you Jon.

Roberts says, well, you tell me, you tell. Bobby, you tell me everything that went on, because I'd rather . . . I told you about eighteen times, says Bobby. He doesn't know anything about James's clothing being removed, and he doesn't know anything about asking James to look into the canal. People can whisper,

151

he says. Jon and youse whisper, you know, everybody whispers. Why would he want to push James into the canal? Why would I want to kill him, when I've got a baby of me own? If I wanted to kill a baby, I'd kill, I'd kill me own, wouldn't I?

Yesterday, says Jacobs, you said your own baby's family, didn't you? What do you mean? Well, you said it, when we were talking to you . . . I know he's me family, I'm not stupid. I don't even know what you're going on about.

Roberts says that when James was found his bottom clothing had been removed. Can Bobby tell them why that is? No. Did Bobby start playing with him? With who? With James's bottom. No. Are you sure, now? Yeah, I'm not a pervert, you know. Bobby begins crying. Well, how would you like me calling you a pervert?

The buzzer goes, and Bobby says he's roasting. He goes to the detention room, and sees his mother. 'He said I'm a pervert, they said I've played with his willy.'

Jon's next interview, his seventh, began shortly after Bobby's. Jon asked if this was the last one. Mark Dale said if he told them absolutely everything they needed to know, it would be.

Jon said he and Robert had not tried to take any other child that day, other than the little boy that the mummy got back. He had never been to the Strand with Robert before, when he had tried to do that. Robert had asked Jon to go the Strand before, but had never mentioned taking little children, there or anywhere else.

The officers go over the route that was taken from the Strand to Walton, and Jon says that they got onto the railway by the wall at the end of the entry opposite the police station. There was a gap there, that you could climb through. They pulled James through the gap, and Bobby, on his knees, pulled James up the slope.

Now, tell me what you do, says Dale, just picture it all in your mind now, yeah. Like you're watching a film, yeah, and you just tell me, in this film in your head, what's happening, because it's easier if you do that, than me keep asking you questions.

Robert opened the paint tin and threw it in James's face, when they were in the middle of the bridge, and then threw the stick he had used to open the tin down between a gap into the road. The paint went into James's left eye, and he cried. He put his hand to his face, trying to wipe the paint off. They were walking then, and Robert said is your head hurting, we'll get a plaster on, and he lifted this brick up, a house brick, and threw it in his face. His face or his head? His head, Jon thinks. James cried and screamed, fell over on his bum, and he got straight back up again. Bobby said to Jon, pick up a brick and throw it, but Jon just threw it on the floor. It was a half brick, and he missed on purpose. Bobby picked the same brick up and threw it again. Jon was trying to stop him doing it. He pulled Robert's coat for a bit. This second throw hit James in the face and made his nose bleed. Jon doesn't know what else happened. Jon picked up little stones, 'cos he wouldn't throw a brick on him. James just kept on getting back up again. He wouldn't stay down. Robert was saying stay down, you stupid divvy and all that. Jon doesn't know why Robert wanted James to stay down. He wanted him dead, probably. Robert took James to the other side 'cos there was loads of bricks there and he kept on, he kept on picking them up and throwing them. Jon was holding Robert back, and Jon took some bricks but missed by a, by a mistake. He means, not by mistake but deliberately 'cos he only picked little stones up, the white ones on the track, and threw them at his arms. Jon doesn't remember what else Robert was shouting. It was last week, he can't remember anything. James was still crying. Jon was dragging Robert off, going leave him alone, you've done enough. Robert threw about ten bricks, Jon only threw six, or five, but he deliberately missed James and hit him once on the arm 'cos he never meant to hit him on the arm. They were house bricks that Jon threw. He hit James twice on the arm, because he wanted to get the bricks at the side of him. Robert said what are you doing, can't you aim properly. Jon said I see double vision, how am I, how am I supposed to aim properly. He doesn't think Robert picked up anything else. Oh, yeah, he picked up this steel bar and hit him once. The bar was bigger than a ruler at school. It was made of steel. He knows that because it was heavy. Robert said it was heavy 'cos Jon had picked it up too and he threw it down dead quick 'cos it was too heavy for him. Jon picked it up because Robert said just feel the weight of that. The bar hit James on the head at the side, and Jon thinks he was knocked out then. Then they threw a few bricks at him, and then they ran away. James was making spluttering noises then, lying on the rail, on his tummy. Jon doesn't know why they ran away. He just said to Robert, don't you think we've done enough now?

Dale asks Jon if he was angry with James when he pulled the hood from James's anorak. No, says Jon, I didn't really want to hurt him, I didn't want to hurt him or nothing 'cos I didn't want to hurt him with strong things, only like light things 'cos, 'cos I deliberately missed him with the bricks, but not with the stones. So you only wanted to hurt him a little bit? There is a pause. Answer the question, says Neil. Dale says why did you want to hurt him a little bit? I mean, I didn't want to hurt him really. Robert probably, I thought Robert, Robert was probably doing it for fun or something, 'cos he was laughing his head off and he grinned at me when I was getting in the car, do you know, when we went to the court. In an evil way.

Jon says he doesn't remember if James was hit with anything else. He did not steal anything in Tandys, and he doesn't think Robert stole anything. Robert pulled James's pants off, and his undies. Jon pulled his shoes off. He doesn't know why. It was last week. He keeps on forgetting.

Just remember, says Dale, I said like a film. Imagine you're watching a film, just like that. Try that and tell us what's going on. I can't see anything, says Jon. Just try and imagine why, what made you pull his shoes off. I don't know, just mad, I went, I just went like that. I just went like that. Just something to do. Were you angry? Dale asks. Because you sort of clenched your fist then. No, I wasn't angry, I was upset.

Robert threw the underpants behind him, then picked them up again and put them on James's face, where there was all blood on. This was after the iron bar had been thrown. Jon wasn't looking then, he was crying, he was too upset.

Jon begins crying. I don't want any more now dad, he's asking me too hard questions. Jon doesn't know what else happened to James. Robert done all of it mainly.

When Bobby's ninth interview began, just before two o'clock on Saturday afternoon, he had decided, as was his right, not to answer any questions. Jason Lee had retired for a rest, and the solicitor from Paul Rooney's, Dominic Lloyd, had taken over.

Bobby didn't want to say his name. Lloyd told him it was all right to say his name. Bob Jacobs asks him if he had spoken to another boy, earlier on the Friday. Yeah, well just listen, says Bobby, breaking his vow of silence, I was told, right, in the paper that the two youths that took James were supposed to have done an old granny over four hours later. The officers say they don't know anything about that, and that isn't what they were talking to him about.

Jacobs tries to steer Bobby into speaking about the abduction of Mrs Power's son. He mentions various shops in the Strand – Mothercare, TJ Hughes – and Bobby says he's heard of them. Jacobs goes through the statement from Mrs Power, referring to the two boys at the purse counter in TJ Hughes. Bobby says he doesn't even know what they're talking about. He's not saying nothing. He then picks Jacobs up over a detail. He says Jacobs has changed the story. Jacobs says he hopes Bobby's not going to pick him up every time he changes stories, because Bobby changes stories as well, doesn't he?

Jacobs ploughs on, through the description of events given by Mrs Power. Bobby quibbles here and there, and finally, when

Jacobs gets to the part where a boy has waved Mrs Power's son towards him, Bobby says Jon could have been making a wave and how was he supposed to hear him say, doing that?

All they want to know, says Roberts, is what happened. Bobby says he never seen Jon do it, but he might've sneaky done it. Bobby wasn't in TJ Hughes, and Jon was with him.

Jacobs then starts to go through the description of the two boys supplied by the mother. A boy with a thin face wearing blue jeans and dark training shoes. Blue jeans? Bobby queries. Well it couldn't've been us, we were in school uniform. The other boy is said to be of stocky build. What's stocky? Bobby queries. It means fattish, says Phil Roberts. Well, it couldn't've been me 'cos I don't eat. Everybody thinks I'm skinny. The boy with a stocky build is also said to have a fat face with a full fringe. I haven't got fat, says Bobby, it couldn't've been me. I haven't got a full fringe. Where's my fringe? And I don't wear jeans.

The interview goes on like this for several minutes, until, finally, Bob Jacobs tells Bobby he is being arrested for the attempted abduction of Mrs Power's son. He explains that it's a new thing Bobby is being arrested for. When do I wear jeans for school, says Bobby.

After the arrest, the officers continue to question Bobby about the incident, and he becomes increasingly awkward. They tell Bobby that Jon has said they planned to throw this boy in front of a car. But we weren't going to take any boy, says Bobby. Well, Jon says you were. So you take everything he says, do you?

Jacobs. And, of course, the main thing is you'd certainly remember if you and Jon planned to take him away . . .
Bobby. I know.
Jacobs . . . and throw him under a car, wouldn't you?
Bobby. You just said in front of one.
Roberts. Well, in front of one.
Jacobs. That's what I just said, then.
Bobby. You said under one.
Roberts. Under, yeah, well, just a play on words, it's just a different,

you just choose the same word again. He just said another, another different word.

Jacobs. So you didn't plan that?

Bobby. No.

They produce the map then, and go through it, marking crosses at the various points Bobby has mentioned. He identifies the fence by City Road, at the opposite end of the entry from Walton Lane, as being the place where they got on to the railway line.

The interview ends, and the next one begins four minutes later. Phil Roberts and Bob Jacobs know they are running out of time now, and they can see that Bobby has become obstructive.

They ask him again about James's clothing being removed, and he again denies it. They ask him if anyone stuck their hand into James's mouth. Bobby denies it.

Bob Jacobs wants to tell what Jon has said. Most probably, says Bobby that I've took everything off him and I've been playing with him. Jacobs asks how he knows that. 'Cos I know he's going to say that. Playing with what? Roberts asks. His privates, that's what you said before. What do you mean, privates, what do you mean by privates, it doesn't matter about the words you use? What I say, says Bobby. What, like his penis, is that what you're saying? 'Cos Jon's not going to own up, is he? Bobby says. He begins crying. They're taking what Jon says. Bobby knows he never touched him.

They again ask Bobby if he touched James's mouth. No. He's told the truth, he's not answering any more. Phil Roberts says that Jon admits taking James's shoes off. Bobby says Jon might've taken his pants off, but Bobby doesn't know 'cos he got down the post. The officers tell Bobby what Jon has said about the removal of James's clothing. Bobby is having none of this. So, in other words, he says, you're taking what Jon says and just ignoring me, so I'll ignore you.

Bobby is asked about the scratch seen on his face later on the Friday evening. He says it was a spot which he had picked. They ask how his face became so mucky with dirty marks.

Bobby. What do you mean, dirty marks?

Jacobs. What I'm saying. You know what dirty marks are, don't you?

Bobby. Like sex marks?

Jacobs. Like what?

Bobby. Sex marks, dirty.

Jacobs. Sex marks?

Bobby. Like dirty words?

Roberts. No, marks on your face.

Jacobs. Bobby, you know what dirty marks are, don't you?

Bobby. Mucky marks.

Roberts. Mucky marks, that's what.

Jacobs. Haven't you heard the word dirty used about anything but sex before? Do you only think about dirty as being about sex?

Bobby understands now. Ask his mum, he says, when they play out they always get dirty. The dirt hasn't come from bricks, 'cos he never touched no bricks. Only little tiny ones they were throwing in the water at the canal.

He is asked about the injury to James's mouth again. He says it might have come off the stick Jon used. It could be like little buds that it caught on and dragged his mouth down. Or the metal bar, 'cos that fell on his head, and then that might have fell on to his face then and pulled it down.

Roberts says he doesn't want Bobby to get angry, but he's got to ask these questions. Did Bobby play with his bottom? No, I never. Okay did you, erm, play with his penis? No. But Jon says that you kicked him between the legs; what do you say to that? No.

Jacobs asks if he or Jon tried to cover the body with stones. Jon did, big stones so you couldn't see his face. He was trying to stop the blood pouring out of his face. Jacobs asks if Bobby helped Jon. Bobby says he stuck one brick on him. It fell off his face. Jon put it on then it would roll back off. Bobby nods his head, yes, he put the brick back on. I haven't got a toothbrush in here, says Bobby. Jacobs says they'll speak to someone about getting him a toothbrush. They end the interview.

Jon's eighth interview had begun at twenty past two. The officers reminded Jon of the point he had reached in the previous interview, where James's clothes had been taken off. Jon said that he and Robert were then pulling bricks onto his face. Covering his face. It was Robert's idea, so nobody can see him. Jon thinks James was moving, because the bricks were moving a bit, like nearly falling off.

Jon then tells how they ran into Walton village, going through the entries until his mum caught them. He thinks they were on the railway for fifteen minutes, ten minutes, five minutes . . . no, not five minutes, that would be too short, wouldn't it?

Mark Dale says he thinks something else has happened that Jon's missed out. He knows Jon doesn't want to talk about it, because he started crying before. But he's got to be brave now, because there's something important he must tell them, and he knows what it is. Jon says he doesn't know. Dale says hasn't he told his mum something today; didn't someone kick him? Oh yeah, me, says Jon, only light, and I punched him light on the reservoir. Didn't you push him and didn't you kick him while you were up at the line? No Robert did. Did he, where? Underneath. Where's underneath? Jon points to his groin. What do you call it, says Dale, come on, it's not rude, come on, let's see what you call it. Willy.

Jon says Robert did that about ten times. He saw his legs going. It was after James's trousers were taken off. So there was something else, wasn't there, says Dale. Oh yeah, says Jon. I forgot it. I told me mum last night everything, but it just came out me mind this morning. Dale says, so you kicked him as well, where did you kick him? The chest and the middle there, and I punched him in his face a few times, light. Did you kick him while he was lying down? No, Robert did, you know, he went like that. Stamped on him? Yeah, not in the face I think it was in the legs or something. Dale says they took a pair of Jon's shoes, and there was blood on them. Jon says he forgot that bit, 'cos he kicked him in the face, and all blood came on his shoes. Jon asks if they took Robert's shoes. They did. Robert kicked him in the face loads of times. Jon only kicked him once or twice. This happened halfway through when Robert was throwing bricks.

Dale asks if Jon had got mad. Must you have been angry to have kicked him? No, I was upset, well, when I got in I was, and I was crying in bed. Well, I bet you were, says Dale, what were your feelings when you were kicking him? Sad, I wasn't angry or I wouldn't have been angry for kick . . . kicking a baby but I've never done it before. Robert most probably did, but I'd never, I'd never done it before.

They speak about the paint on Jon's coat. He thinks James might have touched him on the coat, when he was kneeling down by him, to see if he was all right, to see if his eyes were all right. James said don't hurt me and I went all right. Could he say those words, could he? Dale asks. No, he said, I'm all right, I'm all right, he was too, he was scared of Robert, he wasn't scared of me because I never hit him as much.

Robert didn't kneel down, he was kicking him in the knees and everything and Jon said will you stop it, Bobby, he's scared and all that.

They begin asking Jon about the batteries and when it comes to asking why the batteries were there, Jon begins to cry. He doesn't know. He never put them there. They press him, and he becomes more upset. He says Robert threw them, and Scott says it was a little bit more than throwing them. If he tells them what happened to the batteries it's all over and done with.

Jon is crying. I don't know, I don't know, dad. Scott asks if it's horrible what happened with the batteries. No, I didn't know anything what Robert done with the batteries. Why are you crying then? Because you'll blame it on me that I had them.

Dale asks Jon if he remembers what happened yesterday. When we started talking about all this and you said you hadn't taken James, yeah, and eventually you got very upset didn't you, but you felt better afterwards didn't you, when you told us, and you . . . but you couldn't really tell us at first, could you? Why couldn't you tell us? I'm scared. You were scared, okay, but you got brave didn't you, you eventually managed to come out with it, didn't you?

Jon still doesn't know what happened to the batteries. He is asked if Robert touched James anywhere else. If he did anything else to his willy, other than kicking it. Jon becomes distraught. He doesn't know. He doesn't. He doesn't know. He goes to hit his father. Hey, hey, says Dale, don't go to punch your dad. Jon says me dad thinks I know and I don't, you're saying I do, and I don't. I only know he got killed.

They ask about the bricks placed over the body, and the placing of the underpants. Jon says they're believing what Robert says. Dale says Robert is telling them a story, and they need Jon to tell them one as well. They ask about James's mouth. Jon says he did not put his fingers in James's mouth. Who did? He doesn't know, he never saw nothing. Dale says he's got to admit to himself that he saw everything that happened there, because he was a part of it, so he can't say he didn't see. Jon is crying. He didn't put his fingers in his mouth. He wants his mum. He continues crying and he is inconsolable. He wants his mum. He doesn't know anything else . . . end of interview.

There had been discussion all day about how long the interviews could continue. Unquestionably, they had enough to charge the boys, but could they elicit further admissions, or were the interviews becoming counterproductive as the boys became tired? In any case, they could only hold Bobby and Jon until early on Sunday morning, without charging them. If they continued to interview it might leave the inquiry open to accusations that they had pushed too hard and too far with the interviews. A judge could throw the lot out.

Phil Roberts made it known that he wanted to continue.

It was a frustrating situation, especially with Bobby who had denied so much. There were still so many uncertainties.

Finally, the decision was made. The boys would be charged that evening. The media would be notified, and so too would the Bulger family.

There would be one last session of questioning. The boys would be taken out, separately, and driven over the route to explain exactly which way they had walked with James. It would have been better to walk the route with them, but their safety would have been at risk. They went in unmarked cars, the same people who had been in the stationary interviews, with a back-up car following behind, just in case there were problems. They went at different times, to avoid an unscheduled meeting, and Jon went first.

As they drove down from Lower Lane to the Strand, Jon wanted to know what Dale and Scott would do if there were a whole lot of photographers in the middle of the road taking pictures. Dale said he'd smile, probably. Jon said he'd run them over. He said photographers probably sneaked up on them now. They were good hiders, they go in little gaps and take loads of pictures.

Jon said he was going to sing a song to himself, only they'd be hearing the song all the way through. Dale said he could keep them entertained. They'd have a karaoke. He asked what song Jon had been going to sing. Jon said it was the one thingy sings. He began singing, and carried on, at intervals, over much of the journey.

They drove from the Strand, past the reservoir, through to County Road and on to Walton Lane. Jon saw a boy from school, and pointed him out to his dad. There's Daniel, dad, you know, from school.

He pointed out the various places they had been, the junctions they had crossed. He said he had been in the entry between City Road and Walton Lane when he threw the hood into the tree, not on the railway line that ran alongside it. He said they had got on to the railway line by the fence on Walton Lane, near the bridge, opposite the police station.

Jon wanted to see how many flowers there were on the embankment at Cherry Lane. Dale said they didn't want to be going up there. But they stopped at the bottom of Walton Village, and Jon was able to point out Bobby's house – the one with the policeman outside – and see the flowers on the embankment across the road. Here you are, you wanted to see the flowers. Oh yeah, millions of them.

Jon saw the 'Have you seen these boys?' poster in the window of the chip shop. He pointed it out and said it had Merseyside Police and pictures of him and Robert. George Scott said there were a lot of those around. Jon said you don't need them now, do you. He wanted to know how come his picture was in black-and-white and Robert's wasn't. The officers didn't know.

They began driving back to Lower Lane and Jon said he'd like a drink when he got in. He wanted a Lilt. Then he asked, can fingerprints come out on skin?

Liverpool had been playing at home, that afternoon, to Ipswich, and Bobby's car got stuck in the traffic, leaving Walton Lane for the Strand just after half five. It was a small car and, with five people inside on a cold day, the windscreen was quickly covered in mist, which Phil Roberts, who was driving, struggled to remove.

Bobby was anxious about meeting up with Jon. Where would he be? He wasn't going to be on the railway at the same time was he? Bobby wasn't going if he was. The officers told Bobby they were planning to drive along the route and Bobby wanted to know how you could drive a car on the railway.

Once on Stanley Road they followed the route back to Walton, and Bobby showed them where they had got on to the railway, by the bent fencing in the entry off City Road. Jon got over first then Bobby passed the baby over. Jon grabbed the baby, and then Bobby climbed over, on to the railway.

It had been decided that Albert Kirby should tell Denise and Ralph Bulger that two boys, aged ten, were being charged with the abduction and murder of their son James. Earlier that afternoon Albert and Geoff MacDonald had driven up to Kirkby with Mandy Waller and Jim Green, the two officers who had first dealt with Denise and Ralph, just over a week ago.

On the Monday, Albert had appointed Mandy and Jim to be the inquiry's family liaison officers, and they had spent the week shuttling between Marsh Lane and the home of Denise's mother in Kirkby, where the Bulger family were based.

It had been Jim Green's job on the Monday to tell Denise and Ralph that James's body had been cut in half by the train. He had worried over the words he should use, not wanting them to sound blunt and insensitive. In the end he had asked to see Denise and Ralph privately in the kitchen and said, 'I have to tell you that James's body had been severed by a train.'

Denise had stood there with her head bowed, showing no reaction, and Ralph had stared with what Jim Green would come to recognise as angry eyes. Ralph had simply nodded in response, and neither he nor Denise had asked any questions.

This was the only detail of the injuries that had become public knowledge, and the police had wanted the family to hear it from them first. Albert's decision to keep the other injuries from them had made it difficult for Jim Green, who more or less knew everything because he had attended the post mortem, but had to keep the knowledge to himself in all his dealings with the Bulgers.

As the week progressed the family had become increasingly inquisitive. There was some anger, particularly at moments when they felt the police were not doing their job, not following the right lines of enquiry, or not keeping them informed. The sudden flare of publicity over Snowdrop Street did not help. Why weren't we told? Why are we hearing things from the television? Is this the one? Have you got him?

There had been no time to tell the family of the Snowdrop Street arrest beforehand, and the family liaison officers tried to explain that through the course of the inquiry there might be several such arrests. It would be best not to read too much into them.

One of the many Bulger uncles lived in Walton and picked up various rumours about what had happened and who had been responsible. He had been told that the video footage of the abduction clearly showed the two brothers who had found the body. It was obviously them, why hadn't the police got them? Mandy checked, and reassured the family that they had been eliminated from the inquiry.

On the initial visits, Mandy was served tea in a cup and saucer from the best china. By the end of the week tea was coming in a mug, and they knew without asking that she didn't take sugar. Becoming close to the family, exposed to and touched by the intense emotions they were feeling, was hard enough in itself. It was good, that Saturday afternoon, to be the bearer of positive news.

Albert Kirby spoke to Ralph first, and told him they expected to charge the two boys later that day. Were they sure these were the ones? Oh yes.

Albert asked to see Denise, and was taken upstairs to a bedroom, where Denise sat on the edge of the bed, with a box in front of her containing some of the thousands of cards and letters of sympathy that had been arriving for her and Ralph.

Denise did not at first realise who Albert was, and it seemed to him, as he explained what was happening, that he was talking to someone who wasn't really there. Denise asked no questions of Albert but, back downstairs, the family wanted to know about the boys.

The charges meant that the family was a step closer to getting James's body released for the funeral. The ages of the boys being charged did not make it any easier for the family to focus responsibility for James's death. It was frustrating and incomprehensible. They wanted to know why, but there was no explanation that Albert could offer.

At 6.15 on Saturday evening, 20 February 1993, Detective Inspector Jim Fitzsimmons charged Jon Venables with the abduction and murder of James Patrick Bulger, and the attempted abduction of Mrs Power's son.

Jon sat on a stool against the bridewell counter at Lower Lane Police Station. He was drawing on paper as he waited for the charges to be read. His mother and father were behind him, upset and comforting each other. Susan began crying briefly, and Jon began crying too. Then she stopped, and he stopped. When the charges had been read, and Jim Fitzsimmons had explained them to him in simple language, Jon carried on drawing.

Jim then drove down the East Lancs Road to Walton Lane, to repeat the procedure with Bobby.

Bobby had been playing *Spot Pairs* in the detention room with Brian Whitby, the local police youth liaison officer. PC Whitby had been working at Anfield that afternoon during the Ipswich game, and had been asked to sit with Bobby for a while on his return.

Whitby had been in the station last Friday, 12 February, and had worked out that he had been standing in the kitchen area of the canteen, with its large window directly overlooking the railway barely 50 yards away, at about the time James Bulger was killed. He had been having difficulty coming to terms with this, and was having difficulty coming to terms with the idea that Bobby had been responsible. Whitby had known the Thompsons for years, through his work. Bobby had not been high on his private list of suspects.

They chatted idly as they turned the cards, and Bobby said, 'Can I go home soon, PC Brian? I don't want to be here any more.'

The bridewell was suddenly crowded, for the first time in days, as the interviewing team, the senior officers, the lawyers and the social workers gathered ahead of the charges. The officers chatted and there was some laughter, an air of relief among them. Normally, this moment in an inquiry would be the prelude to a celebratory party back at the station bar. There would be no party tonight at Marsh Lane. Just a few speeches of thanks from the bosses, and some cathartic consumption of alcohol.

Bobby came out of the detention room, and stood briefly, a small figure lost among the grown-ups. It was as if he could have slipped away without anyone noticing.

Then some of the adults left the bridewell, and Jim Fitzsimmons and Bobby took their places opposite each other across the counter. There was no chair for Bobby, who stood with his head slightly raised, peering up at Jim Fitzsimmons. It reminded Phil Roberts of *Oliver Twist*.

When Bobby was charged he said, 'It was Jon that done that.'

Afterwards, his mother, who had been in no state to attend the charges, had to be helped away from the police station. She was in the advanced stages of shock, staggering like a drunk, her whole body shaking uncontrollably, though she was completely sober.

Bobby went back to the detention room and later he fell asleep, while a couple of social workers and a police officer sat there talking. A train went down the railway line, and Bobby sat up. He said, was that a train going past? Yes. Bobby lay down again. I know all the times of them trains.

23

On Shrove Tuesdays in the nineteenth century it was a popular local sport to set a cock loose in a ring with a mob of small boys whose hands had been tied behind their backs. The boys would fight to capture the cock, and the winner would be the boy emerging with the cock held in his teeth.

There was conventional cock-fighting, dog-fighting and bull-baiting, in which a bull was tied to a stake and attacked by dogs, which were set upon it one at a time, one after the other.

The adult game of Lifting was reserved for Easter Mondays and Tuesdays. On the Monday women were free to carry off men, apparently in the hope of finding men with money in their pockets to spend in the ale houses. On Tuesday the men lifted the women and, as one G. H. Wilkinson noted when writing his personal history of Walton in 1913, 'acts of the grossest indecency were committed'. Wilkinson added that the better education of the working classes and the exertions of religious teachers to inculcate more respect had gradually put an end to such disgraceful practices.

Walton was then little more than a small village, still flanked by farmland, nurseries and the estates of the local manor house. It was only at the end of the last century that the village was finally overrun by the creeping city sprawl of Liverpool which, in itself, was a reversal of history.

The sandstone church of St Mary the Virgin in the parish of Walton on the hill was once the Lord's house of all it surveyed. The church has a proud vantage point on the brow of the rise from the River Mersey. It has a 118-foot bell tower, from the top of which, it is said, Blackpool Tower is visible on a good day, some 30 miles away.

The church site, with its ancient circular graveyard, predates Blackpool Tower by at least a thousand years, and for several centuries the parish of Walton extended over 40 square miles, embracing the little fishing community of Liverpool.

The village that developed around the church was a travellers' rest, and policemen with cutlasses sometimes patrolled the outskirts of Walton to discourage the local *banditti* and footpads from highway robbery. The old churchwardens were responsible for dealing with crime, and iron stocks stood in the graveyard for the summary punishment of drunks, debtors and assorted petty offenders.

When Liverpool began developing as a trading port, it no longer wanted to be an outpost of Walton and in 1699, after an argument which had lasted some 50 years, an Act of Parliament finally granted Liverpool its independence as a parish. The Liverpool Corporation's case was set out in a memorial: 'And there being but one Chapel, which doth not contain one half of our Inhabitants, in the Summer (upon pretence of going to the Parish-Church, which is Two long Miles, and there being a village in the way) they Drink in the said village; by which and otherwise many Youth and sundry Families are ruined: Therefore it is hoped the Bill may pass, being to promote the Service of God.'

The said village was Kirkdale, but the legacy of this potential for ruination still persists along Scotland – Scottie – Road which leads out of Liverpool, into Kirkdale Road and on to Walton. There is a press of pubs along the last stretch of Scottie Road. Within a couple of hundred yards, on one side of the road, stand the Foot, the Widows, Dolly Hickey's Pub and Wine Bar, the Parrot, the Corner House and the Clifford Arms; and, on the other side of the road, the Eagle Vaults, One Flew Over the Throstle's Nest, the Newsham House, McGinty's Bar and the Europa.

It was around Scottie Road that the Victorian era delivered some of the worst excesses of poverty and deprivation. The dark, insanitary and thickly populated courts and cellars of Liverpool existed long before Queen Victoria, and the last were not cleared until the 1960s. Yet they achieved a peak of squalor in the mid-nineteenth century, when epidemics of cholera and other diseases were commonplace, and 32 was a ripe old age.

Children, in the language of the day, were ragged street urchins who begged, hustled, robbed and died in sufficient numbers to maintain a high rate of child mortality. They were mythologised in *Her Benny*, a mawkish Victorian novel by Silas B. Hocking in which Her dies, but Benny finds God and is saved from poverty, bachelorhood and death.

This was Liverpool's great moment as an industrial and commercial centre. Unemployment was high, work was often casual, especially at the docks, and wages were low. The Welfare State had yet to be invented and poverty was largely unrelieved.

When the city began clearing its courts and cellars it often replaced them with tenement blocks, known as landings, which became slums in their own right, and were in turn replaced with walk-up flats which in turn came to be classified as slums. The cycle of clearances continued into the 1980s, long after Liverpool's moment had passed, and higher standards of poverty had been attained.

By contrast with Liverpool, Walton was, in the words of an old report, 'free from those atmospheric impurities which injuriously affect animal and vegetable life'. It had the clean air of the Atlantic blowing up from Liverpool Bay, along the route of the so-named Breeze Hill, and it had St Mary's, which it could, and always did, claim as the Mother Church of Liverpool.

Walton developed around the village and the church, predominantly as an area of red-brick terraces; an archetypal Northern landscape of narrow, cobbled streets and flat-fronted houses whose doors opened directly onto the pavement, or bay-windowed properties with front yards barely wide enough to stand in. Back alleys, better known as entries, jiggers or jowlers, threaded between the cramped roads.

It was dense housing, but not so dense as the courts and cellars, and with the exception of the Throstle's Nest estate off Rice Lane, which has long since been razed, Walton's population was spared the greatest indignities endured by the people of Liverpool.

St Mary's was all but destroyed by German bombs in 1941, and was rebuilt in the late forties. The iron stocks have gone, and the last thatched cottage, behind the church, was demolished in the 1960s, along with several other neighbouring houses and buildings, to make way for the Breeze Hill flyover.

There has been some clearance, some redevelopment and the addition of new estates, but the appearance of Walton is broadly unchanged. There is a sense of tradition and continuity which has been lost to other areas of Merseyside. Tarmac has covered the old road surfaces, but cobbles break through in places. Small children sit on the front step and scratch at the pavement, boys and girls play in the streets or roam in groups through the entries.

Many of the houses have been individualised, with aluminium windows, stone cladding, pebble dashing, coats of brightly coloured paint. Still, there is a detectable air of neglect and civic failure in the rough grass and cracked headstones of the churchyard and in Walton Village, which curls down to Walton Lane, and the streets that encircle it to create a distinct, almost enclosed, community. Here the pavements are crumbling, the roads lumpy, pot-holed and patchily repaired.

Many of the shops in Walton Village have closed, the sites derelict. There are still corner newsagents and grocers, a couple of chippies, the video rental, Monica's Cafe, the Mane Attraction Unisex Salon, and the Top House pub, with the Anfield just around the corner.

The Village stands in the heart of Liverpool City Council's County Ward, which is currently represented by one Labour and two Liberal Democrat councillors. County Ward is almost entirely white and primarily working class, though not all the working class are working.

On the City Council's Deprivation Index, Walton is some way below the bleakest areas of Everton and Toxteth, where the unemployment rate is running at over 40 per cent, and fewer than two out of every ten households own either their own home or a car.

County Ward's unemployment rate is just over 20 per cent, rising to nearly 30 per cent among men and young people. The level of unemployment has more than doubled in the last

20 years. Half the households in the area are owner-occupied, though two thirds have neither central heating nor a car. The proportion of single-parent families is under ten per cent, as it is throughout Liverpool, though the ratio in County, and city-wide, has tripled over two decades.

Walton's crime is typically urban, and not significantly high. In any one month some 650 offences are likely to be recorded at Walton Lane Police Station, and a majority of these will be burglaries and thefts of, or from, cars. Criminal damage, shop-lifting and violence will claim a sizeable proportion, with some robbery, a few stolen bikes, and a handful of drug offences. Less than a third of these crimes are likely to be detected, which is a little below the average detection rate on Merseyside. Of those crimes that are detected, about one quarter will have been com-mitted by juveniles, and a majority of those juveniles will be cautioned rather than prosecuted.

The juveniles' misdemeanours will be described on cards, and filed alphabetically in the two-drawer – male and female – card indexing system which is maintained in the Youth and Community Liaison Office at Walton Lane by the two YLOs (formerly JLOs – Juvenile Liaison Officers), Bev Whitehead and Brian Whitby.

PC Whitby is in his mid-thirties, and has two children of his own, a seven-year-old daughter and a boy the same age as Bobby and Jon. His own childhood, though not spent in Walton and perhaps more stable than many, was not so very dissimilar to that of the youngsters he now encounters.

He knows that much of his job reflects the worst of the area – young people in trouble, or causing trouble. He knows it's not all like that. He'll be visiting a school during assembly and only recognise say two dozen faces out of a thousand, as he looks around. He'll go into one classroom and they'll all stand up respectfully as he enters. He'll go into another, and they'll chorus, 'Fuck off, bizzy!'

When he started as a JLO five years ago, he was full of

crusading zeal. He was going to save the children and put the world to rights. At the moment, Brian can think of about ten kids he saw in those early days. Only one has stayed on the straight and narrow. The others have become probably the worst juveniles in Walton.

He's learned to pick out the ones that are going to be a problem. Others will hang their heads when confronted, and cry and seem genuinely remorseful. It's the ones that stare you straight in the eye and deny everything that you've got to watch out for. They've got O Levels in lying before they're ten. They'll be going for the degree.

It usually starts at home, when they're seven or eight, stealing from mum's purse, swearing. The parents'll call the station and say we've tried everything, now can you have a go, have a word with him. One time, a little lad comes into the station with a note in an envelope. He hands it to Brian. 'Dear ofcer, this little bastard of a son of mine has been robbing, can you speak to him, please.' Good enough. So what you been doing? Stealing from me mam's purse. Brian tells him the rights and wrongs, shows him round the cells . . . this is where naughty people go who steal . . . he doesn't do that so much any more, employing the shock tactics, but anyway, he's shown the lad round, and sat him on the desk to give him a final talking-to. The lad says I wanted to buy me mum a mother's day present, and I didn't have enough money. It was two pound fifty, and I only had one pound fifty. That finished Brian. How can he tell the lad off now?

Another day, and Brian's on a home visit. He knocks on the door and a small boy answers. Brian's feeling chirpy, so he says, hello sonny, you the man of the house? Fuck off, I'm only six. He goes inside and speaks to the father. He asks the father, do you know what your son just said to me? Brian recounts the doorstep exchange. Well, what do you fucking expect, says the father. Brian leaves, and finds a big nail under the wheel of his car.

If they're going to make a career of it, the next thing will be trouble at school. There'll be a phone call from the head teacher. Brian will be called in to have a word. In his greener days, he used to go around with a more senior JLO, and they were at a school to see a boy, let's call him Mickey, who's been collecting for charity and pocketing the money. Mickey's from a big family. They're all built like bulldogs, and they're all trouble. Brian's got a bet on that Mickey's going to murder someone.

Anyway, they're up at the school. Mickey's mum's there, the teacher, Brian, and his colleague, who's shouting at Mickey. Suddenly, Mickey keels over, in a dead faint. His mother's over him, get up you little bastard, she's pulling at him, and Brian's concerned, fending her off, trying to give the boy some air. He comes round, and starts crying. End of telling-off.

Two years later, Brian's up at the school to see Mickey's younger brother, who's in trouble for something or other. Brian is giving him what for, when, suddenly, younger brother keels over, in a dead faint. It won't work. Not this time it won't. Brian gets the lad up and carries on, unmoved by his ploy.

There are another two brothers that Brian has dealt with, off and on, over the years. They're only in their early teens now, and often in some trouble or other. People think they're just plain nasty. Cheeky bloody hard-faced kids, Brian calls them.

They were smoking cannabis when they were seven or eight, mixing with older lads, coming on like mini-gangsters: Our mate's doing a five stretch for a blagging . . . pulling the tarts . . . on the skag. The boys have been in and out of care, and used to go missing for days at a time, getting picked up somewhere in the city in the early hours of the morning. There was always some kind of trouble at home, and Brian has been there when one of the boys took a hammer and a snooker cue to his mother. Brian does not know what will become of them, but fears the worst. There's a rumour going round at the moment that they've got a gun. This is information that will need to be checked out.

Brian has been preoccupied lately with the fate of a 12-year-old whom he and social services have been trying to get into secure accommodation, as much for the boy's own protection as for anything else. The boy just can't stop robbing, and the locals are sick of it. When he stole and killed a racing pigeon, allegedly worth £2000, people were coming into the station saying, if you don't sort him out, we will. We'll kill him.

The boy looks like an angel, and is so plausible he can talk his way out of anything. He's forever turning up, miles from home, in some trouble or other. The other day it was St Helen's. He'd had fifty pounds out of a till, and was in the police station. The station sergeant is on the phone to Brian, telling him he seems such a nice lad. Says he's keen on bird-watching. The sergeant gets a bit funny when Brian starts laughing. A week or two before that, the boy is caught in the back of a shop in another centre. A policewoman is called. He cries and cries. He's lost, he can't find his mum, he's frightened. The policewoman takes his name and date of birth, and lets him go. Then it transpires that four other nearby shops have been robbed. The policewoman calls Walton. The name the boy gave is false, but the date of birth is all too familiar to Brian.

No one's counting, but the boy has come to police attention more than 80 times. Many of these will be reports that he's absconded from care homes. None are crimes of violence, and not all are far from Walton Lane Police Station: a policeman is walking into the station one day, and sees the boy wheeling a motorbike out of the yard. It turns out he's just stolen it from round the back of the station, where it had been stored as recovered stolen goods.

Sometimes, Brian can't help admiring the wit and resourcefulness of the youngsters, and the scams they pull. He used to work the director's gate at Anfield on match days. You'd get boys coming along, saying they were from *Jim'll Fix It*, and Jim was fixing it for them to get into the match. Boys trying to slither in under the turnstiles, standing outside wailing that they'd lost their ticket and waiting for some kind soul to come along and get them in, boys that Brian knew lived up the road saying they'd travelled from Speke without a ticket, 'blagging' one from somebody, and then trying to sell it on at an exorbitant price. 'Ere matey, got a spare ticket? No. Well, lend us fifty pence for some ciggies. Like they're seriously intending to pay you back next time they see you.

They mind the parked cars of visiting fans, even of the police officers in uniform, who can't get into the station car park, and have to leave their cars nearby. Brian knows you have to pay. If you said sod off you cheeky little beggars, your tyres'd be flat when you got back. Or they'd've scratched fuck off pigs into the paintwork.

It's a bit of a game, all this, but Brian believes there's a new mood creeping in. More youngsters showing less respect. The other night a boy of about 15 came up to him and pointed at Brian's chest. What's that on your tunic? Brian looked down, and the boy's hand flicked up, knocking off Brian's helmet. Hah, got yer officer. What can you do? You can't give 'em a clip round the earhole.

There's another boy causing a few problems on the street, and Brian's having a word with him. The boy says he goes to one of the local schools which just happens to be the school where Brian is on the board of governors. He tells the boy. The boy says what do you want, a medal? The boy turns to his mates. Give this fella a Blue Peter badge, he's our school guv'nor.

It might only be a minority that's bad, but the minority's getting bigger all the time.

Brian doesn't think the new directive on cautioning is helping very much. Trying to keep kids out of court, penny pinching. There isn't the same flexibility any more. In the old days you could have a word with the boss. Look boss, this kid is stepping out of line a bit, but he's got a good mum, and the offences are very petty, let's try and do something for him. Now it all goes up to the juvenile panel; it's just a paper exercise, and there isn't the scope there was before to work with the kids.

The youngsters have noticed the change too. They've twigged that there's a new leniency, that they can get away with things like knocking a bobby's hat off, and worse.

Take, for instance, a teenage girl, arrested the other day for criminal damage. She smashed a door in after a row with somebody. She'd done exactly the same thing a few days earlier. She's already got two cautions for shoplifting, and seems to be under the impression that she's entitled to three before she gets prosecuted. Her attitude can only be described as cavalier.

It's as if you've got to get two or three cautions under your belt to be taken seriously out there. Everyone looks up to the baddie, and wants to be like them. A few cautions will see you on your way. Go on, smash that window, all youse'll get's a caution.

Nowadays, Brian goes on home visits after an offence has been committed and they're saying, if I admit it, will I get off with a caution? Does that mean I won't have to go to court?

He's gone round to see a 15-year-old about an offence. The youth answers the door and Brian explains why he's there. What the fuck's it got to do with you, the youth replies. Brian says he'll be helping to decide what happens. I've already admitted it, says the youth, I'm going to get a caution. He's standing on the doorstep, verbally abusing Brian, when the father comes out, telling his son not to be rude to the officer. The boy tells his father to mind his own fucking business, and punches him. They're all in the house now, Brian restraining the struggling youth, mother and father dancing round them, saying go on officer, give him a good hiding.

Brian doesn't know what it's all about. They say it's the sixties and the do-gooders, but if you ask him what the difference is between his own son and some of the boys in trouble, he'd say it was care and affection, and teaching them right from wrong. At an early age, Brian would slap his boy's hand if he was naughty. He loves the bones of his children, but he will smack them, and he thinks they do learn from that. Then he sits with his son of an evening, gives him time. They'll go through schoolwork, always have a cuddle. That's what's missing for so many of them. You see families and you think, if you can buy them all these material things, why can't you give them love. Brian sees these kids and, sometimes, he just wants to put his arms around them and give them a great big hug. There's one lad, in a group Brian goes bowling with occasionally. This lad'll be acting all tough with his mates, but Brian'll say, come here, put his arm round him, and the lad'll do it. You can see that he wants to.

That's the main problem. Lack of love and affection. Mothers with four or five kids who say I can't keep an eye on all of them twenty-four hours a day. They just don't seem to have the time or the patience. Brian visits the local youth clubs, and there's a little girl in one of them, about two years old, and she's always running round him. Sometimes she's a bit annoying, to be honest, but she's a sweet thing, and one time, she was more annoying than usual, and the mother told her off, told her to leave Brian alone, and she came back, again being a bit naughty, and the mother just drew her hand back and hit the girl across the face, knocking her head sideways, practically into the door. Hey, hey, said Brian. He was really shocked. You can't go doing that.

He often gives talks at youth clubs and schools, on the effects of drugs and alcohol. There's been some concern lately, that younger children are being used by older children as couriers for the sale of drugs. Mostly cannabis and LSD, being sold in schools as well. Brian's sure the police don't know the half of what goes on.

When he speaks to the youngsters about drugs in his talks they'll all say dreadful, we think drugs are dreadful. And what do you think about cannabis? Nothing wrong with that, they'll say. What about drink? Great. What about LSD? Well, we're a bit wary of that, but we might try it. Drugs to them is crack and heroin, and the rest don't count.

These talks are usually reserved for children of secondary school age. The primary school kids get the Stranger Danger lectures. What do strangers look like, he'll ask the class? They're ten foot tall, with big beards and pointed ears, comes the answer.

Jon was born on 13 August 1982, at the Mill Road Hospital in Everton. His parents, Neil and Susan Venables, who were then aged 29 and 25, were living in an end-terrace house on York Street in Walton, off Rice Lane, a few hundred yards north of St Mary's.

Susan would say her own upbringing had been strict and disciplined. She had one brother, and the family were fans of country and western music. Some of them played in a group. Neil would say that he and his sister had a good time in childhood, and they were spoilt, although their mother died quite early.

When Jon was born, Neil was working as a fork-lift truck driver at the Jacob's Biscuit factory in Aintree, and they already had one son, Mark, born three years earlier in May 1979. Their third child, Michelle, was born 15 months after Jon, in November 1983.

The couple had been married since August 1975, and had previously lived in Roderick Road, a turning off Walton Village, moving to York Street for the extra space after Mark came along.

Early on there were problems with Mark. He had difficulty talking, and when Neil and Susan had him examined it turned out that he had been born with a cleft pallet. The frustration of trying to make himself understood caused Mark to have temper tantrums and when he went to one of the local infant schools it was soon apparent that there were behavioural troubles. At about the time of Jon's birth, Mark was identified as having moderate learning difficulties. He was given speech therapy and began attending Meadow Bank Special School in Fazakerley.

Neil and Susan separated in early 1986 and were later divorced. Neil had lost his job a couple of years earlier, and the strain of this while trying to cope with Mark and two other young children had been too much. Neil at first stayed on in York Street so that he could sell the house, and Susan and the children moved in with her mother. Neil still had a car in those days, and used to take the children out every Sunday.

When York Street sold, Neil moved in with his father, at his father's maisonette in Breeze Close, then rented his own flat nearby on Breeze Hill for a while, before moving into Kirkdale.

Susan left her mother's and went to live in Old Swan, and Jon started at the infants' school in Broad Green. Susan's new place turned out to be damp and none too pleasant, so she and the children moved back in with Neil, who drove Jon to and from school in Broad Green every day. Jon seemed happy at the school, though there were concerns that he was upset and difficult following his parents' split, and he too began to have temper tantrums. He was referred for treatment of a squint in his eye – a problem which would remain untreated.

When Susan's name came up on the council's housing list, she moved into a three-bedroomed house in Scarsdale Road on the Norris Green estate, which was one of the large, modern Liverpool developments of public housing.

There was an incident, in January 1987, when the police were called to Susan's home because the children had been left alone for three hours. Susan had found it difficult to cope with the separation from Neil, and had been treated for depression. Neil also had a history of depressive illness.

Michelle and Jon began attending the Broad Square County Primary Junior School, which was close to Scarsdale Road, in September of 1989, following Jon's seventh birthday. In his first year it was noted that he displayed some anti-social behaviour in class, which was annoying but nothing too serious. Sometimes, he would go home complaining of being bullied by a gang of lads at school. In June 1990 he was referred to an educational psychologist, and seen by a trainee who reported that Jon seemed uninterested and unable to concentrate. He stared into space. He seemed unable to cope with the pressures on him.

Neil was on the move again, going back to York Street to share with a mate, and he'd often spend a couple of nights at Scarsdale

Road, occasionally baby-sitting if Susan wanted a night out.

There was still concern over Mark, who continued to have sudden temper tantrums. This is not unusual among children with learning difficulties, but it led to the involvement of a social worker, who made arrangements for respite fostering. Mark began spending one weekend of every month with a foster family, and this helped to reduce the number of tantrums.

In the following year, Michelle also began to show learning difficulties, and she joined Mark at Meadow Bank Special School. Jon moved up to Year 4 at Broad Square, in a class of 24 pupils, and in the first term there were no particular problems.

It was after the Christmas holiday, in January 1991, that his class teacher, Kathryn Bolger, began to be concerned. Jon was acting very strangely. He would sit on his chair, holding his desk in his hands, and rock backwards and forwards, moaning and making strange noises. When the teacher moved him to sit near her at the front of the class he would fiddle with things on her desk and knock them to the floor. He would sometimes bang his head on the furniture, so hard that the teacher was sure it must be hurting him. Jon cried and said he was being picked on out of class. He occasionally ran out of school, and someone would be sent to his home to find him. He wouldn't do anything he was asked, and his school books were empty of work. Jon was marked down as a low achiever; the teacher was sure he was capable of doing more.

Jon's behaviour began to be disruptive at home. He was abusive towards his mother, and the social worker, who had initially been supporting the family over Mark, now found his attention directed towards Jon. There seemed to be problems with other children in the street where Susan was living. Jokes about Jon's brother and sister being backward, some bullying of Mark and Jon by older boys, and a lot of name calling: 'shit, big ears, fucking prick, divvy'. The social worker believed that Jon was experiencing peer group pressure, and was also feeling excluded by, and jealous of, the attention being devoted to Mark and Michelle over their special needs.

It also appeared that Jon copied Mark's behaviour.

Susan was visiting Broad Square School regularly to discuss the difficulties with Jon, but there was no improvement, and his teacher, Kathryn Bolger, was finding it hard to cope with him. She reported all the incidents to the head teacher, and began keeping her own log of Jon's misbehaviour. The parents of other pupils started to complain that Jon was a disruptive influence in the class.

In March there was a weekend trip to North Wales for Jon's school year. The teacher did not want to take responsibility for Jon on the trip. The social worker's offer to go along and take individual charge of him was refused, and Jon did not go to North Wales.

His behaviour deteriorated, and became increasingly bizarre. He would revolve around the walls of the classroom, pulling down displays and other objects. He would lie down and wedge himself between the desks. He would cut himself deliberately with scissors, cut holes in his socks, and stick paper over his face. He would stand on desks, and throw chairs. He threw things across the classroom at the other children, and once, when he was put outside, he began throwing things down the corridor. On another occasion he suspended himself, upside down like a bat, from the coat pegs.

In fourteen years of teaching, Kathryn Bolger had never come across a pupil like Jon. The burden of looking after him in class, coping with what she saw as his attention-seeking behaviour, gave her some stress and anxiety.

The school told Susan that Jon could not sit still for a minute, and she said he was the same at home. He was hyperactive and his sleep was disturbed. He was again referred to the School Psychology Service, and Susan took him to see a psychologist at the clinic in Norris Green. She wondered if Jon's diet might be causing his hyperactivity, and the psychologist said this was possible. A special diet might help. The psychologist suggested another referral to a more senior colleague.

Susan was supplied with a diet sheet by a social worker, which cut out food with such additives as artificial colouring. She never pursued the second referral, and tried the special diet on Jon for a while. It did not seem to make much difference to his behaviour, and eventually she gave up.

Neil had moved into a flat in Walton Village, and wasn't seeing so much of his ex-wife and the children. He left the schooling to Susan, and thought the problems with bullying were just part of growing up. He saw them all on Sundays for a while, and then didn't see Susan for a couple of months, until she came down to Walton Village and started talking about the difficulties she was having with Jon at school. Neil agreed with Susan that it might be best if he changed schools.

Finally, in class one day, not long before the end of the school year, Jon got behind another boy and held a 12-inch wooden ruler to his throat. The boy began going red in the face, and it seemed to the teacher that Jon was trying to choke his classmate. It required some effort from the teacher and a colleague to free the boy from Jon, who seemed so strong. Jon was taken to the head teacher's office, and did not complete his final term at Broad Square.

With the help of the social worker, an approach was made to Walton St Mary's Church of England Primary School, and the head teacher, Irene Slack, was asked if she would accept Jon as a pupil because there were problems at his current school.

Irene Slack was concerned by the background to the transfer request, but said she would take him on condition that Jon behaved himself and went into a class below his proper age group.

Walton St Mary's was in Bedford Road, which was just across County Road from St Mary's Church. It was an old Victorian school building which now shared some 260 pupils with a branch infant school over towards Walton Village.

Irene Slack had been the head teacher for eleven years. The

evolved philosophy of the school was that the pupils should be taught to be tolerant of other races, religions and ways of life; to understand the independence of individuals, groups and nations; to be active participants in society and responsible contributors to it; to be given the ability to function as contributing members of cooperative groups; to be aware of self and sensitive to others.

That latter awareness was the aim that Irene Slack regarded as being the most important. Do unto others as you would like to be done unto yourself was the rule.

Jon entered at the start of the new school year in September 1991 and joined class 4D with Bobby, who was also being kept back a year because of his slow learning progress. Perhaps because of this mutual distinction, they gradually became friends.

The class teacher, Michael Dwyer, was in his fifties and held firm views on discipline. He had taught in schools that catered for what used to be known as maladjusted children, and soon recognised the symptoms of maladjustment in Jon, who sometimes ignored Dwyer's instructions, or walked around the class in the middle of lessons and collapsed in a heap over his desk when he was being defiant.

Dwyer responded by trying to create a structured environment for Jon, showing him what work was required, and what behaviour was acceptable. The system was fine in the classroom, but broke down in the unstructured playground, where Jon often got into fights. On one occasion, Dwyer caught him picking on a younger and smaller boy. Dwyer asked Jon how he would like it if a bigger boy began fighting him.

In class, Bobby seemed shy, quiet, an under-achiever, though Dwyer noticed that he could be sly, and sometimes made the bullets for others to shoot. Like Jon, Bobby would become involved in playtime fights, but Dwyer could not say that either of the boys was remarkable as a trouble-maker or a problem child.

Throughout that year there was a little concern over Bobby's truancy, but no such difficulty with Jon. It appeared that he was settling down in his new school, and his behaviour at home was improving, though the social worker was still worried that Jon felt he was being overlooked because of the attention being given to Michelle and Mark. Jon did not get on well with Mark, and occasionally they would fight. That summer the social worker arranged a holiday for Jon and Michelle, through the charity KIND, Kids In Need and Distress.

The problem of Jon being bullied in the area around his Norris Green home seemed to have subsided, and he had a group of friends there with whom he was always out playing, though Susan noticed that he seemed happier in the company of younger children.

When he played out Jon was usually involved in football, riding around on his bike or games such as hide and seek and British bulldog. Sometimes his was the only bike, and they would give each other piggy rides on the back. Sometimes they sat on the stairs at another boy's home, and told each other jokes and ghost stories.

Jon liked computer games, and was a big fan of Sonic the Hedgehog. At home he had a Commodore C64 that plugged into the television, a Sonic watch and some ordinary hand-held games.

When he first started at St Mary's, his dad used to pick him up and take him home to Norris Green every day. Then Jon began staying over at his dad's a couple of nights a week. It was on one of those nights that Bobby called for Jon, asking for him to play out. Jon told Neil that Bobby was just a boy from his class at school, but the boy in the flat below Neil said that Bobby came from a bad family. Neil told Jon not to play with Bobby and, after that, Neil would chase Bobby if he called at the flat.

The beginning of Jon's new school year in September 1992, five months before the killing of James Bulger, was marked by his graduation from short grey pants to long black school trousers.

At about this time his parents decided to try and revive their relationship, and began living together at Neil's home for half the week. Neil's father had died in June, and Neil had moved back to his father's flat in Breeze Close. He and Susan had taken the children on holiday together, to Pwllheli Butlins in North Wales, and had decided to attempt a reconciliation. Susan started going to Breeze Hill with the three children on Thursday, and staying over until Sunday.

It was little more than five minutes' walk from Neil's new home to school for Jon, who usually made the journey there on his own, and might be met at the gates by his dad for the walk back. Every Friday Mark and Michelle were taken to Norris Green to meet the minibus that took them to Meadow Bank, and when they came back to Norris Green in the afternoons, they were met by Neil or Susan for the return trip to Walton.

Sometimes, when Jon became too difficult for Susan, he would stay with his father throughout the week. Otherwise, he would travel to school from Norris Green and back again on his own, on the 60 or 81 bus, because Susan had to look after Mark and Michelle.

Jon and Bobby were now in 5R with 26 other pupils, the boys outnumbered by 18 girls. The teacher, Mrs Rigg, did not find Jon and Bobby any more trouble than many of the children she taught, though she found it advisable to keep them apart, placing their desks at either end of the classroom.

Jon was not generally naughty, but he could be disruptive, awkward and lazy. Bobby was fairly easy to handle, but was always ready to tell tales on the others, and would never admit to doing anything wrong himself. There were no signs that the teacher noticed in either boy of violent or aggressive tendencies.

Joan Rigg developed a soft spot for Jon. She could see that he knew when he was misbehaving but carried on anyway, as if he didn't care, as if he wanted the attention. When she confronted him he would hang his head and avoid her eye. When Bobby was challenged he would turn meek and, apparently, cry to order. Joan Rigg felt that Bobby was shrewd, streetwise and always aware of what was going on around him.

Neither of the boys' classwork reflected the advantage of being a year older than the other children. She ranked them both in the lower half of the class. Still, she believed that when she taught the class the parable of the Good Shepherd, Bobby and Jon would have got the message that it was important to be kind to people and protective, even towards strangers.

Other members of staff who came into contact with the two boys formed differing impressions of them. Lynn Duckworth, the dinner lady who supervised the playground during lunch breaks, often had to reprimand Jon for being a nuisance to the other children. The standard punishment was to be made to stand facing the wall for a few minutes.

The first couple of times this happened to Jon he turned round and butted his head against the wall before falling down and flailing his arms. The dinner lady paid no attention and eventually Jon stopped doing it, but she thought the boy had a problem, and shouldn't have been at the school. By comparison, Bobby seemed quite normal and likeable, and was never very difficult.

One of the longest-serving teachers, Ruth Ryder, who had been at the school for 22 years, knew Bobby as a quiet, non-verbal child who was a little bit crafty and calculating; always quick to deny any misdeeds and shift the blame elsewhere; a bit manipulative and influential, in his own way, and capable of getting others into trouble. With Jon, Bobby was definitely the leader, the more streetwise of the two, while Jon seemed more immature and easily led.

In most of his dealings with Ruth Ryder, Jon was very quiet and submissive. But on one occasion, when she was telling him off in front of a class, Jon began holding his hands across his face in an odd, aggressive manner, as if shielding himself. He put his head to one side and turned away to the class, giggling.

It was this type of behaviour, together with the tantrums and the telling of lies, that led another teacher, Jacqueline Helm, to the conclusion that Jon was emotionally disturbed.

Helm taught Bobby's kid brother, Ryan, and though she never actually took a class with Jon and Bobby she formed the impression that they were both disruptive influences in the classroom and not very popular with the other pupils. Despite this, she often felt sorry for Jon who had a sweet air about him and yet managed to earn a reputation as a trouble-maker.

The head teacher, Irene Slack, was forever speaking to Jon about his fighting. There was no doubt, in her mind, that Jon had a short temper and an aggressive nature, and once the other pupils picked up on this they went out of their way to wind him up.

Irene Slack could only describe Jon as odd, and given to inappropriate behaviour. He always avoided eye contact when she spoke to him, showed very little emotion and appeared able to turn on the tears as he wished. Though Jon had responded to the firm and disciplined approach of his previous teacher, Michael Dwyer, it seemed that he had been able to take advantage of the different teaching style of Joan Rigg, and make a nuisance of himself.

In spite of this, Irene Slack thought Jon was more open and more likely to tell the truth than Bobby. It was Bobby who would be the dominant one in the friendship, and though he was quiet and seldom a problem in class, Slack shared the consensus that he was cunning and a liar.

Some of their fellow pupils noted that Jon and Bobby sulked and swore behind the teachers' backs. Many of the pupils thought they were all right, and not too much trouble. Bobby would sit quietly in class, help others with their work, and be helped by them in return. He would chat about what he'd seen on television.

But he and Jon also had a reputation for picking on people and bullying. They called the overweight boy names like Fatty and Sumo, and imitated a Japanese wrestler whenever they saw him. Bobby threw gravel in his face.

Jon was aggressive with the juniors, and 'clotheslined' the girls in the playground, running past and knocking into them with his outstretched arms. He and Bobby would push the other children around, telling them to get out of the way.

Even the tallest boy in 5R, who called himself the cock of the class because he told the others what to do, had trouble with Jon, who called him big lips. He offered to fight Jon after school. Jon just ran away, shouting abuse. Another boy thought Jon and Bobby were weird. They never talked to the others. They were like a little gang.

Their principal notoriety, however, was for sagging. There was the time Bobby had asked to go to the toilet in class. He was gone for ages so Mrs Rigg sent Jon to go and get him. They never came back. They must have both run out of school, and one of them had written MAT down the side of the mirror in the boys' toilets, which was probably short for Matthew, who was one of the boys that Jon didn't like, and liked to bully.

Mrs Rigg took the register every morning and every afternoon. The 1992 autumn term consisted of 140 half-days, and Bobby was absent for 49 of them. Jon was missing for 50, though ten of these were accounted for by holiday. There were five half-days when both boys were absent at the same time.

Truancy was something of a rarity in the local primary schools, though it was not unheard of. Walton St Mary's was not locked and barred during school hours, but the doors were kept closed, and you could only gain access by ringing on a bell and waiting for a member of staff to answer. It wasn't necessary to call a member of staff to leave the school, but still, you had to be pretty determined to escape. It was easier, of course, not to turn up at all.

Bobby sometimes sagged with his brother Ryan, or his friend Gummy Gee, who was two years younger than Bobby. Both boys told the teachers that Bobby bullied and threatened them to go with him.

189

Irene Slack had known Bobby's family for several years, and had often presented the various child care agencies with information regarding the hierarchy of bullying that appeared to exist among the Thompson brothers, who had all been through the school: an elder brother picking on the brother below him in age.

There had been six brothers in all – with the recent addition of a seventh, baby Ben – and now the problem seemed to be repeating itself with Ryan. As Irene Slack told Bobby, he might have made the decision to opt out of school, but she did not want him spoiling Ryan's life . . .

Ann and Bobby Thompson had married at St Mary's Church in Walton on 11 December 1971. They were both eighteen. In fact, it was the day of Ann's eighteenth birthday.

Both came from local families and were known in the Walton area. Ann was brought up around Netherfield Road. She was the middle child of three, with a slightly older sister, and a brother some six years her junior. In childhood, being the middle one meant being left out and treated differently. It was her sister who got the days out to New Brighton and the lovely new black leather Bible for Sunday School. Her sister was the lady; her brother was the boy her parents always wanted and got spoilt because he was the baby; Ann was the gobshite, the hard-faced cow in the middle.

They went to Sunday School one Easter, Ann and her sister, with dresses mum had made and whitener on their shoes. Ann won a prize, a Bible. It was just a plain brown Bible, but she was made up, because she'd won it, and no one had to buy it for her.

They had these dresses, stripey, the sister's was blue and white, Ann's was red and white. Every time Ann wore hers something would happen. She'd have a nosebleed or fall over and run blood all down it. One day she was running up the road with a cane and she tripped and stuck the cane in the roof of her mouth. Into the hospital at the top of the road, dress blooded again.

Ann was always up the hospital. Whatever it was, she caught it. Never one of the others. Tonsils, adenoids, the lot. She was playing out once and had terrible pains in her side. She got dragged indoors and the doctor came round, and said it was appendicitis. Ann's dad went with her in the ambulance. If you are fuckin' lyin' I'll kill yer, he said, I've gotta go to work tomorrow. The pains stopped when she got to the hospital. She was terrified going home, waiting for the beating.

Her dad was a lorry driver, head convener for the corporation, and liked by all. He was always in the pub, standing rounds of drinks, buying Tambourine sherry by the bottle. To Ann he was like Jekyll and Hyde, always shouting and lashing out at her at home.

When she was about five she used to get bullied by a girl in the street. Hit 'er back, hit 'er back, Ann's dad would say. Ann would get hit by her dad, for not hitting her bully.

Ann and her sister had got their pocket money, only the sister had spent hers. Ann bought some crisps for herself and a friend. Her sister saw them with the crisps and wanted them and told their dad. Dad said give your sister some and Ann said no, she's spent her money. So Ann got hit for buying some crisps for her friend.

When she was older, Ann would look back and be unable to remember anything good in her childhood. If her parents loved her they had a funny way of showing it. If she ever got treated by them, bought presents at Christmas, she could not remember.

The only kindness she would recall was from her dad's friend. When he'd been round there'd always be money hidden in the house for her to find. She asked her dad for money once, for sweets for school, and he battered her.

Dad's friend bought her a china doll. Porcelain. Ann loved it, and kept it in her pram. She had all these steps to get down, so she called her dad. Dad will you take the pram down the steps. No. So she did it herself, dropped the pram, and smashed the china doll's face. She was heartbroken. They took it to the doll's hospital and fixed it up, but it was never quite the same.

Ann used to lie in bed, listening for her dad coming in drunk. She slept terribly, nightmares, sleepwalking, the lot. She woke up one night, literally standing on the headboard of the bed, bashing the wall with her hands.

Another night he pushed Ann's mum into the girls' bedroom. He had her over the sister's bed, and mum was screaming to Ann, get the police, get the police. Ann was in bed and when she got out he went for her and she took a battering for going after the police. Ann and her mum never spoke about it afterwards. They never spoke about any of it.

She was older then, about fifteen or sixteen, and was seeing Bobby, her first boyfriend, who was to become her husband. They'd met while she was still at school. Ann would not remember why she was attracted to Bobby. She could only think it was because he was the first fella who ever paid her any attention. The sooner she got married the sooner she could leave home.

Ann's dad didn't like Bobby very much and when he came round to say they were getting married, Ann's dad said he'd give it twelve months before they divorced. Bobby asked for his permission and he said, you look after 'er, now piss off 'ome, lad, piss off 'ome. When Bobby had gone he kicked Ann round the house. You're pregnant, aren't you? I'm not. She wasn't. He took the belt to her.

Ann was running away once, to Bobby, and her dad came after her and caught her on some steps by the pensioners' home, near the Hermitage pub. He threw her down the steps – only three steps – and split her head open. He dragged her home, past a lot of people who did nothing, and as he walked he said, just look at these houses and look at these trees. 'Cos you're not gonna fuckin' see them again. I'm gonna kill you when I get in.

He got her on the floor in the kitchen, by the back door, and used his old army belt with the big buckle.

Ann was working by then, doing wiring at Plessey's. Three

pairs of tights, black tights, for Monday morning, so no one'd see the marks on her legs.

She could not remember her sister or brother being beaten. It was always the cheeky hard-faced cow. Who knows, perhaps she enjoyed it. If he told her she was to be in by nine she'd always get back at five past, pushing her luck, asking for it.

There was one night when she was ten minutes late. Right, he said, do you want to stay in for a week or do you want a hiding? The thought of staying in a week was unbearable. I'll have a hiding. So he battered her and he said for bein' so fuckin' hard-faced you're stayin' in for a week as well. And she had to.

Ann didn't go out places too often because there wasn't much point if you had to be in by nine. She wouldn't usually bother getting dressed up to go out, and it was a rare day if she looked at herself and felt good going out the door.

It was about a week before the wedding when she went to the Wookie Hollow 'cos Gerry Marsden was on. She made the effort that night, and actually got a kiss off Gerry Marsden. She didn't get in till gone midnight, and her dad was waiting up to take it out on her, because he'd said be in by eleven. Still, that kiss almost made it worthwhile.

Bobby saw the marks on Ann's legs and he knew, but they never discussed it. There was no one to tell, and what was there to tell? Plenty of people got battered.

Ann's mother was always too afraid to do anything, except one night when two of her husband's mates brought him home and he was polatic, really gone, and they said where do you want us to put him, and Ann's mum said there, in the garden. So they put him in the garden, and that was where he woke up the following morning. Ann felt good about that.

On the day she got married he gave her a whisky and said, I'm made up you're goin' the right way. Just like Jekyll and Hyde.

Horrible.

He always drank in the Anfield, which they all called the bottom house, and Bobby's family drank in the Walton Hotel, which was the top house, and eventually got renamed the Top House because that was how everyone knew it.

Ann and Bobby got engaged in the top house, on her seventeenth birthday, and were in there after the wedding at St Mary's. It was like a second home and of course they were all back there for that first Christmas, when Ann and Bobby were newly-weds. Bobby said come on, we'll go and see your dad in the Anfield.

Ann put two fingers in her throat to show how she felt, but they went anyway. Her father bought her a drink and put his arm around her in front of all his mates. Here's my baby daughter, like he was dead proud. Ann was heaving.

(After the trial, after her son had been convicted of murder, Ann phoned her parents to tell them a few home truths. Her dad was sobbing down the phone. I'm sorry I battered yer. I'm sorry. Ann felt nothing for him. In fact, though she was crying too, she quite enjoyed his distress.)

Ann wore white for the wedding. She had made the dress herself. She had always played grown-ups when she was little, with her dolls and her pram, and she always thought being married, being a mum, would be just like a fairy tale. She wanted two boys and a girl. The boys would look after the girl, because no one had ever looked after her.

Looking back, she thinks she was rather stupid in those early days of the marriage. Shy, young . . . too young to have kids, probably. Bobby was only her age, but he always seemed older and more mature.

Bobby was the third youngest of eight, four boys and four girls, and his father had died when he was still a child. The paternal role had been taken on by the elder brothers, and they were strict in imposing discipline.

The Thompsons were a Walton family, and Bobby had attended Walton St Mary's School. Like many other local kids, he played on the railway line by Walton Lane. There was an upward slope of the track near there, for trains coming out of the docks. Freight trains with heavy loads would trundle slowly up the hill, and the kids could leap on, and help themselves to the cargo.

Ann and Bobby started married life in a flat in Birchfield Road, off Walton Village. Then they moved in with his mother for a while, still in Birchfield, and paid key money to a landlord to get a house of their own, across the road.

It was while they were at his mother's that Ann fell pregnant for the first time, with David. In the ensuing nine years she would have five children, all boys: David, Peter, Ian, Philip and little Bobby, who was born in Fazakarley Hospital on 23 August 1982. Ann convinced herself every time that it would be a girl. It just never happened and she kept on trying. She reckoned big Bobby wanted a football team.

Those nine years were difficult and Ann felt no more accepted by most of big Bobby's large family than she did by her own. At weekends she'd sit looking out of the window, watching her husband go off to the top house with his family. There was no one to mind the kids, so she stayed at home. There was no telly, which might explain all the babies, but didn't help when she was stuck indoors on her own.

Big Bobby was always in the pub and when he came home after he'd been drinking he'd be aggressive and sometimes violent. It was a volatile marriage from the start. The wedding certificate got shredded in the first week.

As far as Ann was concerned, if you argued with Bobby you argued with all the Thompsons, his mother included. She had a miscarriage after David, at three months, and was five months gone with the next pregnancy when they were all round his mother's arguing one Saturday night after going to the pub. Ann said she could keep her bloody son. Go on, she told Bobby, hide behind yer mother. He and his brothers flung Ann down the hallway and jammed her in the door and she lost the baby not long after.

One night Bobby dragged her down the street, coming home from the pub. She'd had all that with her father, and didn't need it again. Only once, in that first year, did Ann leave him and go back to her mother. Bobby came round and fetched her and she never walked out again.

He'd come in drunk with a takeaway and shout for Ann to fetch him a fork. When he'd finished he'd say now go an' wash it, and she'd say go an' bloody wash it yer bloody self, and he'd drag her through the kitchen by her hair, fill the sink up and push her face in the water. Then she'd go up to bed and he'd come and beat her for going to sleep.

Bobby was an apprentice electrician and, even when he was doing jobs on the side, there was never very much money. Ann gave up Plessey's when the kids came along. They just had to make do, but it was hard to cope.

In 1977 David, then aged four, was placed on the child protection register for physical abuse. He was seen with a black eye and a burn mark and he said his mum had pushed him against a door, hitting his head. Ann said there was an innocent explanation and the allegation of abuse was not substantiated. When there was no repeat of the incident, David was taken off the register, in 1979.

Philip had just been born, in November 1978, when Ann took an overdose of Valium and ended up in hospital. There was nothing exactly she could say that triggered the attempt at suicide. She didn't even plan it particularly. She just couldn't take any more, and did it.

She saw a psychiatrist the next day and he said, you going to do this again, and she said no, and went home and that was that. Social services arranged for the boys to go to nursery, which helped take the pressure off Ann.

The kids were always getting shouted at and battered. Big Bobby would put his face in theirs. See the evil in me eyes, twat. Wallop.

It was funny, when the Ripper case was going on, they all used to joke how big Bobby looked like Peter Sutcliffe, with his dark beard and his eyebrows that met in the middle. There *was* something in his eyes, too. He wasn't really like the Ripper, of course, but it was funny all the same.

He told the kids once he was puttin' 'em in a home, 'cos they were gettin' out of hand. He put them in his van and drove round to this big old house and said there's the home, that's where yer goin' if you don't behave. It was just a house, not really a home, but that kept them quiet for a week or so, the thought of going to this place that didn't exist.

When David got older, big Bobby caught him smoking and he told him if he caught him again he'd make David eat them. Next time he found David with ciggies he made him put them in his mouth and chew them. He didn't actually have to swallow them.

The family moved from Birchfield to Belmont Road after little Bobby was born, and life became more stable, Ann and big Bobby growing more used to each other, and each other's little ways.

Bobby had been camping as a kid, and one week he said why don't we borrow our Val's tent and give it a try, and if you like it we'll get a bigger tent. He had a Cortina then, so they loaded it up with the camping gear and the boys and went off to Mostyn in North Wales for the weekend.

They all fished and cooked and everyone liked it, so they got the bigger tent and started going regularly, first to Wales and later to Formby Point, and to a caravan site at Banks, just north of Southport, where they had a clubhouse and country and western nights with live bands.

Bobby was a better electrician now, taking on bigger jobs, rewiring houses, usually on the side, cash in hand. There was a bit more money to go round. He did a job at a place with a big old caravan in the garden. The man had just bought a new one, so he gave the old one to Bobby in part payment, and he towed it home and put it outside the house.

They cleaned the caravan out, took it to Formby Point a few times, and, at the end of the summer they really went to work on it. New cupboards, new curtains, re-covering all the seats . . . Bobby picked up some royal-blue ship paint, knock-off, and they kept it in the caravan toilet before they started painting.

Ann and Bobby were at their allotment one day and when they came home someone had driven off with the caravan. A neighbour had noted the registration of the car that took it, so they told the police. When the police finally found the car, not far away, on the Walton Lane estate, it had been painted royal blue. The caravan was never recovered, so it was back to the eight-berth tent.

The camping and the fishing went on for about four years. Ann was almost happy then. It was always good to get out of the house, and in the long school holidays they took to staying in Banks. Bobby would go off to work, and Ann would stay there with the boys and the doberman they'd got, whose name was Rocky. At weekends they'd be in the country club, sometimes dressed up in big cowboy hats and all.

At Banks Ann and Bobby met Tommy and Melanie from Salford. They'd take turns in each others tents, playing cards at night and having a drink.

In the last summer, the summer of 1988, Tommy brought another couple over and said, this is Barbara and Jack, I've been tellin' 'em about yer family and the kids, an' how we all have a crackin' laugh.

Barbara and Jack didn't stay over the whole summer but they came and went at weekends, and all three couples were very friendly. One week Barbara came with watches for the boys and Ann said, isn't that nice of yer but yer shouldn't be spendin' all yer money on the kids like that. Barbara said, oh I've got loads of money and no one to spend it on. Her daughter was grown up with a baby and she had two boys in the army. Her and Jack had a nice house in Oswaldtwistle, near Blackburn.

After that, Barbara was always bringing things in. A bottle of vodka for when they played cards, other gifts for the boys. They were at a car boot sale on the Saturday, and Barbara said to Ann, look, I've bought this watch for big Bobby 'cos he hasn't got one, has he? Ann said, no, but yer all right, I'll get 'im it. No, said

Barbara, I've got loads of money, and she gave Bobby the watch.

The following weekend she came into the country club with her camera, taking pictures of all the kids. Come on, she said to Ann, you get in the middle of 'em. Ann was 18 stone by this time. She'd started ballooning at Plessey's, when she had money to spend on sweets for the first time. They used to tell her it was puppy fat, but she was a bit old for that now. Ann didn't want her picture taken, thanks very much.

In the end Ann posed with Bobby in their straw hats and with the fish they'd caught that day. Ann with her nine-pound pike.

Ann and Bobby went home that week and on the Thursday night, before he went off to play darts, Bobby said, we won't go to the campsite this weekend, eh? Ann said, bloody right we will, I've got them kids all week an' that's my only break an' I enjoy goin' the country club.

So they went and on the Saturday Ann met an elderly woman she knew at the site who said, what's wrong with Barbara today, she's awful funny; I've just been over to see her and she's all of a flutter; I'm sure she's goin' through the change or somethin', 'cos when I asked what was the matter she said, nuttin', I'm just thinkin' of what I'm gonna do.

In the club that night, Barbara had brought a bottle of rum, and the only one that drank that was big Bobby. It still never clicked with Ann. She was pouring it out, and she and Bobby danced, which didn't bother Ann because they always danced and, being that big, she preferred to keep her seat.

At the end of the evening, Bobby got drink spilt on him. They're all bladdered and, next thing, off comes his shirt and his pants and he's sat there in his boxies. Ann had a pint in front of her. She said, 'ere, yer might as well take them off an' all, and threw the pint in his lap and walked out.

She was just getting into bed when Jack turned up, saying you'd better get round to those two, they've pissed off together. Don't act silly, Ann said. She'd never known Bobby go off with anyone. But Jack said she'd better do something, so Ann threw her coat on over her nightie and her dressing gown and walked round by the club and there were Bobby and Barbara kissing and cuddling as they came out of the door.

Just leave her alone, Bobby tells Ann, just leave her alone. Ann grabbed at the sleeve of Barbara's dress and it just came off in her hands, so she flung it and as Barbara was looking round for it, she grabbed at the dress again and pulled the front away so everything was showing.

Jack appears with a knife. I'll bloody kill yer, I'll bloody kill yer. Don't be stupid, says Ann, go and put yer knife away. It's not the first time she's done it, you know, Jack said. You're the fifth family she's split up, but she'll be back. Twelve months and she'll be back. He got in his car and drove home to Oswaldtwistle. Bobby and Barbara took a taxi and went off together. Ann was left with six kids, an eight-berth tent and a van she couldn't drive.

In the morning, as soon as it was light, Ann phoned Bobby's mother and asked for Al to come and fetch them. His mum said, oh, our Robert wouldn't have buggered off with somebody. I'm tellin yer, 'e 'as, said Ann.

At dinner time, while she was still waiting for Al, Bobby turned up with Barbara and put her in the front of the van and said, if you touch 'er I'll fuckin' kill yer. I'll just leave youse all here. He started collecting all the stuff. They were all going to drive back from Banks together in the van. Ann had been up all night, turning it over in her head. If I could get that lead round her neck as we're drivin' along, let's see what he does then. But she sacked that and grabbed the teapot instead, lunged forward and embedded it in Barbara's head. The last thing she saw was all the blood, then Bobby grabbed her and she woke up on the floor, and he drove off, leaving her with the kids again. The kids were in a right state by this time.

Eventually, Al arrived and took them home.

Bobby was back in the house that night, and stayed there for six or seven weeks, sleeping on the couch, during which time he more or less locked Ann in the house. If she went anywhere he'd take her there and back again. She got out one day when he didn't lock the door, and went round to tell his mother. Our Robert wouldn't do a thing like that, she said. Ann walked back home through Walton Village.

She had to take one of the boys to the clinic, so she told the nurse what'd been happening, and the nurse sent her to the Family Service Unit. She was feeling really paranoid, so they gave her some Temazepam and Diazepam, but they only seemed to make her more depressed.

It was Sunday, 16 October 1988 when Bobby left for good. He'd sent one of the boys out for a copy of *The Sport* earlier in the week. Bobby never read *The Sport*, but he looked through it and said, load of bloody crap that, go an throw it in the bin.

Ann later convinced herself that Barbara had put a message in *The Sport* for Bobby. He went out on the Friday night and came back at three in the morning. He'd been cross all day and Ann was fuming. She stood there ironing his clothes and on the Sunday she said, there's yer clothes, now piss off, and he just packed it all up and went. He told Ian he'd be back for him on Tuesday, but the only time any of them ever saw him after that was once, at his mother's funeral.

As he was walking out the door Ann gave him her wedding ring. 'Ere's somethin' to remember me by. Ann's brother had just come back from Cyprus and given her a bottle of Ouzo, so she opened it and drank the lot, straight down. It never touched the sides, and it didn't make her drunk, and it didn't make her forget.

Bobby had walked out on a thousand-pound electricity bill and a five-hundred-pound gas bill. Ann had a fiver in her pocket. She went to the benefit office and sat there crying. They gave her a crisis loan.

A week later, on Saturday, 22 October, Ann and the boys went round to her parents', and when they returned home the house was on fire. It was said to have been caused by an electrical fault

– which was an unhappy coincidence, but only a coincidence, given big Bobby's trade.

They were put into a hostel in Toxteth for a few weeks and, at first, Ann barely knew what day it was. She couldn't remember the fire or anything. It was about a fortnight before she came out of it and washed her hair and did it up, and began to feel better. The man who'd booked them into the hostel saw Ann and said, my God, I wouldn't have given tuppence for yer when you came in, and now look at yer.

It was January before they were rehoused, at 223 Walton Village. Peter, the second eldest, couldn't bear the hostel and had gone to stay with his nan, big Bobby's mum. It wasn't long after they moved into the Village that someone from social services came round saying Peter was being mistreated at home, and that Ann was beating her kids with a stick.

Ann ushered all the boys into the room and said to the people from social services, here, if you can find one bruise on any of 'em . . . she made all the boys strip off and stand in a line.

The weight fell away from Ann. She developed asthma, which she was told was psychosomatic, though it stayed with her. She had a lump on her breast, which terrified her, until she got it checked out, and it was non-malignant, just fatty tissue. She began drinking, seriously drinking, starting at home in the morning, and into the top house, or Top House as it was by now, for the rest of the day.

When she went home at night and got into bed she'd see faces crowding round, laughing at her. It wasn't anyone she knew, just faces. She'd lie there sweating and sweating, and unable to sleep. She decided she'd better stop taking the Temazepam and the Diazepam, so she did, and the faces went away.

Her friend Monica helped out with the kids. Monica would go into the pub and say, come on, come 'ome an' 'ave somethin' to eat. Piss off an' leave me alone, Ann would say, I don't wanna know. She'd just sit in the corner and drink, or take it out on the dartboard.

They'd always had darts in the Top House. Bobby had started a team there and when they'd moved to Belmont Road Ann had played in the Ladies' Prem for the King Charles pub team. She'd been good, playing competitively, but now when she got on the oche she went blank with the tension, and couldn't throw. Now she just played killer with some of the others, and sometimes she threw so hard her darts got embedded in the barrel behind the board. That was the anger coming out.

Occasionally, someone, a fella more often than not, would say something. You should be ashamed of yerself, in 'ere with yer kids at 'ome. Slag. They'd never said that when she had a husband of course. When you put a loaf on me table, Ann would tell them, then you can order me about. Until then, mind yer own fuckin' business. If they persisted, she'd hit them.

Most of the time she couldn't get drunk, though it wasn't for lack of trying. It was just like drinking through it, and coming out sober the other side. She kept a bottle under her pillow, and woke up with it most mornings for the best part of eighteen months.

The older sons were left in charge at home, and sometimes hit the younger ones, sometimes with sticks. They began sagging, hanging out with other lads in the area, getting involved in petty crime. Bobby and Ryan were still in the infants', displaying no outward signs of the domestic difficulties.

After their dad left, Philip asked Ian who he'd rather be with. Ian said his dad, and Philip told Ann, who was upset and started giving Ian a hard time. Ian already felt he was getting a hard time at Walton St Mary's school, singled out as a Thompson by the staff, because of the reputation for truancy and misbehaviour earned by his elder brothers.

Ian was suspected of some petty theft at the school. His younger brother, Philip, was seen there with bite marks. He sometimes said he was being bullied by Ian.

When the group of boys he was going around with began thieving and smoking dope, Ian stopped seeing them, not wanting to get involved.

Peter was the first one into care. It seemed to Ann that he had been hit the hardest by their dad's going. Peter said David had locked him in the pigeon shed and chained him up. David was arrested and Peter was examined. There were no charges. Ann was sure he was lying, and said he'd be best off in voluntary care until he learned to tell the truth.

David left home and came back again, and continued to live there periodically. He got probation for robbing a motorbike. Ian moved on to secondary school and Bobby and Ryan started at Walton St Mary's. As the next eldest, Ian was left in charge, with responsibility for making sure Bobby and Ryan got up and ready for school, and getting them there in time, before going to school himself.

Philip went out early, came home late at night, and was always sagging. He began doing drugs, sniffing aerosols and all sorts. He was picking up a string of cautions for petty offences. Once he was seen and caught coming out of the window of a local solicitors' office with several thousand pounds' worth of computer equipment. He had been looking after Bobby and Ryan at the time, and had taken them with him on the job.

On another occasion there was a fire at an abandoned property in the Village. A sooty-faced boy emerged from the smoke claiming that Philip and another lad had started the fire, and Philip was picked up and taken to Walton Lane Police Station. Ann was notified, and went to the station, going in on the bounce, blaming the police for picking on her boys. Her Philip wouldn't start a fire. It was always the Thompsons that got the blame. You wouldn't do a thing like that would you, Philip? Mum, it was me, I was there. There were no charges.

Philip was suspected of an indecency offence involving two small children, but the case was dropped, the allegation unproved.

In the end, he was getting so out of hand that Ann took all his clothes and tore them up and burnt them, everything except his school uniform, in an effort to keep him at home. Yer fuckin' bastard doin' that to me clothes, said Philip. He climbed out the window and went round his mate's and took his mate's mum's trainies. She came knocking for Ann and told her they'd cost fifty quid.

When Philip came home Ann got him on the floor with Ian and told Ian to hold his hands while she got the trainies off his feet. Philip wriggled free and pulled a knife out and went for Ian. Ann marched him down the police station, and Philip went into voluntary care.

Ian got on well at secondary school. He was likeable, popular and academically bright. His head teacher identified him as one of the cleverest pupils in the school, and he was student of the year.

Gradually, as he continued to take responsibilities in the family, Ian began to exhibit behavioural problems at school, being cheeky and argumentative with the staff and, finally, he was excluded from school, after threatening a teacher with a chair during a row.

Ann met a man over the road, in the laundrette, and began a relationship with him – he was another Bobby – which led to another pregnancy. She stopped drinking altogether then, and baby Ben was born in May 1992.

Things seemed better at home for a while, and Ian felt his burden of responsibility had been lifted. As it turned out, the respite was short-lived and, in October, a week before the fourth anniversary of big Bobby's departure, Ann swung at Ian with a cane she kept to threaten them all, and hit him on the arm.

Ian decided he'd had enough, and, after seeing a social worker, he went into voluntary care at a residential home round the corner from 223 Walton Village. This was the first social worker involvement with the family for some months, because of staff sickness.

Little Bobby went round to see Ian at his home one evening, not long after his arrival. Bobby showed Ian what he was carrying, which was a green bulb and a red bulb attached to a plastic disc by wires. The eyes of a troll doll, Bobby explained. A troll with illuminating eyes. Ian asked Bobby where he'd got it from, and Bobby said out of a troll. Ian asked Bobby if his mum had bought it, and Bobby said no, he'd robbed it out of the Kwikkie. He'd robbed it just to get the eyes. This did not seem strange to Ian, because Bobby was always messing around with electrical things, taking them apart carefully with screwdrivers and knives, just to get at some small component inside.

The staff at Walton St Mary's discovered that Bobby and Jon were going robbing when they sagged, and did their best to respond. Irene Slack could never get the truth out of Bobby, but on one occasion, after he and Jon had been seen shoplifting while they should have been in school, she lost her temper and shouted at him. Bobby admitted what they had been doing. It was the only time Irene Slack ever got him to admit anything.

She was concerned about Ryan, who was beginning to notch up his own tally of unauthorised absences. Ryan said Bobby threatened to break his glasses if he didn't sag, and was always complaining to his teacher, Jacqueline Helm, that Bobby punched and kicked him when they were at home. Ryan was enthusiastic at school but it seemed that Bobby's bullying was making him miserable.

John Gregory, Walton Lane Police Station's community liaison officer, had already spoken to Bobby and Ryan about truanting, and, when he came to the school with Brian Whitby in mid-November, to give one of their Stranger Danger talks to the pupils, they were asked to give another truancy talk to Bobby and Ryan. Brian Whitby told them it was wrong to sag, and asked them if they knew why. Because we get into trouble off Miss Slack.

Ten days later, one Thursday when the caretaker was away ill and there was no one watching the gates, Bobby and Jon were overheard plotting their escape, and ran out of the school when the lunch break started. They were later seen on County Road, robbing again.

Jon was supposed to be staying at his father's that night, and Neil had been at the school to meet Jon when he came out. He called Susan and eventually they went to the police to report Jon missing. Neil went round in a Panda car, looking for Jon, but he was finally found by Susan at about half past ten, playing out with Bobby in Walton Village.

Jon said he'd been enjoying himself and had forgotten the time. He didn't seem very bothered by the upset he'd caused. His mum smacked Jon, and sent him to bed. He was grounded for a week.

His parents had noticed that he was always asking for things, saying that they thought more of Mark and Michelle than they did of him. Neil thought this might be because the other two were together at a special school, and always going out on trips and excursions. Jon actually asked once if he could go to Mark and Michelle's school, because of all the things he could get. Neil told him he couldn't go there because it was a special kind of school. He told Jon he wasn't being left out, and made an effort to try and compensate with trips and treats.

Neil had owned a video recorder for a couple of years, and regularly rented films for himself and Susan to watch in the evenings, after the children had gone to bed. He would also rent videos for the children, and sometimes respond to requests from Jon.

Neil was member number 4548 at the Videoscene rental shop on County Road. It was only a pound a night for each tape at Videoscene, and he usually went there in the late afternoon to choose a film, returning it at lunchtime the following day. He had joined the club at another shop, Video Gold, in Hale Road, but their rental was two pounds a night, and this was a bit too expensive.

When he was renting videos for himself, Neil liked horror or action adventure movies such as *Ricochet, Manhunt, Dolly Dearest, Predator 2* and *Freddy 6*. He wouldn't let the children see these films, though Jon sometimes got up early in the mornings and went downstairs by himself, and turned on the television and the video. It was possible he could have seen them then.

Jon and his brother and sister saw films such as *Hook*, *Critters*, *Bill And Ted's Bogus Journey*, and *Turtles 2*. Jon really liked *Goonies*, and would watch it all the time, but if he asked for a film it would usually be a martial arts movie, such as *Suburban Commando* or *Double Impact*, both of which he saw. Sometimes, Jon imitated the karate kicks that they used in those films.

The day after they had run out of school, Jon and Bobby were told off by Ruth Ryder, who was deputising for Irene Slack as head teacher.

Joan Rigg told them they were making their parents unhappy, upsetting their schoolwork, and making her unhappy, because they had broken her trust. Bobby began crying and promised he'd never do it again, and would try harder with his schoolwork. Jon promised too.

Michael Dwyer was asked to speak to the boys and Bobby told him they stole from shops while they were playing truant. Jon told him Bobby stole from shops. They said they also went to the reservoir, and Dwyer pointed out the risks they were running. Someone might take them and injure them, or they might drown, he said, apparently unaware that the reservoir was a grassy hill.

At the following week's staff meeting they discussed Jon and Bobby's truanting, and decided on a containment policy. The boys would be separated in different classes, and not allowed out at playtimes, when they would again be kept apart, under supervision.

Susan Venables went to the school with Jon to discuss the problem with Irene Slack, who tried to explain to Jon that what he was doing was wrong, and left it to Susan to shout at her son.

There was also a meeting with Ann Thompson, who said Bobby had run off from home the night before, and she had hidden his shoes so he wouldn't do it again. She said she would collect him from school herself in future.

Ann took Bobby to Walton Lane Police Station for another talking-to. The cells were pointed out to him. That's where you'll end up if you don't behave.

In his bedroom at home Bobby was building up quite a collection of trolls. Most were bought for him, but some were thieved on his excursions down County Road. Sometimes Bobby robbed so much in the Kwikkie that he had to throw it all behind the freezers in the shop, and collect it later, or just abandon it. Often he was robbing for the sake of it, and not because he particularly wanted the things he stole.

People who knew him did not think of Bobby as a violent boy. Ian Thompson thought his little brother was frightened of his own shadow. He just occasionally tried to act big, that was all.

Once, Bobby was playing up at the Top House, running in and out of the doors, making a nuisance of himself. When the landlady challenged him he said fuck off you twat, and ran away calling out, you cunt, you slag. Another time, the landlady found Bobby and a little blond-haired girl hiding under the seats in the lounge. They started fooling around, saying they were with their dads, and, not long after they had gone, Bobby came back in and said a glass had been smashed outside. The landlady said she was going to tell his mum.

Despite the mischief he made, Bobby could be well-behaved at home, attentive towards Ben, helping his mother with feeding and caring for the baby, spending ages in the kitchen baking cakes. He and Ryan appeared to be close to each other. Bobby was always sucking his thumb and at the same time rubbing his ear between the thumb and first finger of his other hand. He'd sit on his mum's lap and suck his thumb and rub her ear. At nights he and Ryan would sometimes lie together in bed, and Bobby would suck Ryan's thumb instead of his own.

Bobby and Kelly, the ten-year-old daughter of Ann's friend across the road, Lesley Henderson, were like boyfriend and girlfriend. They often played out together, sometimes with Kelly's seven-year-old brother, Christopher, with whom Bobby was protective and sensitive, defending him when he was picked on by bigger boys.

When he was not sagging, robbing or skitting, Bobby was often out on his rollerboots in the neighbouring streets. On match days at Everton he contributed to the local kids' protection racket of minding cars. There was always a white BMW parked outside his house, and Bobby was in charge of it, receiving a small reimbursement in return for the car being in one piece when its owner came back from the game. Ian was down there one evening, from his care home, and was standing by the BMW while Bobby was elsewhere. Ann came out and 'kicked off' at Ian, thinking he was doing Bobby out of his job.

In the first week of January there was a series of minor disturbances at Ian's care home. Two of the young female residents stayed out overnight on the Sunday, and in the early hours of the Tuesday morning, the police were called to help the staff impose some order. There was a row between a few of the residents and the police, and the officers went back to the station, followed a short time later by Ian and three other teenagers shouting abuse. After Ian spat at one of the policemen they were all arrested for disorderly conduct, though later discharged. In the early hours of the Wednesday morning, two of the women were found by police under the Breeze Hill flyover. They dropped an eight-inch knife when the police appeared. They said they wanted to stab the police. Later that day another girl took an overdose of paracetamol, and had to go to hospital.

An officer who knew Ian went round to the home to try and calm things down. It seemed that one of the first policemen who had gone to the home had asked Ian his name and, on hearing it, had said, oh, right, you're one of those Thompsons. Ian had kicked off at this insult, and now, explaining it to the officer who knew him, Ian seemed upset and a bit weird. The officer asked Ian if he was all right. Yeah, said Ian. No, he's not all right, said one of the other residents, he's taken 20 paracetamol. Ian was taken to hospital. He survived.

Philip got picked up by the police two or three times after Christmas on suspicion of various offences he hadn't committed. He and David were held for the burglary of a flat which was rented by a friend of David's. The friend had gone away, and given David the keys to look after it. David had been in hospital with pneumonia over Christmas and was still recovering.

Then Ian and Philip were stopped and held. Philip had a bottle of 25 paracetamol in his pocket, and when he was released he took the lot. He went into hospital and came out and took another overdose. Ian took another overdose. Ann had both of them in hospital in the same week. A neighbour came round and said Philip had nicked his tracksuit off the washing line. Unlikely, said Ann, he's in hospital with an overdose.

Ann had never again thought of taking too many pills. Not even after big Bobby went. Especially after big Bobby went. She wouldn't kill herself over him.

For Bobby and Jon, 1993 did not begin auspiciously at Walton St Mary's. They ran out of school at lunchtime on their first day back. Jon was returned later in the day by his parents, who had found him nearby.

The containment policy was maintained, but one afternoon towards the end of the month the school received a phone call from the Strand Shopping Centre. Ryan was in the manager's office there, alone and in tears. His class teacher, Jacqueline Helm, went down to collect him, and Ryan explained that he had been bullied into sagging with Bobby and Gummy Gee. Bobby had told Gummy to hit Ryan if he refused to go with them. They had gone down by the canal, and Bobby and Gummy had run away and left Ryan on his own.

The last video rented from Videoscene on Neil's membership before the killing of James Bulger was *Child's Play 3*, which was taken out on 18 January 1993.

Child's Play 3 tells the story of a Good Guy doll, Chucky, which comes to life possessed by the soul of a psychopath, the

Lakeside Strangler, and embarks on a series of murders: 'Don't fuck with the Chuck'. There are seven killings, played out in vivid detail, including a long close-up of a man's face as he is being strangled, a barber whose throat is cut by his own razor, and a youngster whose body explodes when he jumps on a live grenade.

The film climaxes at a fun fair, inside the ghost train. The rail tracks are wreathed in dry ice, and surrounded by various objects of gothic horror. Chucky's face is stained with blue paint from an earlier war game battle with paint guns, and as he pursues his intended victims across the tracks – 'This is it kid. End of the line' – half of his face is chopped away by the Grim Reaper's scythe. Chucky loses various limbs, before being shredded in a wind machine.

On 26 January, Bobby and Jon were thought to be sagging with another boy. Someone from the Education Welfare Office went round to the home of Susan Venables the following day. There was no answer at the door and the EWO representative left a letter, which never received a reply.

At around this time – he would later be unable to remember the exact day, only that it was the end of January – a man was shopping in the Strand during the lunch break from his work at the Girobank, and saw two boys standing outside TJ Hughes, looking excited and lively as one of them tapped on the glass front of the store. The man thought they were up to mischief and he stopped to watch them. The boy tapping on the glass was evidently trying to attract the attention of a small child, a toddler, and was beckoning him towards the door of the shop. The child walked forward a few paces, and then went back to his mother. The two lads made off.

Several weeks later, at an identification parade, the man picked out Jon as one of the two boys he had seen.

On 4 February, Ann went to the school for a network meeting with the staff, a social worker and an Education Welfare Officer. The School's usual EWO had been off sick since May, but there was emergency cover provided by another EWO, Julia Roberts, who had been involved with Bobby's family in the past. At the meeting Ann agreed that the only sure way to get Bobby into school was to take him herself. She'd already padlocked the back door and screwed the windows down to stop him running off.

In spite of the problems, Bobby was due to begin secondary school next September.

Bobby and Jon's supervision and separation at school continued. They were even watched when they went to the toilet. Jon was often in the classroom next to Jacqueline Helm's, when he was kept in, and she always made a point of talking to him, touched by his sweet air.

On Thursday, 11 February, Jon was with Jacqueline Helm, helping her lay out paints in class. She told him he was such a good and helpful boy and asked him why he couldn't behave like this all the time. Jon agreed with her that it was wrong to sag. She asked him why he did it, then. I don't know, said Jon.

24

Over the weekend after they had been charged, the identities of Bobby and Jon became an open secret in Walton. One man, the father of a boy who usually sat next to Bobby in class, heard the names while he was out in the village and went home to tell his son. The boy said that Bobby and Jon used to ask him to sag off. They used to say, do you want to be in our gang, we're going to kill someone. The boy went quiet for a while and then said, I'm not sitting next to him on Monday.

On Monday, and throughout that week, the school was besieged by the press and unsettled by its new notoriety. Another classmate sat in Bobby's chair and bounced up and down, singing, I'm in the murderer's seat, I'm in the murderer's seat.

Reporters stood at the school gates hoping to interview the children, and barraged the head teacher with phone calls. Some pretended to be parents who had lost a copy of their child's school photograph and wanted to acquire a replacement.

The photograph which included Bobby and Jon was hanging from a wall in one of the school corridors. The mother of a pupil took the tabloid shilling to try and steal it. When she discovered that the picture was fixed to the wall, the newspaper supplied her with a small camera, and the mother practised with it, timing herself to remove the camera from the pocket of her anorak, hold it to her eye, snap the picture and return the camera to her pocket. When she had got the timing down to about 12 seconds, the mother went round to the school to meet her boy, and he led her to the corridor where the school photograph was hanging. She had her hand in her pocket, poised, but the school was one step ahead. The photograph had already been removed.

Bobby and Jon remained in custody at their respective police stations until Monday morning, when they were driven to Bootle, to appear at South Sefton Magistrates Court. The two boys fidgeted their way through the remand hearing, which lasted for two minutes, and then left the court and Liverpool. They would be taken to separate secure units, where they would spend the next year of childhood.

The route from the court was lined by a thicket of television crews and a small crowd of local people, some of whom ran forward offering physical and verbal abuse. There were six arrests in the mêlée, but the tightly framed images of hatred on the television news seemed to exaggerate the scale of the incident.

The boys' parents, Ann Thompson and Neil and Susan Venables, never returned to their homes. Removal teams went in to take their possessions into storage, and the families were rehoused by social services. There was much secrecy and paranoia: fear of being found by the media, the greater fear of some faceless mob, or a vengeful maniac with a petrol bomb.

Ann spent several weeks with Ryan and Ben in a flat attached to a residential home for the elderly, before being moved into a small house on a large estate, not far from Bobby's secure unit. She kept Ryan with her at home, unwilling to let him go to school because he might accidentally disclose their secret.

Neil and Susan Venables were reunited in their efforts to deal with what had happened, and moved together to a house in a quiet street near Jon's secure unit. Susan sent a thank-you note to the police at Lower Lane, a Hallmark card with a front picture of flowers and the printed words,

A message can't really convey
The gratitude that's sent your way . . .
But may these words somehow express
Warm thanks for all your thoughtfulness.

Alongside the message, Susan wrote, 'We would like to thank all the staff at Lower Lane Station for the kind thoughts and respect we received from you. Without your help I know we would not have coped, we will never forget you. God bless you all. Thanks so very much once again, Sue Neil Jon.'

On the first Saturday in March the boys were collected from their units by police officers from Merseyside and taken to an identification suite at Longsight Police Station in Manchester, to stand on identification parades. Bobby went first, in a line with eight other boys, and was pointed out by two women who had seen him in the Strand, an assistant from Animate, the pet shop on County Road, and the two boys who had been playing with handcuffs on Church Road West.

Jon waited in the detention room with his father and a couple of police officers. He asked his dad if Pauline was going to be there. 'Pauline saw us, I think.' His dad didn't know. 'Pauline, a friend of my mum's,' Jon explained to the officers. He asked one of them if they had seen *Crimewatch*. They asked what about. 'The James Bulger thing.' Yes. 'What did it say?' Then Jon wanted to know if the woman with the black dog was there for the parade.

When he was taken out to begin the parade, Jon began crying and became very distressed. He was taken back to the detention room, but could not stop crying. He wanted the door opened, to let in some fresh air. Why do I have to do it, he said to his dad, I've told them it was me. His parade was abandoned.

On the way back to his unit, travelling in an unmarked car, Jon asked why they couldn't have a police car. I know, he said, 'cos people might look and say there's that murder boy. Then he said, 'Me and Robert might get set free 'cos only two identified Robert and that was out of twenty.'

They tried again the following Saturday, and again Jon became upset and worried, waiting at Longsight for the parade to begin. An officer walked him round the station, trying to calm him down, but it was no good. Jon could not go through with the parade. The police decided instead to conduct the identification parade by video. They would film Jon, and eight other boys, and show the sequence to witnesses. Jon was told he would have to be recorded, walking up and down the corridor. 'Is that because they saw me walking in the Strand?'

The video recordings were made that day, and shown to witnesses a week later. Jon did not have to attend this time, but his solicitor was there to monitor fair play. Jon was picked out by one of the two women who had also recognised Bobby at the Strand, by the owner of the DIY shop on County Road, and by the man who had seen two boys tapping on the window of TJ Hughes in late January, apparently trying to attract the attention of a child.

Towards the end of March case conferences were convened at the Merseyside offices of the NSPCC – the National Society for the Prevention of Cruelty to Children. Bobby was discussed at nine thirty in the morning and Jon at eleven o'clock. No members of the boys' families were present, but the head teacher of the school was there, along with numerous social services' representatives, an education welfare officer, and a detective from the Merseyside Police child protection unit.

The conferences were intended to examine the boys' backgrounds and look for any possible connection between abuse they might have suffered and the offences with which they had been charged. Bobby's conference was told of the violence and neglect in his mother's childhood, and his father's strict upbringing in a fatherless household. All the known indications of physical abuse in Bobby's family were considered. The police questioning of Philip over the allegation of inciting a gross indecency was mentioned.

There was no direct evidence that Bobby had been abused by his mother or his elder brothers, and he had seemed happy enough three months ago when seen at a local social services' Christmas party. A social worker said that the recent period, before the killing of James Bulger, had been more stabilising for Ann and her family. She had been gaining insight into the needs of herself and her children, acknowledging difficulties and showing the motivation to address them; and she had begun to involve herself in areas such as schooling, in which previously she had felt uncomfortable and intimidated. Despite the absence of social work involvement in the months preceding the autumn of 1992, because of staff sickness, Ann had since been receiving support in coming to terms with her own childhood, her husband's departure, parenting skills, budgeting, together with the day-to-day dysfunctional aspects of a family.

The conference concluded that, despite features of neglect and emotional abuse, the physical abuse of Bobby could not be substantiated and no link could be established between his background and the alleged offences. He would not be placed on the Child Protection Register.

Jon's conference heard that both his parents had been involved in raising the children, despite their divorce, and was told of the feeling that Jon's behaviour was affected by his jealousy of the attention given to his elder brother, Mark. There had been no child protection concerns involving either Jon or his siblings, and there was no indication that Jon had been abused.

There was one reference, in Mark's medical history, to his being violent towards Jon, and there was the suspicion that physical chastisement was used on Jon as a form of punishment for his misbehaviour, though there was no evidence that this went beyond what could be called reasonable.

If there was any vulnerability to physical abuse, this could have been in the evenings, when Susan Venables had difficulty settling the children down, and stress might have led to abuse, though, again, there was no evidence of this. It was felt that Jon's parents had struggled to maintain a consistent method of parental control, trying different means in response to his difficult behaviour, and sometimes allowing him to get away with things that would otherwise have been punished, while the attention was focused on Mark.

There was concern that Neil Venables had allowed Susan to take the major role in disciplining and caring for the children. Jon had lived with his father, but Neil had found it hard to cope and sent Jon back to his mother. The head teacher was asked if Jon had ever behaved in a sexually inappropriate manner in school, but said there was no suggestion of this, or any indication of physical abuse.

Despite the concerns, and in the absence of any firm evidence, the conference decided it would not place Jon on the Child Protection Register.

Though it was not articulated at the case conferences, there was some worry over the conflict of interest between the judicial process in which the boys were now involved, and their needs as disturbed or damaged children. Any programme of psychotherapy or counselling could not begin in advance of the trial, because it might produce information which could prejudice or influence the case. The delay would only make the task of helping the boys that much harder. Like many defendants, young or old, in cases of serious crime, they would suppress and deny what had actually happened. The longer this went on, the deeper the truth would be buried, and the more difficult it would be to make progress with rehabilitation, which would involve acknowledging what had really taken place, and coming to an understanding of why it had happened.

Bobby had sat through seven hours and six minutes of taped police interviews without making any admission of his participation in the abduction and killing of James Bulger. He had said nothing since to suggest otherwise, and, irrespective of the truth, his lawyers had no option but to act on their client's instructions. He was saying he was not guilty, and this position could not be tested, by anyone around him, until the evidence was put before a jury at the trial. Bobby would not be unique if, despite his guilt, he convinced himself of his own innocence.

While Jon had made admissions to the police, and had said, 'I did kill him,' he was now blaming Bobby for the offences, as were his parents, who would say that Jon had been led on by Bobby. Jon could not bring himself to talk about events on the railway line. It was an understandable way of trying to manage the unmanageable, but it was also a form of denial.

When he had arrived at his secure unit, Jon had been given a cover story, ostensibly to protect his interests with the other residents. He was told to say he was twelve, not ten, and that he had been caught 'twoccing', which was car-stealing: taking without the owner's consent. It was a further encouragement to deny, and a reminder, as if any was needed, that the actual offences with which he was charged were too awful to be confronted.

Jon's solicitor, Lawrence Lee, visiting his client for the first time, told Jon, it's all right, son, we're going to tell the judge you were mad when you did it. This attempt to speak in the language of children reflected the belief that Jon might be able to run a defence of diminished responsibility, in which psychiatric evidence could play a crucial role.

The Crown – in the guise of the Merseyside Crown Prosecution Service – was also interested in expert evidence. In making its case against the boys it needed to counter the presumption in law that, at the age of ten, the boys did not know that what they were doing was seriously wrong. It also needed to counter any suggestion that the boys were unfit to stand trial, or that they were 'mad': suffering from diminished responsibility.

John Brighouse, the CPS's special casework lawyer, contacted the defence and requested that their clients be seen by Dr Susan Bailey, a consultant adolescent forensic psychiatrist from Prestwich Hospital in Manchester. Bobby's lawyers refused and Jon's agreed. Dr Bailey first saw Jon's parents in May and went on to interview them over two sessions. She conducted seven clinical interviews with Jon over the next four months.

On 14 May, the boys stood side by side in the dock at Liverpool Crown Court, formally entering 'not guilty' pleas to the charges and hearing that the trial was fixed for 1 November, at Preston Crown Court. Jon was hyperventilating for most of the brief hearing, and a social worker clutched at his leg for support. The public gallery was empty except for Sean Sexton, the local solicitor representing the Bulger family. Neil was the only parent in court, sitting surrounded by bulky plain-clothed policemen.

There had been some debate about a possible venue for the trial, which could not be held in Liverpool because 'feelings were running high' and because of the difficulty of finding a jury that had not already made up its mind about the boys' guilt. It had been suggested that the trial might be held at the Old Bailey in London, but the Honourable Mr Justice Morland, who was the presiding judge of the Northern Circuit, decided he would hear the case in Preston, which was a more practical alternative to Liverpool, and would enable the boys to return to their units every evening.

In her twelve-page psychiatric report on Jon Venables, which was delivered shortly before the start of the trial, Dr Bailey recorded Neil and Susan's view of their family background and Jon's childhood development. She said that there was no history of epilepsy, alcohol abuse or mental health problems. Susan told Dr Bailey of the stress and anxiety of caring for Mark when he was an infant, and how this had contributed to the separation from Neil. They had told Jon that they could not get on together but were still friends. Neil continued to see all the children.

Jon had been overactive at school and at home he would run around and play in the garden, but he was not aggressive. He had been bullied at school by boys who lived nearby and who bullied Jon and his brother Mark at home. Jon showed no anger or antagonism towards Mark, and never expressed any unhappiness about the time and attention Mark had required because of his learning difficulties. Jon was protective towards Mark and Michelle and understanding of their special needs.

Susan had been very worried about the bullying and had told Jon to stand up for himself, but he worried about his eye and his squint. She had complained to the school, and was told Jon was throwing things in class. He was suspended for two days because he had been throwing things and lying on the floor, refusing to get up.

Eventually, Susan decided to keep Jon out of school until they got rid of the bullies, so that Jon would no longer be a victim. It was then that he changed schools. Jon had been brilliant at first, in his new school, with the discipline and structure provided by a male teacher. In his current year, with a female teacher, he had begun associating with Robert and truanting. Jon had felt sorry for Robert because he had no friends at school. The police and other local families had warned them to keep Jon away from Robert, who was trouble and renowned for thieving. Jon had been bullied by Robert.

The only stealing Jon had done was taking cigarettes from his mother's handbag, and that only because lads in the street had threatened him.

Jon bit his nails and shared with his mother a fear of bees and wasps. He slept with the light on and used to have a distressing recurring dream in which the spotlight from his eye operation was focused on him. Since being charged and held in secure accommodation, Jon had been observed to line his toys along the side of the bed, to keep things away at night. He had told his mother of flashbacks, particularly an image of blood coming out of James Bulger's mouth. The memories would not go away when he tried to push them to the back of his mind.

He had been having bad dreams and good dreams, but could not remember the bad dreams. In a recurring good dream he rescued the victim by snatching James and returning him to his mother. This was worse than the bad dreams because he couldn't make it real.

In his interviews with Dr Bailey, Jon was able to settle, sit still and concentrate. If the subject became uncomfortable he would fidget or hide under his sweater. About the offences he would only say that Robert had suggested they sag off and go to the Strand. He was unable to talk further about what happened, and became tearful and inconsolable when the subject was raised. He told Dr Bailey to ask his mum and dad. He said the only people he could talk to about it were the police. Dr Bailey noted that, at times, especially when speaking of Robert, Jon would use the same phrases his mother had employed.

He showed no evidence of any hallucinatory or other unusual experiences, and there was no indication of obsessive or compulsive phenomena. He had not presented with any clinical evidence of a depressive illness, though he had appropriate anxieties about the forthcoming trial. It was unfortunate, Dr Bailey observed, that Jon had been advised to disguise his age and offences at the secure unit. This had hindered him in coming to terms with his situation.

Jon's three magic wishes were to be out of his secure unit; to turn the world into a chocolate factory; to live forever, with enough money, and to have no accidents or illnesses. His choice of a partner on a desert island would be his mum, if he could take only one person, but, otherwise, mum, teddy, dad, brother, sister and nan.

If he could go back in time, he would return to the offence so it didn't happen. He could be happy if it hadn't happened.

Going forward in time, to twenty, he would like to be living with his mum and dad and have a job as a mechanic. He was fearful that he would go to prison when he was eighteen and stay there until he was 40.

Asked about his understanding of death, Jon told Dr Bailey that when pets or people die that fact can't change, they cannot come back. Good people go to heaven where there is Jesus, Mary, God and disciples, all in white. Naughty people go to hell.

Jon liked watching cartoons such as Bugs Bunny and Daffy Duck which he recognised as make-believe. He liked the soap operas, and their characters were his favourite people on television. His favourite film was *Goonies,* which he liked to watch every day, rewinding to see the funniest parts again. He also enjoyed *Police Academy, Home Alone* and *The Incredible Hulk.*

He told Dr Bailey he would make believe it was only acting when he saw 'naughty things', by which he said he meant blood or fighting. He would turn his face away and put his fingers in his ears if, in the *Rocky* films, someone was punched and blood came out. He watched Kung Fu films which his dad got out on video; when he saw them he thought they were real, and he would cry. If he could be anyone out of the films, Jon would be Sylvester Stallone/Rocky, because he was rich and he was nice. He'd like to be Sonic the Hedgehog from the computer games, because he ran fast and saved his friends.

Dr Bailey's behavioural analysis of Jon's problems was that there was no evidence of any organic factors in infancy which might have affected his development. He had been reared in a supportive family setting and, in early childhood, had been described as a happy boy who functioned normally in a playgroup setting. Between the ages of four and seven he had functioned normally within the home and within education.

When his parents separated they had taken joint responsibility for the children, with active support from Susan's mother. Styles of parenting had differed, with Susan presenting as more direct and immediate in her responses. Jon's behaviour and achievement in school had deteriorated but, significantly, he had responded best when set limits and boundaries. The bullying was linked to remarks about Jon's eye defect and his brother's special needs. Both Jon and his parents had stressed the bad influence of Robert, in the months before the offences, when Jon began to play truant and become involved in minor anti-social acts.

Jon always stressed that he had no problems in his family, and no frustration with regard to the time and attention his 'less able' siblings needed and received. It was apparent to Dr Bailey, from her interviews with Jon, that he wanted to please his mother, and it was very important that his parents thought well of him.

His parents had spoken to her of the cognitive and emotional difficulties they had experienced, trying to come to terms with what had happened. Neil showed more overt distress and fearfulness. Susan expressed her feelings through the pressure and depth of her speech. They had been asking for, and needed, more professional support than they had been receiving. They had remained supportive towards Jon, and non-rejecting of him. At times, however, they were understandably overwhelmed by the situation in which they found themselves.

Dr Bailey said she could not comment on the offences, but Jon continued to lay the blame on Robert. She concluded that Jon was fit to plead and stand trial, was not suffering from any mental disorder, was of average intellectual ability, had a clear understanding of right and wrong, could understand the concept and permanence of death, and could distinguish between fantasy and reality. He had remained consistent in his accounts of both neutral and emotive topics, typically denied anything negative about himself or his family, but expressed anxiety about his future.

Dr Bailey had fulfilled the role required of her by the Crown, but there was nothing in her report to support the family social worker's view that Jon was jealous of the attention given to his brother and sister, which had made him feel neglected. There was no mention of his tantrums, or the possibility that he had copied Mark's behaviour. Scant reference was made to the more extreme behaviour he had presented at school and the aggression he had displayed.

The report did not refer to any instability that might have resulted from Neil and Susan's separation, the ensuing moves from one home to another, and the apparent on-off nature of the couple's subsequent relationship. There was no suggestion of any emotional, verbal or physical conflict between Neil and Susan, before or after the separation, or the impact this might have made on Jon. No mention was made of their depression or its possible effect on Jon.

There was a brief reference to the different parenting styles of Neil and Susan, but no exploration of this, or the possible effect of inconsistent parenting on Jon. Dr Bailey had noted that Susan had smacked Jon 'out of worry' on the night James Bulger was killed, but there was no reference in the report to any inquiry about physical punishment of Jon.

Dr Bailey had made a concluding point about the theme of denial in her interviews with Jon, but there was no indication in the report of any disparity between the family's view of itself and other information that was then available. Dr Bailey had concluded that Jon could distinguish between fantasy and reality, but had noted from her interviews with Jon that when he watched Kung Fu videos he thought they were real, and would cry.

In October the CPS made a second request, for Jon to be seen by a consultant psychologist, Marion Preston. She spent the day with Jon at his unit towards the end of the month, carrying out a series of recognised tests which were designed to assess Jon's intellectual functioning and his current emotional and psychological status.

They sat together in the school room of Jon's unit, where

225

he normally went for one-on-one teaching. Marion Preston had been told that Jon might be distracted, but she found him engaged and responsive, only once stopping to ask his social worker, who was sitting quietly in the room, what book he was reading. Jon was affable and cooperative, making appropriate jokes, in particular about his being overweight.

The first two tests, of Jon's intelligence, scholastic aptitude and literacy, suggested that he was of average ability, with some underachievement, probably linked to his difficulties at, and absence from, school. The third test, the Bene Anthony Family Relations Test, was designed to explore a child's feelings towards his family and him/herself. Jon chose his mum and dad, his brother and sister, and his nan as his family. The test included a Mr Nobody, to whom the child could assign qualities that were not felt to apply to anyone in the family.

Jon allocated more items to Mr Nobody than anybody else, and they were mostly negative associations. Nobody scolded Jon, disliked him, frightened him or thought badly of him. He did not think badly of anyone in his family, or hate anyone, or feel like being violent towards anyone. He did not get fed up with anyone in his family, he did not want to annoy anyone, and no one in his family made him angry.

Marion Preston noted that Jon gave very few items to himself, particularly anything in relation to positive feelings. He indicated that his parents were over-protective, and that his mother paid too much attention to him. He attributed many positive feelings to his mother and suggested that his brother, Mark, was sometimes a bit too fussy and spoilt other people's fun. He expressed positive feelings about his sister, Michelle, with the one negative note that he felt she was never satisfied.

Marion Preston's report said that the test indicated a high level of denial of any negative feelings, both from Jon to his family, and from his family to Jon. The only positive item he gave to himself was that this person was nice. Mr Nobody was given anything associated with kissing or close contact, his mother given cuddling, being near to and giving hugs to Jon. There was no indication of physical contact with his father, other than that he liked his dad to tickle him. Jon's picture of family life was that his mother was warm and giving, his father less emotionally demonstrative; there were never any arguments, disagreements or difficulties between any members of the family. Marion Preston said this was an unrealistic view of family life, with clear denial of any problems or difficulties.

The next test, the Child's Depression Scale (Revised), was designed to examine feelings of unhappiness and sadness, inadequacy and low self-esteem, boredom and withdrawal, psychosomatic illnesses, preoccupation with death or illness and problems with aggression, irritability or temper outbursts. Jon's test gave no clear pattern of response, and no indication of clinical depression, though there was a recognisable denial of negative feelings and of many problems, particularly in relation to his family. He was above average in preoccupation with sickness, feeling tired a lot of the time, not liking waking up in the mornings, experiencing some sleep disturbance, and feeling uninterested in doing anything at the moment. There was some acknowledgement of feelings of guilt.

The Culture Free Self-Esteem Inventory measured self-perception and self-esteem, and also included a lie scale to indicate defensiveness. Jon's test gave him a low self-esteem, in the bottom 22 per cent of children, but because he had found it difficult to make up his mind when scoring some of the categories, Marion Preston said the results should be treated with some care. By contrast, Jon had suggested that he was happy most of the time and believed he was as contented as most boys and girls. He did not think his parents thought him a failure, they did not make him feel he was not good enough, and they did not dislike him. He felt that he did well at school, persisted at his work, liked school, and felt that teachers thought he did well. This was particularly in relation to schooling at his secure unit.

Jon's lie score was relatively high, and Marion Preston said this was in keeping with the degree of defensiveness shown in other tests. He was continuing to deny any difficulties, notably to do with his family.

The final test was the Revised Children's Manifest Anxiety Scale: 'What I think and feel'. Again, Jon did not show a high level of anxiety, except in relation to what was going to happen to him. He felt people were going to tell him he did things the wrong way, and he was aware that a lot of people were against him. There was a high lie score in this test, too, consistent with faking good, and relating, the report said, to an idealised view of himself.

With the tests completed, Marion Preston tried to approach the subject of the charges with Jon. He immediately became subdued and uncommunicative, and put his head down on the table in front of him. He said he hated Robert because Robert made him do it. He said he was sorry about what had happened, but refused to discuss it further.

Staff at the unit told Marion Preston that in general Jon behaved himself and was very little trouble. With the increased attention he had been receiving – the expert assessments, the interviews – he had begun discussing his feelings with the residential care workers, but had not disclosed any details of the offences at length. He had recently regressed in some of his behaviour and had soiled himself twice, which had not been happening when he first went to the unit.

Marion Preston's report concluded that Jon was of average intelligence with no deficits in intellectual functioning. He had presented an unrealistic view of relationships within his family, but had shown some awareness of his current difficulties. Throughout the tests he had demonstrated an understanding of right and wrong, and had known the right thing to do when confronted with a moral dilemma.

Marion Preston believed that Jon was repressing and denying many of his emotional concerns. It was not altogether surprising, she reported, but it indicated an awareness on his part of what needed to be considered, and he was consistent in this over the four hours of testing. It was likely that Jon would require treatment by an expert psychiatrist or psychologist to help him to address the very difficult circumstances surrounding his offending behaviour, regardless of the outcome of proceedings against him. The final line of the report stated that Jon Venables presented as a capable young man, who would require treatment and support for some time to come.

Jon's lawyers also commissioned their own report from another child psychiatrist. There was no evidence here of any abnormality of mind, nothing to suggest he was unfit to stand trial, nothing that might support a defence of diminished responsibility.

It had been noted that, on many occasions before the sessions with one expert or another, Jon had been seen alone by his father for a quiet chat. Perhaps it was a natural way of offering reassurance, but it caused some concern among case workers from the various social services.

There was also persistent talk of the possibility that Jon had seen *Child's Play 3*. The police had been round to the video stores used by both families, and collected lists of the films they had rented. Albert Kirby insisted that the police could make no connection between the killing and the watching of videos, but the content of *Child's Play 3* (the last film on Neil's list) was, at the very least, a bizarre coincidence.

Eventually, Jon was asked directly if he had seen the film. His sheepish denial – I don't like horror films – left many who saw and heard it with the impression that he had watched *Child's Play 3*.

Bobby had once seen two minutes of *Child's Play 2*, walking into the room when some of his elder brothers were watching the video. Ann had come in and ushered Bobby away. Ann really didn't like horror films.

Bobby's lawyers maintained their client's position. There was no need for any expert evidence because Bobby hadn't committed the offences. Unlike Jon, however, Bobby was able to talk about what had happened. His solicitor, Dominic Lloyd, sat with him in his room at his unit over several sessions, going through the evidence that had been presented by the Crown and eliciting from Bobby his own version of the killings.

Bobby told his solicitor of a sequence of events that matched the account he had given in his interviews with the police. The assault began with Jon throwing paint at James's eye, and ended with Jon throwing the fishplate, the big metal thingy, as Bobby called it.

Bobby watched Jon remove James's underpants and lay them carefully over James's face. Bobby did not know why he had done this, but assumed it was because the blood coming out of his mouth looked horrible. Bobby did not like looking at the blood. You could still see it pumping out underneath the underpants every couple of seconds, so Bobby started putting bricks round the head so that bricks could be put over the face. He only tried to cover James's face so that he would not have to look at the blood any more.

Bobby was certain he had not kicked James in the head.

Sometimes, as he spoke of the killing, Bobby would bow his head and cry quietly, almost unnoticeably. He would fidget constantly, kicking off his shoes, removing his socks and knotting them into a soft cosh. He messed with the polystyrene bust in his room, smearing it with crayon colouring for make-up, defacing the eyes, nose and mouth. He played cassette tapes of Patsy Cline and Diana Ross, which had been given to him by his mother. He twisted and styled the hair on the heads of his trolls.

Bobby's collection of trolls now outnumbered those he had hoarded in his bedroom at home – which had been removed by the police as potential evidence. The new trolls had been brought for him as gifts, mostly by his elder brothers and his mother, who visited him regularly.

Ann's eldest son, David, had just moved into a flat in Liverpool, setting up on his own for the first time, when James Bulger was killed. He had been shopping with Bobby, buying paint to start decorating the flat, the day after the killing. Following the arrests he too had been forced to leave Liverpool, and was now with his mother, helping her out with baby Ben as he had once helped with his other younger brothers.

Peter, the second eldest, was living in Yorkshire with a girlfriend and working as a trainee manager for a supermarket chain. He couldn't visit so often, but spent long hours on the phone, talking to Ann.

Philip and Ian had moved together from a care home in Walton to a care home in Derbyshire. Ian had taken another overdose after Bobby's arrest, and both he and Philip had become involved in some fighting and stealing at their new home, which led to arrests and charges of assault and theft.

Ryan had become increasingly isolated at home and showed increasing signs of disturbed behaviour. Ann would still not run the risk of sending him to school, and would call him in from the garden if he became too chatty with neighbouring children. He had the run down the side of the house on his bike, and that was it. Always a chubby child, he was swelling to even wider proportions as he loafed around in the house.

Ryan was bedwetting regularly, and set a small fire in his bedroom. He seemed almost envious of Bobby's room at the unit and the attention he was receiving. Ann's fear that he would spill the beans on his family's notoriety was replaced with the greater terror that he would do something – 'something terrible' – to get looked after like Bobby.

Ben's father remained in contact with Ann, passing on to her a proposition from *The Sun* which appeared on the doormat of his home in Walton: 'We'd like to talk to you. Naturally, you'll be compensated for your loss of time.'

No one – not even *The Sun* – knew the whereabouts of Ann's husband, Bobby Thompson senior. Little Bobby and his brothers all remembered the anniversary of his departure; it was five years this October. Neither they, nor Ann, had any contact with him, and he had apparently severed all ties with Walton.

Bobby senior was in complete ignorance of events for months, until a small advertisement appeared in his local newspaper: 'Will Robert Thompson, formerly living in Walton, please call this number urgently . . .' He saw the advertisement and dialled the telephone number. It was a direct line to a reporter from the *Daily Mirror*. 'Did you know your son's on this James Bulger murder charge?' No, he didn't know. Bobby senior put the phone down and called Merseyside Police.

Two of the case officers, Phil Roberts and Jim Green, went out to meet him and explain the charges Bobby was facing. They took a one-page statement from him, outlining the brief circumstances of his separation from Ann, and his limited contact with the family – once in five years. They advised him to contact Dominic Lloyd, his son's solicitor. Lloyd was at first suspicious of the call. Press activity was intense in the weeks before the trial, and pretending to be Bobby's dad might simply be an effective way of extracting information. Persuaded that this was not a hack in paternal clothing, Lloyd arranged to meet Bobby senior one night at a pub in Southport.

He turned up with Barbara, the woman he had met at the campsite just up the road, and for whom he had left Ann and the boys. He said he had not kept in touch with the family because there was just no talking sense with Ann. He said he'd like to visit Bobby. (This was vetoed by social services because it might further disturb Bobby in the run-up to the trial.) Like his wife and his sons, Bobby senior was shocked at the news of his son's arrest, and incredulous that his lad could be involved in the killing. None of them could believe or understand that he was capable of such violence.

The Crown's forensic evidence clearly demonstrated that the patterned mark on James's cheek came from a shoe, and had been caused by a stamp or a kick. It was the imprint of the upper part of a shoe. The D-ring lace holders, and the lace itself, were visible in the imprint. There was equally no doubt that it was Bobby's shoe.

The defence sought its own expert forensic examination. The expert consulted William J. Bodziak's book, *Footwear Impression Evidence*, which considered marks left on skin according to the force connected with a blow. It was arguable that a lighter blow would be more likely to leave a clearer imprint such as the mark on James's face. It would be more difficult to argue that the mark had not been caused by a kick, and impossible to argue that it had not been caused by Bobby's shoe.

This was the single most damning piece of forensic evidence against either defendant, and it undermined Bobby's assertion that he had taken no part in the attack. If the jury believed the forensic evidence, they would be unlikely to believe Bobby.

After hurried discussion at this late stage, and with some misgivings from all concerned, including Bobby, who did not think of himself as a nutter, Bobby's lawyers decided to submit their client to a psychiatric assessment. They chose a Consultant Child and Adolescent Psychiatrist from the Tavistock Clinic in London, Dr Eileen Vizard. The Crown was notified of this change of approach, and responded with a renewed request for Dr Bailey to see Bobby. She travelled to his secure unit, but he refused to be seen by her.

Dr Vizard saw Bobby on Saturday, 16 October, two weeks before the start of the trial, and five years to the day since Bobby senior had left his family. Dr Vizard took with her a colleague, Colin Hawkes, a probation officer who specialised in working with adolescent and adult abusers. She also took a toy train set, several toy cars and some dolls. The assessment interview lasted four hours, and her report, delivered on the fifth day of the trial, ran to 27 pages.

Dr Vizard would have liked to have videotaped the interview, but this was vetoed by Bobby, who also asked that his case worker from social services sit in for reassurance. They gathered around a low table in a staff meeting room at the unit. It was warm in the room, but Bobby wanted the windows closed in case someone from the media, or elsewhere, was eavesdropping.

Bobby was asked if he knew why Dr Vizard and Mr Hawkes had come to see him. He said, to see if I'm a nutter . . . to see if anything was playing in my head when it happened. That's right, he was told, but they were also interested in finding out if he needed help as a result of having been present when James Bulger was killed.

When it became apparent that Dr Vizard would be doing most of the talking, Bobby turned his chair to face her. She and Colin Hawkes observed in their report that he maintained good eye contact and that, from time to time, he drummed or tapped with his hands on the arms of his chair. The drumming accelerated when the questions became difficult or worrying, and at times he was humming anxiously under his breath. He sometimes shifted in his chair in a rocking motion or curled up in the chair like a smaller child. On one occasion he sucked his thumb.

They spoke about going to court, and Bobby was asked how he felt about the trial. He became hesitant and looked across at his case worker. It seemed as if he was looking for reassurance. He said he was most afraid of all the crowds but, as the windows of the van were opaque, his fear was not so great. He was asked what he would say in court, and replied, not guilty. He said he knew he would come back to his unit, whatever the verdict, and began tapping more vigorously on the arm of his chair when asked how long he thought he might have to remain in secure accommodation. That's not for me to guess, he said.

Already, as their report observed, Dr Vizard and her colleague saw Bobby as an articulate boy of reasonable intelligence who was spontaneous in his speech and communication. He spoke rapidly at times, but was coherent and rational, and understood all the questions. At times it almost seemed that he was of better than average intelligence, his responses being carefully gauged for his interviewers.

They moved on to talk about Bobby's family and drew up a family tree, with Bobby showing an accurate recall of names, ages and events. The report explained how Bobby had perceived his father as a consistent source of control in the family until 1988, when he had suddenly left home and had not returned.

It was Bobby's recollection that they had all been camping together when his father returned from a visit to the pub to say that he was leaving. Bobby looked sad as he said he couldn't make any sense of it. He seemed to be actively reliving the experience of rejection by his father, though he then tried to deny that his father's departure had caused him any significant distress. He said things in the family got looser afterwards, and his mother needed a lot of help from social workers so she could cope. I'm surprised she did cope, with all of us boys on her own.

He seemed keen to talk about his mother, and told of her asthma and the trapped nerve in her hand which was going to need surgery. Dr Vizard said she understood that his mother had a temporary problem with drinking too much after his father left. Bobby found this subject difficult, and at first denied any problem. Then he said she did drink at one time, but, like, only three nights a week, when she would go straight to bed on her return from the pub.

Bobby sounded defensive now and, for the first time, dropped eye contact with Dr Vizard. He picked up a toy lion and began playing with it on his leg and on the arm of the chair. The lion was made to scratch and attack the arm of the chair angrily. Bobby said he wasn't bothered whether his mother drank or not and, anyway, she doesn't touch a drop now.

They stopped then for lunch, and the train set was laid out on the table. After they had eaten, they discussed Bobby's weight, and he said he'd put on a lot, and was now eight and a half stones: I was like a matchstick, compared with what I am now. He said he took no exercise at the unit because the other boys were much older and the gym equipment was too heavy to use.

He slept fairly well, and would ring the buzzer when he had

nightmares, so that a member of staff would come and comfort him. He described a recurring dream in which he was chasing someone through the street and ran into the road where he was hit by a car. The car hit him on the front, no, on the side. As he spoke of the dream Bobby began fanning his face with his hands as if it was making him feel hot and bothered. He looked agitated and asked his case worker to open the windows. He said that whenever he had the dream he would try not to go back to sleep again, in case the dream returned. He now looked distressed and red-faced, and looked anxiously around the room.

Dr Vizard told Bobby that sometimes nightmares were linked to painful memories and it helped to talk through these issues. Bobby said he tried to keep his mind off his dream. Again, he looked around the room, as if he would like to escape. When Dr Vizard said it was helpful to talk about bad memories, as well as painful dreams, Bobby leaned forward and touched the toy railway track. He seemed to be anxiously humming or muttering under his breath.

There were three cloth dolls on the table with the train track. Dr Vizard explained the idea of using these toys to help Bobby give his account of James Bulger's death. A Jon doll, a Bobby doll, a James doll. She asked Bobby's thoughts about James. How do you mean, the baby? Bobby put his hands over his eyes and began to cry. They told him it was understandable that he should cry. There were bound to be strong feelings involved when someone had been present at, and perhaps taken part in, the death of a child.

Dr Vizard said it would help to cry, and Bobby reacted angrily through his tears. Well, how does this help me? If they were going to help him they needed to know how he felt when James Bulger was killed. Bobby was crying bitterly. How does it help to make it all come back? I don't want to do it. He was given a tissue by Dr Vizard, to wipe his tears.

She and Mr Hawkes said they realised how difficult it was

236

for Bobby to talk about the killing, but it was also difficult to understand what had happened, because Jon said Bobby did it and Bobby said Jon did it. Bobby said, that's the truth.

They began to move the dolls on the track, Bobby holding the Bobby doll, and Dr Vizard holding the Jon doll, asking him where she should place the James doll. Bobby said he was holding Jons hand and that Jon and the baby were about five yards ahead of him as they walked along the track. Dr Vizard asked what happened next and, with a flicking gesture of his wrist, Bobby said Jon had thrown paint in one of the baby's eyes. Dr Vizard coloured the James doll's left eye and cheek with blue marker pen to show where the paint had stained.

Reluctantly, in response to Dr Vizard's request, Bobby used the dolls to show how Jon had thrown a brick at James. He demonstrated with the James doll how the baby fell backwards into a sitting position. He showed how Jon had thrown another brick as James tried to get up. He became increasingly involved in moving the dolls to represent the assault, dolls and track being dislodged from the table as he tried to position them correctly, determined to show his version of events. Jon had thrown three or four more bricks and then the iron bar.

Occasionally, Bobby paused, staring at the scene before him, as if lost in thought. He seemed genuinely upset by this process of reliving the assault. Sometimes, he corrected Dr Vizard's positioning of the dolls.

Bobby moved the dolls to show how Jon had dragged James across the tracks and placed him face upwards across the rail. He said Jon continued to throw bricks which hit James on the head and body. Dr Vizard asked Bobby where he had been standing and what he had been doing. He said, I tried to stop him, pulled him down once or twice but he was getting more angry. Bobby placed the Bobby doll behind the Jon doll and wrapped the Bobby doll's arms around the Jon doll's body, showing how the two fell backwards onto the track by James. Bobby said, Jon got up more angry, I don't know what he was angry about. I tried to get up after he squashed me because he fell on top of me. My back was all squashed.

Bobby then spent some time trying to demonstrate how Jon had placed bricks around James's head. The James doll would not lie still and be held by the bricks positioned against it. He was asked to show how James's lower clothing had been removed by Jon, and the James doll was dislodged from the bricks as he did so. Bobby said Jon had placed the underlayer on James's mouth.

Dr Vizard asked what else had happened and Bobby said, I'm trying not to watch him. He didn't join in the assault because he wasn't that kind of person. He didn't speak to Jon because he was so shocked he said nothing.

Bobby could not explain the alleged disturbance of James's penis, which Dr Vizard said had puzzled her. Jon took the pants off, I was trying not to look, said Bobby. It could have been caused by the bricks, or Jon's kicking, though he had seen most of the things Jon did.

Dr Vizard asked Bobby if either he or Jon had touched or interfered with James's genitals. Bobby looked away and said, no. He sounded defensive and angry. Dr Vizard said it was difficult to understand why two boys should take a young child away, physically damage him and then take off his trousers. She wondered if it had been the intention of either Jon or Bobby to sexually abuse the little boy and whether this went badly wrong, with the result that they became angry and tried to silence him.

Bobby listened, head down, playing with some toy animals. He seemed unsurprised, or unmoved, by the idea that there might have been a sexual motive. He looked directly at Dr Vizard and said, angrily, I didn't touch him. He looked down and shrugged his shoulders when Dr Vizard suggested Jon might have interfered with James while Bobby wasn't looking: I dunno, I didn't see what he did when I looked away. I was shocked, wasn't I.

Dr Vizard said Bobby's description made Jon's behaviour sound very strange and beyond explanation. Bobby looked up and said, he is a strange boy. Bobby seemed annoyed when Dr Vizard asked if there wasn't anything else he could have done to stop Jon: I couldn't hold him all night or throw him off the railway bridge. I couldn't move him off the railway.

Bobby said he didn't know where the blood on his shoes came from. He responded irritably to Dr Vizard's suggestion that it was James's blood: yes, it's not just started raining blood, has it. There must have been so much blood that it seemed like rain, said Dr Vizard. Bobby nodded and looked down. He said the assault ended when Jon just stopped, all red in the face and staring at the baby. They slid down the lamp-post and didn't speak afterwards.

Dr Vizard pointed out that Bobby had said nothing to explain the impression of his shoe on James's face. Bobby said he hadn't kicked James and didn't have a clue how the mark got there. At Dr Vizard's request he again used the Bobby doll and the Jon doll to show his struggle with Jon. Dr Vizard suggested he might have stamped on or kicked James's face in this struggle. Bobby didn't know: I'm not concentrating on what my feet are doing, I'm putting all my pressure on him, my feet are going all over the place.

Bobby was asked what he was thinking when he left the railway line. He said he was thinking, what on earth did he do that for, he's an effing bastard. He thought Jon would get a good beating for what he had done. Bobby didn't think he would get into trouble because he hadn't done anything.

Why had James's body been placed across the track? Bobby said, it's not up to me to think why he put the baby on the track. Then he added, so it would get cut up. What was the point of that? Bobby looked uncomfortable. He said, repeatedly, that he didn't know. Then he said, some people might say it would give an excuse.

When he was asked what kind of little boy James had been, Bobby said, all little boys are nice until they get older. James had been quiet, in comparison with baby Ben, although he was asking, where is my mother, every three minutes.

Dr Vizard noticed that Bobby had the Jon doll in his hand, swinging it to and fro. She asked him if Jon had ever tried to steal a baby from its mother before. Bobby had never seen him. He said, Jon doesn't like being around babies. I do. Bobby left the room to go to the toilet.

When he came back he was asked how he felt James Bulger's death might affect him as he grew older. Bobby thought he might end up lonely, never able to go out. People would always keep their children in sight, in case they might disappear. Dr Vizard's colleague said people might fear Jon and Bobby, and see them as very dangerous to children. Bobby sighed, and began knotting the arms and legs of the cloth doll he was holding.

He said he never had any angry or violent thoughts about children. Dr Vizard said he might be afraid of describing such thoughts. Bobby suddenly pulled his legs up onto the chair and began sucking his thumb, banging the cloth doll against the side of his chair. He was like a much younger child. Dr Vizard said it would be better to let such thoughts out, rather than bottle them up in his mind where they might cause him more distress. Bobby sighed several times and did not reply.

With the interview coming to an end, Dr Vizard and her colleague told Bobby that they believed he would be helped in future by being able to talk more openly about what had happened in the past. They thought he had more to say about his actions and feelings and that, perhaps, important aspects of James's death had not been shared during the interview. Bobby had held back some facts and been honest about others.

He responded angrily, saying he had told them one hundred per cent of his actions and ninety-nine per cent of his feelings. He said he now felt angry with Jon and would like to ask him why he killed James. He would like to give him a slap. Dr Vizard said he seemed much angrier than that, and wondered what he really felt about Jon. Bobby agreed, chuckling, and said he would like to kick his face in. Dr Vizard suggested he pick up the Bobby doll and the Jon doll, and Bobby smiled as he used the Bobby doll to kick the Jon doll.

Finally, what would he like to say to James, if such a thing was possible. What, say to the baby? I don't know. Bobby went quiet and became tearful. Eventually he said, I feel sorry for him.

He was told the meeting had ended, and quickly became more relaxed, playing unselfconsciously with the dolls and the train set.

In the summary of their report, Dr Vizard and Colin Hawkes first addressed Bobby's current state of mind and his fitness to stand trial. They wrote that he had presented as a boy of average intelligence, fully orientated in time and space, with no signs of any formal mental illness such as psychosis or a major depressive disorder. In a boy who had been described as underachieving academically, it was interesting to note his flashes of quick intelligence, and the ease and eagerness with which he used the play materials.

His affectual responses – feelings – had been varied and seemed to relate, more or less accurately, to whatever he was describing or demonstrating at the time. He cried readily, and genuinely, when asked what he thought about James. He went from bitter sobbing to an angry exchange when it was suggested that describing his feelings might be helpful.

It had been made clear at several points during the interview that Bobby intended to repress or hold back all conscious memories and feelings about the murder. It was also clear that this was a great effort and that his emotional responses would break through and be expressed in some way. In terms of body language, Bobby had been active during the interview. He had gone to the toilet when distressed, moved around in the chair, and sometimes seemed to feel trapped. Despite these indicators of such feelings as anxiety and anger, there had been an impressive sense that Bobby was able to contain his feelings and responses to the killing, so that the same story always emerged. There was no real sense that he would allow himself to relax and speak freely.

It was a complex picture, but Bobby's feelings, his body

language, sleep disturbance, bad dreams and anxiety about allowing recall of the crime could be understood in terms of the symptoms of post-traumatic stress disorder after being present at or involved in the killing of James Bulger. These symptoms would have worsened over the last eight months, in the absence of any skilled therapeutic help, and limited Bobby's capacity to testify in his own defence.

The report relied on the American Psychiatric Association's diagnostic criteria, DSM-III-R, for diagnosis of Bobby's state of mind. He had experienced an event outside the range of usual human experience (a murder), which was the defining criteria for post-traumatic stress, and the symptoms Dr Vizard and her colleague had observed in Bobby conformed to the Assocation's classification of the disorder. The report said it should be made clear that there was no reason to think Bobby suffered from the disorder before the crime.

With the limited information available to them about Bobby's background and his schooling, and in the absence of a psychological report (Bobby had refused to see a psychologist), Dr Vizard and Colin Hawkes could only make a clinical assessment of Bobby as having an Academic Problem and a Conduct Disorder.

The former was appropriate, because there was no mental disorder to explain Bobby's underachievement. The academic problem seemed to be linked to a pattern of truanting which was item A 13 in the DSMR-III-R definition of Conduct Disorder, Undifferentiated Type. He was also known to have been stealing, to tell lies and to have been physically cruel to people, all of which were part of the definition. The report said that Bobby's weight increase since arriving at the unit suggested he might have been finding solace in food, in a way which probably related to his high levels of anxiety about his past behaviour and its future consequences.

The report said that questions could and, in the opinion of its authors, should be asked about why such a young child was not seen and assessed by a psychiatrist or psychologist, following his involvement in such a horrific crime. In the absence of any such examination comments about Bobby's mental state at the time of the killing could only be speculative.

Still, it could be argued that, before the offences, there was a body of evidence that suggested emotional and behavioural disturbance in Bobby and might have merited the attention of an expert. It seemed likely that there were conflicts, doubtless relating to home and school life, in Bobby's mind which drove him to participate, in a very calculated way, in the offences.

Assessing Bobby's current and future needs, the report suggested that Bobby's emotional and physical development was being impaired by his placement at the unit which, in the opinion of the authors, was quite inappropriate for such a young boy. He had no same-age peers and his main activity was playing video games on his own. The unit gym was equipped for older boys and he could not join in physical activities, nor find flat, open spaces inside the unit on which to play roller boarding or other active games.

Dr Vizard and Colin Hawkes were concerned about Bobby's increase in weight. It was not, the report stated, a trivial matter, and had implications for his future physical health. Clinical experience suggested that obesity in children was often associated with the early onset of puberty, for which Bobby should receive counselling or therapy.

They were gravely concerned over the absence of any therapeutic work with Bobby or his family since the arrest. There might or might not have been legal advice about the need to avoid compromising or contaminating Bobby's defence by pre-trial therapy, but Bobby's best interests needed to be actively considered alongside his status as an alleged juvenile offender. In the opinion of the report's authors, Bobby's capacity to instruct his lawyers and testify in his defence had been impaired by the residual, untreated symptoms of post-traumatic stress.

He had not been able to express his feelings about the alleged offences and this might be more difficult in the future. It was also likely that his family's attitude towards Bobby and the offences would become fixed in a legal perspective and it would be harder for the family to benefit from therapy.

There was an immediate need for Bobby and his family to be helped to begin talking about the offences and the likely effects on the rest of his life. The report also recommended that Bobby should not be allowed any unsupervised contact with younger or vulnerable children, because of the serious risk of Significant Harm which he posed.

25

Monday, 1 November 1993 was not the first time Bobby and Jon had been to Preston Crown Court. They had been driven there in police vans, one after the other, on Sunday, 3 October, to familiarise themselves with the setting in which they would be tried for murder.

The court had been busy making accommodations to the ages of the defendants and the infamy of their alleged crimes. Two rooms had been set aside – one, the female officers' rest room – where the boys could go with parents and social workers in the breaks between sittings. Already, court staff had been turning the lights on in these rooms early in the morning, so that new activity would not be identified and associated with the boys by press photographers outside the building.

A wooden platform nine inches high had been knocked together and painted black. The boys would sit in chairs on the platform in the dock, so that their view would not be obscured by the dock's brass rail.

The usual rows of free-standing chairs in the public gallery had been replaced by seats that were screwed to the floor, in case anyone was tempted to throw them.

The boys' visit, that Sunday morning, had been unusual, and unlike all their subsequent daily trips during the trial. The vans had not entered the court complex, but had pulled up at an outside door. The boys had taken a few steps along the street to enter the building.

The Wednesday of the following week was the day of Home Secretary Michael Howard's rabble-rousing speech on law and order to the Conservative Party Conference. The speech was widely reported in Thursday's national newspapers.

The front page of Thursday's edition of *The Sun* gave a single left-hand column to Michael Howard. SUN SPEAKS ITS MIND. YES, CRIME MINISTER.

It was, said *The Sun*, a joy to hear a tough-talking Home Secretary say he couldn't give a damn if more people ended up behind bars. Never mind three cheers, he deserved one hundred and three for yesterday's declaration of war on the muggers, robbers and rapists who made our life hell. Bail bandits, young yobs the law couldn't touch, guilty men freed because they stayed silent in court. They were all about to be whacked with a very large stick.

The rest of *The Sun*'s front page, alongside this column, was consumed by a photograph of Jon, carrying a lollipop, being led into Preston Crown Court by a policeman with his hand on Jon's shoulder, taken the previous Sunday. Jon's face had been digitalised and was obscured by fleshy cubes. It would have been contempt of court to identify him. SUN PICTURE EXCLUSIVE: Arm on shoulder, lollipop in hand, the boy accused of Jamie murder. Continued on Page 12.

Page 12 described in some selective and spurious detail the boys' luxurious lives in their units as they awaited trial. Page 13 was two more photographs from Preston. One of Bobby and another of Jon, again with their faces obscured. They were, respectively, captioned: Good life . . . one of the boys charged with Jamie's murder, escorted here by a PC, has put on weight.

Sweet treatment . . . the second accused lad clutches a lolly as he is led into court to view the dock where he will sit.

It appeared that *The Sun* had waited four days to use these pictures, alongside its comment on the Home Secretary's speech. It was not unreasonable to speculate that someone had been compensated for their loss of time in betraying the advance information of Bobby and Jon's trip to Preston to *The Sun*.

There was no opportunity for snatched photographs on 1 November, when the vans drove straight through the open gates of Preston Crown Court and into the secluded courtyard. A handful of people stood still and silent at the gates as the vans passed by. There were legions of press photographers and television news crews. There were eleven people queuing for seats in the public gallery.

Bobby and Jon were led to their respective rooms. There they sat, waiting. They were not in the dock when Court One rose at ten o'clock to greet the Honourable Mr Justice Morland for the first time in the trial.

Who's Who 1993

MORLAND, Hon. Sir Michael, K.t 1989; Hon. Mr Justice Morland; a Judge of the High Court of Justice, Queen's Bench Division, since 1989; Presiding Judge, Northern Circuit, since 1991; *b* 16 July 1929; *e s* of Edward Morland, Liverpool, and Jane Morland (*née* Beckett); *m* 1961, Lillian Jensen, Copenhagen; one *s* one *d*. *Educ.* Stowe; Christ Church, Oxford (MA). 2nd Lieut, Grenadier Guards, 1948–49; served in Malaya. Called to Bar, Inner Temple, 1953, Bencher 1979; Northern Circuit; QC 1972; a Recorder, 1972–89. Mem., Criminal Injuries Compensation Bd, 1980–89. *Address:* Royal Courts of Justice, Strand, WC2.

The Lord Chancellor's Department in London had earlier issued a press release, announcing that the judge would address the media at ten o'clock on the first morning of the trial. It was like a summons to appear, and the court was overflowing with journalists. There were more media representatives than press seats, so it was standing room only for the judge's address.

Morland, who was not yet fully robed, outlined the orders he had drawn up, which would restrict reporting to protect various interests and avoid prejudicing the trial.

It was no longer R – v – T and V, Regina versus Thompson and Venables. It was R – v – A and B (two children). For the purposes of reporting, Bobby was now Child A and Jon was Child B.

Nothing which was said in court in the absence of the jury could be reported before the verdicts were given. The boys could not be identified, and neither could any child witnesses. No witness or defendant, or any member of their families, could be harassed, followed or interviewed until after the verdicts.

To cope with the sheer volume of press interest, a court annexe had been set up at Crystal House, a high-rise office building across the square from the court. Morland and the Lord Chief Justice had discussed the possibility of providing a video link from Court One to the annexe. It had never been done before in a criminal trial, and they decided not to do it now. A sound link had been set up instead and, Morland explained, the annexe was now subject to the same rules as the court. No tape recorders, no laptops, no bleeping pagers, no mobile phones.

Morland excused himself if he seemed schoolmasterish. He said he would be happy to help if there was a problem. Any breach by anyone of the orders should render that person liable to a substantial term of imprisonment and a fine. There was a short break, for everyone to find their seats and settle down. The judge went out, and came back in again.

In accordance with ancient ceremonial tradition, Morland was now wearing a long red gown, with black sash trimming, and a horsehair wig. He carried a pair of white gloves and a folded black cloth. It was the same black cloth cap that judges had once put on their heads to pass a sentence of death. It was 162 years since John Any Bird Bell had been sentenced to death in Maidstone, the last child to be hanged for murder. The concessions to informality introduced in modern youth courts would not be allowed at this trial.

At twenty to eleven, Morland said, 'Let the defendants be brought up.' Bobby and Jon emerged from the cell area below the court, up a row of steps leading into the dock. They were led by a bullet-headed prison warder with tattoos on his arms. There were four chairs on the nine-inch raised platform. Jon took the first and his case worker the second. Bobby's case worker took the third chair and Bobby the fourth. Later that day Bobby and his case worker swapped seats. Boy, adult, boy, adult. And, with one exception, these were the positions they kept for the duration of the trial.

The judge spoke to the boys. 'Are you Robert Thompson?' Bobby held up a finger, as if he was answering the register in class. 'Are you Jon Venables?' A nod from Jon.

It was immediately apparent that the benefit of the raised platform on the floor of the dock was double-edged. It gave the boys a clearer view of the court. It also gave the court a clearer view of the boys, raised up in the brass-railed dock like a pair of caged animals, where they could and would be subjected to the most intense scrutiny.

Both boys had grown, upwards and outwards, since their last public appearance in a court. They looked significantly older, and bulkier, than 37 weeks ago when James Bulger had been killed. Jon, puffy-faced and anxious, as if he was between tears, wore black trousers and a black jacket with two vents. Bobby, his head newly shaven, looked dressed for school, and was indeed wearing his school tie under a grey V-necked sweater. His neck was crammed into a size 14 shirt. His counsel suggested, privately, that he had the appearance of a butcher's boy, and someone recommended the purchase of some bigger shirts. Tomorrow Bobby would be in size 15.

Bobby began as he evidently intended to continue, giving nothing away if he could help it. His face revealed no sign of distress, anxiety or any other emotional reaction. This was to be swiftly interpreted as the impassivity of an unfeeling psychopath, or the boredom of indifference.

The boys had been followed up the stairs by Neil and Susan Venables. Ann Thompson had not come to court, because she could not cope with the thought of being there. She was severely stressed, was taking a cabinetful of pills, and had recently begun seeing a psychiatric nurse. Talking to the nurse had brought all the pain in her past to the surface.

All three parents had sought the support of Aftermath, a voluntary group set up to help the families of those accused of serious crime. Aftermath had tried to bring Ann and Neil and Susan together but, as with their sons since the arrests, there was more mutual antipathy between them than any sense of shared suffering.

Neil and Susan could not sit in the dock with their son and walked out of it, through a gate, following the aisle that ran the length of the court in front of the public gallery. They walked round to the far side of the dock, and sat in a pew next to Jon, where Aftermath's Shirl Marshall was waiting to take Susan's hand in hers.

Their walk had taken them past the front left row of the public gallery which was filled with members of the Bulger family, including James's father, and flanked by the family liaison officers from Merseyside Police, Jim Green and Mandy Waller. Neil and Susan Venables, he in a grey flecked suit, she in funereal black, kept their eyes to the floor. They sat down, shoulders hunched over, heads bowed, Neil's face drawn skeletal tight. They exuded an aura of abject humiliation and shame.

There were 48 seats in the public gallery, and only eight of them allocated to the Bulgers. It was not always full, but there would usually be only a scattering of empty seats. Many were taken by foreign journalists and assorted members of the British media who were passing through. Others went to law students, lecturers, curious Preston people and a young man from London who'd had a difficult childhood and was thinking of writing a novel based on the case.

The gallery was separated from the rest of the court by an iron rail. After the rail came the aisle, and after the aisle a long central pew of press seats which backed on to the dock. To the left sat the Merseyside Police, Albert Kirby and Jim Fitzsimmons in the front row on a cushion which Jim carried to and from the court every day.

Behind Neil and Susan, on the immediate right of the dock, sat three representatives of Liverpool City Council Social Services. In front of Neil and Susan were defence solicitors and their clerks, and, in front of them, two long rows of pews, with junior and leading counsel for the prosecution on the left, Bobby's counsel in the middle, and Jon's on the right.

There were more press seats on the far right and, in front of these, facing sideways into the court, the jury box, which was three rows of tiered pews. In front of the jury box were two short pews which were the last six seats of the court's allocation to the media – 38 in all. These six were to be the most sought-after location; the only seats with a full frontal view of Bobby and Jon, from where it was possible to take notes of their every twitch and fidget.

The jury box faced the witness stand, across the court. Between the box and the stand was the court's clerk, facing the dock, and towering over the clerk was the high bench, running the length of the court, behind which, in an even higher chair with an enormous back, sat the judge. The judge sometimes had his own clerk sitting near him for company and assistance with handling files. The judge's clerk swore in some of the witnesses. He had a booming Scottish accent and a thick beard. He was a dead ringer for James Robertson Justice in the *Doctor* films.

Dotted around the front of the court were microphones, loudspeakers and video monitors. These high-tech accoutrements sat uneasily amid the oak-panelled archaism of the court. It was only ninety years old, but it could have been centuries.

Preston's judicial worthies of times past were depicted in a series of full-length portraits around the walls of the court.

Henry Wilson Worsley-Taylor, KC, MP; Sir Harcourt Evarard Clare, Kt; Thomas Batty Addison ('the terror of the criminal') ... any one of these might have been the berobed fellow beneath the wig trying Bobby and Jon.

The jury, chosen at random from Preston's electoral roll, was sworn in without challenge. There were nine men and three women, all white and predominantly middle-aged. A couple were younger men, and only one did not appear to have dressed for the occasion. There was a straight-backed, silver-haired chap in a smart blazer with a breast-pocket handkerchief. He looked like a jury foreman.

Once sworn, they were dispatched to the jury room, so that the judge could hear applications from counsel. Bobby's QC, David Turner, rose to address the judge, to argue that the trial should be abandoned.

TURNER, David Andrew; QC 199; a Recorder of the Crown Court, since 1990; *b* 6 March 1947; *s* of James and Phyllis Turner; *m* 1978, Mary Christine Moffatt; two *s* one *d Educ.* King George V Sch., Southport; Quens Coll., Cambridge (MA, LLM). Called to the Bar, Gray's Inn, 1971; Asst Recorder, 1987–90. *Recreations*: squash, music. *Address*: Pearl Assurance House, Derby Square, Liverpool L2 9XX. *T*: 051-236 7747. *Club*: Liverpool Racquet.

In the language of the law, Turner was making an abuse of process application. He was, he said, seeking a stay of proceedings because a fair trial of these defendants was now impossible. The abduction and death of James Bulger had led to what could only be described as saturation coverage in the media. The reporting of the early stages had gone far beyond the usual reporting of a criminal case. This was because the public had been asked to become deeply involved in the investigation itself, highly emotive language had been used in articles, and the case had coincided with a government initiative on the treatment of young offenders, and become part of a public debate.

Turner said that abuse applications usually resulted from a delay in the proceedings reaching court. He referred to the summary by Mr Justice Garland in the case of three police officers who had been charged with misconduct over the Birmingham Six inquiry. Though delay had been the principal issue in that case, Garland's summary had suggested that publicity alone could be a free-standing ground for appeal. The burden of proving unfairness rested on the defendant. It was a matter to be decided on the balance of probabilities.

Turner said he would contend strenuously that the volume, nature and quality of the national publicity was so powerful as to make a fair trial impossible. There were four categories of publicity: first, when an editor expressed an opinion of guilt by headline, comment or innuendo; second, publishing an express view of a politician or church leader that the defendants were guilty, or establishing that as the only inference that could be drawn from the article; third, publishing material that was wrong, misleading or prejudicial; and, fourth, publishing sensational or highly prejudicial material.

Turner went on to cite examples of each from a file of 243 copies of articles from national newspapers. It was not, he said, an exhaustive compilation: What sort of monsters could do that to a child; new police pic shows evil lads who murdered toddler; crime beyond evil; how killer children are caged. There were references to leaders in the *Daily Telegraph* and *The Times*. There were quotes from Kenneth Baker and the Archbishop of Canterbury. There were inaccuracies such as James being tossed like a toy and being dragged screaming and bleeding to his death. It's them, *The Star* had said before the boys were charged. *The Express* had reached the mother of the child the boys had allegedly attempted to abduct and had her saying, they nearly slaughtered him as well.

Turner said that after this barrage of publicity, much of it prejudicial, it would be impossible to have a fair trial.

Many people in court had not anticipated this application. The litany of quotations from and references to articles gave considerable substance to his argument. Albert Kirby was soon sitting forward, resting his elbow on his knee, chewing his nails. It was unthinkable – wasn't it? – after all this time and money and effort, that the trial should end before it had begun.

Jon's QC, Brian Walsh, stood to support the application. He had been ill before the trial and at one stage his junior counsel, Richard Isaacson, had been going to take over. The judge had said this was not a case for a junior counsel. Walsh had undergone an unpleasant operation with a local anaesthetic, and recovered in time to appear.

WALSH, Brian, QC 1977; a Recorder of the Crown Court, since 1972; *b* 17 June 1935; *er s* of late Percy Walsh and Sheila (*née* Frais), Leeds; *m* 1964, Susan Margaret, *d* of late Eli (Kay) Frieze and of Doris Frieze; two *d. Educ*: Sheikh Bagh Sch., Srinagar, Kashmir; Leeds Grammar Sch. (Head Boy 1954); Gonville and Caius Coll., Cambridge (BA, LLB; MA 1992). Pres. Cambridge Union Soc., 1959. Served RAF (Pilot Officer), 1954–56. Called to the Bar, Middle Temple, 1961 (Blackstone Scholar, Harmsworth Scholar); Bencher, 1986. Joined North Eastern Circuit, 1961; Leader, 1990–. Member: Circuit Exec. Cttee, 1980–; Gen. Council of the Bar 1982–84 and 1990–; Mental Health Review Tribunal, 1986–. Member: Court, Leeds Univ., 1988–; Cttee. Yorks CCC 1984– (Chm. 1986–91); Governor: Leeds Grammar Sch. 1977–; Leeds Girls' High Sch., 1978–; Pres., Old Leodiensian Assoc., 1983–85. *Recreations*: golf, cricket, eating. *Address*. Park Court Chambers, 40 Park Cross Street, Leeds LS1 2QH. *T*: Leeds (0532) 433277.

'The stream of justice', said Walsh, 'should run as purely and unpolluted as possible'. What had been published already in this case, he submitted, poisoned that stream. The consequences were on the heads of those who had published.

The Crown QC, Richard Henriques, said that never in the history of criminal trials had a trial been stayed because of adverse publicity. There was always a lot of in-depth reporting in advance of murder trials. The real issues were not affected. The real issue was between the two defendants. Twelve fair jurors, seeing two eleven-year-old boys in the dock, would deal with this case as all juries do.

The judge said that in his judgement the test he had to apply was that no stay should be imposed unless the defendant could show that owing to the extent and nature of pretrial publicity he would suffer such prejudice to the extent that no fair trial could be held. The judge said it was right that he should refer in some detail to the media coverage. When the judge said this, there were those in court who thought he was seriously considering granting the stay. Wiser observers suspected it meant the opposite. He was simply being seen to have weighed the merit of the application.

Saturation was the right word for the media coverage, said the judge. Matters of opinion had been canvassed on page after page and, while the criminal investigation was proceeding, the nature of reporting went way beyond what was normally done by the media before defendants are charged and the trial begins. It was not a case where the publicity had been merely local. There had been widespread comment and articles containing alleged information about the case and the background of the defendants. There was much strength in Mr Turner's submission that editors had expressed opinion and comment and suggested by innuendo that the defendants were guilty. Publicity had been misleading, prejudicial and, in a number of cases, highly sensational.

The judge went on to cite many of the articles in Turner's 243-page file. He said the publicity had not merely been at the time of death. As recently as a few days ago *The Sun* newspaper had published photographs of the boys in the custody of police officers. Their faces had been disguised but . . . the judge quoted the headline referring to Jon and his lollipop.

The extent and nature of the publicity at pretrial in this case had caused him very considerable concern. But he had come unhesitatingly to the conclusion that it had not been established that on the balance of probability either of these two defendants would suffer serious prejudice to the extent that no fair trial could be held. It was not a case where the defence was raising alibi issues. The issue was whether the Crown could establish joint enterprise, whether one or other of the boys was proved to have been the killer and whether one or the other had proved against them the necessary intent for murder to be established.

'Having considered all these matters I am not satisfied there cannot be a fair trial.' Application refused. Court rise for lunch.

After lunch, David Turner asked the judge to remove two photographs from the bundle of 54 pictures which the Crown would be submitting in evidence. These were a sequence of photographs depiciting the route the boys had taken with James and pictures from the scene of the killing itself, including close-ups of James Bulger's head injuries. It was the Crown's duty to present these as evidence, but the Crown would also appreciate the emotional impact of these photographs on the jury, as would the defence. The photographs, numbers 47 and 48, which Turner asked to be omitted, were two close-ups of the head. The judge said there would be no omissions.

This concluded business between judge and counsel. The jury could be recalled and, suddenly, the trial was beginning. Morland told the jury that the case had generated a substantial degree of media attention. 'You must remember to decide this case solely on the evidence produced in court, and only on that evidence.'

There had been a great deal of advance speculation about the length of the trial, which finally settled on around four weeks. With all those days stretching ahead, it was expected that the trial would begin gently, moving gradually from arcane legal discussion into the facts of the case and the difficult detail of the killing.

Now Henriques was on his feet and making his opening speech for the Crown. He spoke with gravity and resonance and without resort to dramatic overstatement. There was no need. It soon became apparent that his narrative outline would spare the court no detail.

HENRIQUES, Richard Henry Quixano; QC 1986; barrister; a Recorder of the Crown Court, since 1983; b 27 Oct. 1943; s of Cecil

Quixano Henriques and late Doreen Mary Henriques; *m* Joan Hilary, (Toni), (*née* Senior); one *s* and one step *s*. *Educ*: Bradfield Coll., Berks; Worcester Coll., Oxford (BA). Called to the Bar, Inner Temple, 1967. Mem., Northern Circuit. Council Mem., Rossall Sch. *Recreations*: bridge, golf. *Address*: Ilex House, Woodhouse Road, Thornton-Cleveleys, Lancs FY5 5LQ. *T*: Cleveleys (0253) 826199. *Clubs*. The Manchester (Manchester); North Shore Golf (Blackpool).

'James Bulger was two years and 11 months old when he died. He was the only child of Ralph and Denise Bulger.

'These two defendants abducted him from his mother in a shopping centre in Bootle. They walked him some two and a half miles across Liverpool to Walton village – a long and distressing journey for a two-year-old.

'James was then taken up onto a railway line and was subjected to a prolonged and violent attack. Bricks, stones and a piece of metal appear to have been thrown at James, and he was kicked in the face and body. He sustained many fractures of the skull.

'Death resulted from multiple blunt force injuries to the head. There were several lacerations. At some point James's lower clothing was removed. His body was put across the railway line and some time later his body was run over by a train which cut it in two. Death occurred prior to the impact of the train.

'The Prosecution alleges that the two defendants acting together took James from the precinct and together were responsible for causing his death.

'Both defendants are now eleven years of age. On the 12th of February they were ten years old, both having been born in August 1982. They both intended to kill James or to cause him really serious injury. They both knew that their behaviour was seriously wrong.

'Not only is it alleged that they abducted and killed James, but that prior to abducting James they tried to abduct another two-year-old.'

These opening words were themselves an outline of the more

detailed account Henriques would give in his speech. It was the case against the boys which the prosecution would spend the next three weeks presenting. It was the Crown's version of what had happened to James Bulger, in all its terrible minutiae. The outline had an immediate impact on those in court, a tightening of the tension of the first day. Neil Venables held his head in his hands. Susan had a white-knuckle grip on some tissues. It wasn't necessary to look at the members of the Bulger family to imagine how they felt about what was soon to be described.

Bobby had earlier kicked off his shoes and removed his sweater. Now he fidgeted and sighed heavily. Jon had not previously been able to confront what had happened. Now it was coming and he had no choice. He moved his hands restlessly and looked desperate.

By the time Henriques's narrative had taken the boys out of the Strand with James and onto Stanley Road, Jon was crying openly, burying his face in the adjacent shoulder of his case worker.

Henriques told the jury he was going through the evidence in detail because it would show that both boys had been involved, that it was a joint enterprise. He said 12 February had been an ordinary school day on Merseyside when all ten-year-olds, including the two defendants, should have been in school. Then he began the description of the boys' day, through the accounts of the various witnesses who had seen or encountered them. He spoke of Toymaster and the tins of paint, and the paint that was later found on their clothing and on James Bulger. It would, he said, form an important part of the prosecution case.

He described the early attempt at abduction and the abduction of James: 'Denise believed that James was by her side – but she looked down and he was gone.' He referred to the sightings and timings on the Strand's security video.

Out on to Stanley Road, and into the journey. At the reservoir, Henriques mentioned an incline. Bobby leant over and whispered to his case worker, who held up his hand at an angle. That's what an incline is.

Away from the reservoir, along to County Road, and through to the entry alongside the railway line. Down to the end of the entry by Walton Lane. A witness who had seen a youth carrying a child who was laughing. That, said Henriques, may well be the last time that anyone, other than the defendants, saw James Bulger alive.

It was between 5.30 and 6.45 that James Bulger was stoned and beaten to death before being placed across a railway line. Henriques described how the body was found by four boys, and described the scene that greeted the police on the railway line. He mentioned the patterned bruise on James's cheek, the result of a severe blow. He told the jury they would hear more of that severe blow.

There was the blood on the boys' shoes and the forensic tests that showed it was James's blood. There was the head hair on the lace of Bobby's right shoe, and the forensic test that showed it was James's hair. There were the stains of blue paint, including the mark on the sleeve of Jon's jacket, and the forensic tests that showed it could well be the mark of a small hand stained with paint.

The boys were arrested six days later and they were both interviewed. The jury would hear the interviews.

Henriques stopped then, and it was the end of the first day of the trial. The court would only sit from 10.30 to 3.30 each day, with breaks in mid-morning and mid-afternoon, and an hour for lunch. This was in deference to the attention span of two eleven-year-old boys. It was an approximation of their school day.

That night, Jon was in distress at his unit, shouting at his dad. The following morning he was hysterical, before coming up into the dock. His face was flushed and puffy, his eyes red and tired.

Henriques was still on his opening, going through the content of each of the interviews for the jury. He said they demonstrated the boys' fluent capacity to tell lies. Each defendant changed ground to meet the circumstances. As the police disclosed the evidence, so each made further admissions. They demonstrated a progression from total ignorance of events, to partial knowledge, through to placing as much of the blame as possible on their co-accused.

Bobby was quoted. I wouldn't hit the baby, I wouldn't touch him. Henriques told the jury that, when considering whether or not he knew this was seriously wrong, they would bear in mind those words.

Jon was quoted. I said it's a very bad thing to do, isn't it. Henriques told the jury to bear this in mind when deciding whether Jon knew what he was doing was seriously wrong.

In order to prove murder against either of these defendants, Henriques said, the prosecution must make sure that the defendant in question played a part in causing the death of James Bulger. Participation might vary from actually delivering the fatal blow, or some of the blows, to a much lesser role of intentionally giving encouragement to the other by his mere presence. In the present case, he submitted, both defendants played a part in causing James Bulger's death.

It must also be proved that the defendants knew that death or serious injury would be inflicted on James. Because they were under 14, the jury had to be sure that they knew what they were doing was seriously wrong, rather than naughty or mischievous.

'Some criminal acts are more obviously wrong than others. These crimes are most seriously obviously wrong, not merely to a ten-year-old but to a child of perhaps half that age or even less.'

In due course the prosecution would point to the gross nature of the acts, to the defendants' conduct and demeanour after the events and their manner and demeanour during the interviews. The jury would hear from people who taught the boys at school, including a teacher who taught religious education and had sixteen years' experience of teaching maladjusted pupils. He taught them right from wrong.

The closing words of the opening speech were: 'You can properly be satisfied that each of them knew it was seriously wrong to take a young child from his mother, to try to do so, and to use such extreme violence on a child of such tender years.'

The jury were given files of folded plans and maps depicting the Strand and the route. Then they were given the ring-pull folders containing copies of the 54 photographs. Henriques led them through the photographs. Again, they were taken on the journey.

Photograph 1 showed the escalators at the Strand and by photograph 24 they were looking at the reservoir steps. Photograph 25 also showed the reservoir steps. 38 was the hood of James's anorak, in the tree where Jon had thrown it.

Henriques paused after 43. The remaining photographs are unpleasant to look at and I advise you to steel yourselves. Here were the scene-of-crime pictures, showing the two halves of the body, and the close-ups of the face and head. A woman juror began crying. Susan Venables began crying. Jon leant over, looking anxiously at his mother, asking if she was all right.

The first witness was called, one of the assistants from Clinton Cards. She was asked to describe trolls, for the benefit of those who were unfamiliar with them. She said they were miniature dolls with ugly faces and straggly hair. She was a chirpy woman, seemingly undaunted by her appearance in court. When she had given her evidence-in-chief she was offered to Turner and Walsh for cross-examination. Brian Walsh asked her to agree that it was the smaller boy – Bobby – who had been doing all the talking during her conversation with the boys. She was happy to agree to this.

It took five more days and 42 more witnesses to take the Crown's case from Clinton Cards in the Strand to the entry opposite Walton Lane Police Station. Every known moment of the day, and the journey, was recalled and pored over in the finest and sometimes most painful detail. The witnesses were young, middle-aged and elderly, all of them ordinary people from Bootle, Walton and elsewhere on Merseyside. Some had apparently dressed for court, others came in their regular clothes. Some spoke clearly and confidently. Some were so terrified that their bodies shook and their mouths went dry. The judge was always solicitous. Would you like a glass of water? Do you think you might be more comfortable if you gave your evidence sitting down? He gathered up his gown and swept over to the witness box, offering assistance with the search for locations on maps and plans when witnesses became confused.

Many were clearly very emotional. James Bulger had passed them by. If only . . . if only . . . Sometimes it seemed that they had made these if onlys real in their own minds. Their evidence would veer wildly from the statements they had given to the police, eight months before. David Turner and Brian Walsh would do their best to steer the witnesses back to their original recollections. Or at least try to imply to the jury that all was not quite as accurate as it should be. Walsh, in particular, would often sound patronising, as he tried, helpfully, to suggest that the passage of time could play tricks with the memory.

I'm not going senile at 51 years of age, someone retorted angrily. It was a red-headed woman in a big black-and-white checked jacket. She was very nervous, but she was not about to let some smart-arse barrister put one over on her. There was not always the reverence for their authority which Turner and Walsh might more readily have expected, and even exploited, from witnesses not born and raised in Liverpool. The rounded, educated, voices of counsel rubbed uneasily against the colloquial patter of the witnesses. There was the unmistakable conflict of class.

The mother of the child that Bobby and Jon were accused of attempting to abduct said in court that it looked as if Jon had been enticing her son to follow him. This was not something she had originally said in her police statement. In cross-examination, Brian Walsh asked her to look at her original statement. When it was handed to her, the mother said, stroppily, well, do you want me to read it? Walsh pointed out that she had not contacted the police until four days after the incident. He suggested that if she had not heard the news of James Bulger's killing she would not have contacted the police. She said she didn't think that anyone of that age could kill anyone. Then she began crying.

Another mother giving evidence said that one of the boys had spoken to her son, when he approached the boys while they were playing with a fire hydrant door at the Strand. This was much more damaging to the defence than her original statement, in which she said her son had gone up and spoken to the boys. She said the boys had stared at her, and had been mumbling to each other. She hadn't mentioned those incidents either, in her statement.

David Turner, cross-examining, asked if she was sure the boy had been talking to her son. Well, his mouth was moving up and down, she said. Clearly, the mother was getting upset. There were more questions and, when the woman carried on speaking, Turner tried to talk over her, to restrict her answers. Henriques stood up and pointed this out. The judge said, I'm sure, Mr Turner, you will be careful not to interrupt the witnesses. Turner said he wasn't aware he had, but he apologised, and was more careful with witnesses after that.

It was the cabbie who had been waiting outside the Strand who provided the first evidence of any violence towards James, with his description of a boy in a mustard jacket – Jon – who had jerked James up to carry him. Brian Walsh cross-examined the cabbie and asked him to confirm that the boy in the mustard jacket did not seem to be someone experienced in lifting a small child. The cabbie was happy to agree this, but it was difficult to see how it advanced Jon's defence.

Brian Walsh cross-examined several witnesses on geographical points, apparently trying to establish where they had been when they saw or spoke to the boys. These too, were puzzling interventions.

The full impact of the case – and the publicity that had surrounded it – on some of the witnesses was expressed in the evidence of the woman who had been travelling along Breeze Hill on the 67 bus when she had seen the boys swinging James between them. She had told the police in her statement, ten days after the killing, that she had commented on the boys' actions to her daughter, sitting beside her on the bus. She thought the passenger sitting behind them might have overheard her remarks.

In court she gave evidence that she had shouted, what the friggin' hell they doin' to that poor kid, and the whole of the bus had turned to look. David Turner pointed out that this was not in her statement. She said the police didn't put it in. She had shouted. She would never forget the incident. But it didn't find its way into your statement, said Turner. The woman said she didn't know why not. 'I came here to give evidence and I've come to tell the truth and that's what I'm doing.' Do you feel emotional? Turner asked. 'I'm emotional because of what happened to that little boy.'

'Maudlin Liverpool shite,' muttered someone, a Liverpudlian, in the court.

Turner spent considerable time cross-examining the witness who had seen a boy – Bobby – giving James a persuasive kick, while he was driving past in his van, looking in his mirror. His evidence did not vary significantly from his earlier statement, and he would not be persuaded that he might not have seen what he said he had seen. Turner tried everything. The heavy traffic, the whereabouts of the boys in relation to the van, was it a quick glimpse in the mirror? It was more of a stare. Which mirror? The interior mirror. I suggest to you there was no kick. There was.

More than any other witness, the elderly woman who had been walking her dog on the reservoir, and spoken to the boys, seemed burdened by guilt and if only. She had been subjected to considerable local publicity at the time of the killing, when it was thought she might have been the last person to see James alive. She wasn't, but she was plainly troubled by the memory and looked very unhappy, giving evidence.

She had told the police at the time that she had asked the boys if they knew the child. They had said they didn't and she had told them he should have some attention for the visible bumps on his head. The boys had said they would take him to the police station, and they had walked away. In court, giving evidence, the two bumps had become 'this huge big lump . . . this terrible lump'. She said she thought all three children were brothers. They had told her they were going home, and she had told them to hurry up, and show their mum the lump.

When Turner stood he immediately told the woman, please understand that in cross-examination, he was not suggesting she was anything other than truthful, but . . . She denied telling the police she had asked the boys if they knew the child. She denied saying they had told her, no. She was sure one of them had said they were going home, and that she had told them to hurry up. Turner said her statement showed completely different words. That wasn't what she had said, she said. But it was in the statement, and wasn't the statement more likely to be correct? How do you mean? Wasn't it more likely to be right because it was taken nearer the time? No, said the woman. The judge asked why not. 'Because I didn't say that to them.' It was made clear that she had signed the statement as a true and accurate record of what she had said. She had even signed one or two small alterations. Still, standing there in the witness box, she would not concede the original description of her encounter.

Brian Walsh followed David Turner and fared no better. He even offered the woman a way out: perhaps she had confused her own statement with that of her friend, who had also been a witness. Was that an explanation? 'No, I don't think so.'

All the Crown QC, Henriques, had to do was guide the witnesses through their evidence-in-chief. It was the defence who had the problem. They were doing well if they could hold the witnesses to their original police statements. The problem, it gradually became apparent, was that there was no defence to speak of. Walsh and Turner could emphasise the minor role of their own defendant in these various encounters, and emphasise the major role of the other defendant. They had little else to work with.

After only a handful of positive identifications among the many witnesses, Bobby and Jon were rarely referred to by name in the court. Bobby was the short one, the chubby one, the round-faced one, the one in the black anorak, the one with the skinhead haircut, the one with the skinhead haircut that was beginning to grow out, as several witnesses described it, showing careful attention to hair style. Jon was the taller one, the one with the longer hair, the one wearing the beige or mustard-coloured anorak. Sometimes the descriptions became muddled. It didn't seem to matter very much.

No one spoke to the boys. Apart from brief, whispered exchanges with their case workers or their lawyers – 'How many more witnesses are there, Mr Walsh?' Jon could be heard to ask – they seemed to be taking no part in the proceedings. Between the first and last days of the trial, not a single word uttered in court was addressed to them. It was difficult to believe that they could concentrate on, or understand, more than a tiny proportion of what was going on around them. Their understanding did not seem to be a priority of the court. The abstract descriptions of the boys by the witnesses only reinforced the idea that they weren't actually there, or need not, or should not, have been there, as child participants in an adult ritual.

Don't be surprised to see men with red noses juggling balls in the court, someone said. It was not just the presence of the media that created a circus-like atmosphere. It was the men – they were all men – in wigs and gowns, the formality and theatricality of the language and the procedure.

The family of James Bulger had a right to expect, and to see justice. Retribution for the killing was an important component of the ritual, but it was not the only, nor even the major consideration. It was hard to square the desire for due process, the playing out of the full majesty of the law, with the ages of the two boys in the dock.

The trial was likened to the mediaeval case of a pig – 1386, Normandy – which was tried and hanged for infanticide. It had torn the head and arms of a child, and the child had died. The pig faced a tribunal and was sentenced to be mangled and maimed in the head and forelegs, before being executed. It was dressed in male clothing for the public hanging in the town square.

Sometimes Bobby and Jon would seem to be engaged by the procession of characters through the witness box, if only by displays of emotion, tension or distress. Occasionally, if Bobby was being mentioned, Jon would look cautiously in Bobby's direction, and snap his head back if Bobby turned to meet his glance. When Jon was mentioned, Bobby might do the same.

They never held each other's eyes and nothing was shared between them, though there was one moment, after they had been toying with paper tissues, when both boys simultaneously produced identical tissue-creations, like knotted hankies, which they together smoothed out across their knees. Like all their behaviour in court, this was capable of being interpreted in some way or other. Perhaps the boys were only there for the benefit of the media, who scrutinised, analysed, enlarged and invented their activities.

Constrained by the trial, trapped in their chairs, there was no room for normal childlike behaviour. No nipping off to kick a ball around, no being excused to go to the loo. No robbing or sagging. Instead, Bobby and Jon fidgeted; rolled and unrolled their ties, played with tissues, fiddled with their hands, shifted around in their seats. This was especially so in the afternoon sessions, when their concentration was spent.

Jon fished around in the pockets of his jacket and bit his nails. It had initially looked as if he might be unable to survive the ordeal of the trial. But, after the first couple of days, he appeared to adjust to the routine. He moved his fingers, as if playing a computer game in his head. He glanced anxiously around, particularly towards his mum and dad when they were showing signs of distress. The lawyers, near him, noticed that Jon was keen to catch their eye, to receive a warm response and a smile, which he would eagerly return.

Bobby slumped back and stared at the ceiling; he sighed and asked his care worker the time and was shown the care worker's wrist watch. He unravelled the overlong sleeves of his oversized shirts, which dangled from his hands like those of a straitjacket. He did not, as one tabloid writer suggested, stare out members of the jury. As many others suggested, he showed no emotion – though this was probably not, as many implied, because he was feeling no emotion. Bobby sucked his thumb and licked his fingers, and some who observed this ascribed very specific explanations of childhood disturbance. There was a theory that Bobby sucked his thumb because he had been orally, sexually abused. Who knows? Perhaps he sucked his thumb and licked his fingers because he was very insecure. With these two boys, who had done so much and given away so little, anything was possible, and the speculation unbounded.

In the queue coming back into court one lunchtime – all journalists and members of the public had to walk through a metal detector and be frisked with a scanner – a reporter stepped into the doorway and met two colleagues. Phew, he said, I just saw a kid outside who looked like Robert Thompson. It really spooked me. The reporter did not notice the two representatives from Liverpool Social Services standing behind him, all their worst impressions of the assembled media confirmed in an instant. They complained to the court, and the judge made a general announcement about the need to exercise caution when using the boys' names outside the courtroom.

In court at the end of one session, a writer up from London leant on the rail of the public gallery and watched, as many did, while the boys were led down to the cell area: two lumpy, awkward figures, almost waddling down the steps. He's such a sweet boy, that one, said the writer. That other one, he's a little thug: the fatty. There was not much sympathy in circulation for the boys, but what little there was went to Jon, who looked so troubled and had shown such distress, which could be described as remorse. It was only later, after his interviews had been played in court, that people began to point out the coldness, the cruelty, that they believed they saw in Jon's eyes.

By the consensus of counsel, Denise Bulger was not called to give her evidence in person. Her statement was read to the jury on the third day, and was followed by the screening, on the television monitors, of a compilation from the Strand's security video.

It lasted for some 20 minutes, during which time, for the only time, the court sat in total silence. An arrow had been added to the images, to indicate the position of the boys, and James, in the footage. The arrow darted from one side of the screen to the other, and everyone in court did their best to follow it. The boys were little more than streaks of colour. The jury asked to see the last few minutes again, watching James's exit from the shopping precinct, with Jon at his side, and Bobby just in front, looking back as he walked ahead.

Other witnesses, whose evidence was not contested, were also not called, and had their statements read. Again, by agreement, Graham Nelson, who had identified Jon as one of two boys he had seen at the Strand in late January, was not called, his statement not read.

When the last witness had been called, on the seventh day of the trial, Henriques began entering the exhibits. As he numbered and itemised each one, a police officer held it up in a thick polystyrene bag. When it came to exhibit 34, the metal bar, the fishplate, the judge asked if he could see it. My Lord, said Henriques, this is one exhibit we'd rather like to have handed round, if we may.

The judge took the bar and, having felt its weight, passed it on to a clerk so that it could be held by the jury. The judge told the jury the bar was extremely heavy. Do not drop it on your big toe, because it might cause some damage, he said. One woman juror declined the offer to hold the bar. The press watched all this with fascination, and took full notes.

The bloodstained bricks, the bloodstained stones, the various pieces of James's clothing that had been found at the scene, a tin of Humbrol paint . . . all were held up for inspection, though none were passed round. The last items to be entered were the clothes Bobby and Jon had been wearing on the day. Jon's jacket was produced from its bag, at the judge's request. It was mustard-coloured, and very small. It looked in need of a clean. The paint stain mark of a hand, which was probably James's hand, was just visible.

Forensic scientists were called to explain the part each exhibit had played in the killing of James. The pathologist described the scene that had greeted him when he was called to the railway on Sunday the fourteenth, and the results of his post mortem. Henriques asked him if it was immediately apparent that the head had sustained multiple injuries. Yes, said the pathologist, Alan Williams. He went on to describe the shattering of James's skull, and outlined the many injuries, one after the other. He could not isolate a single blow as the cause of death, because there were so many.

As he had described in his report, Williams said the foreskin of James's penis appeared abnormal, and was partially retracted. He said it was not normal in a child of that age, and would require pulling back or forceful retraction. This was the only indication of any sexual assault. At the time the police had interviewed Bobby and Jon, they believed that the batteries might have been inserted into James's rectum. There were no admissions from the boys, and there was no reported evidence of any injury to support this. Forensic tests on the batteries had also failed to produce any result.

The presence of the batteries at the scene, like so much else about the killing, remained unexplained. Throughout the trial it was the source of much rumour and speculative theorising. Albert Kirby privately expressed the view that the batteries had been inserted and said as much to social services case workers after the trial. Jon had said something similar in an account of the attack he had given his mother.

The extent to which sexual assault had been part of the attack, and perhaps even the motive, was a difficult issue. It had probably tormented James's family, but, if the killing is ever to be explained, it cannot be ignored or hidden away. It is possible that other injuries, particularly to the mouth, are indicators of sexual assault. The extreme reaction of both boys to this area of questioning during the interviews – 'They're trying to say I'm a pervert' – is significant. If the boys did do this, it had almost certainly been done to them, one or other of them, or both, at some stage in their brief lives.

Susan and Neil Venables were not sitting in court for these unpalatable sessions with the scientists. Ralph Bulger had given up some days earlier. He made it known, through his solicitor, that it was all too much to bear. The jury, every one of them, looked colourless and strained.

Much of the reporting of the trial began to seem prurient in its concentration on gruesome and disturbing detail. BBC local radio on Merseyside began warning its listeners that they might find some of the following trial report distressing. In the newspapers, the story shrank, and slipped down the pages.

Bobby and Jon sat in the dock playing with tissues. The forensic evidence linking them to the scene, and the killing, was overwhelming. Their counsel could make little headway with the various experts.

Phil Rydeard had examined the boot mark on James's face. He conceded, in response to a question from the judge, that it could have been caused by a light impact. But it was the result, he was satisfied, of a dynamic action. He did not think a fall forward on to the shoe could have produced that bruising.

The prosecution had intended to follow the forensic evidence with the boys' teachers. Jim Fitzsimmons had spent many hours taking statements from staff at the school, describing the boys behaviour in and out of the classroom, and the material had been served as part of the Crown's case.

At the end of the seventh day of the trial, when the last forensic expert had been called, the jury were dismissed, and the judge and counsel discussed the issue of *doli incapax* – which the judge referred to as *doli capax*. Morland said he believed the bulk of the teachers' evidence was inadmissible, because it was hearsay. The only evidence that was admissible was expert opinion that the boys knew right from wrong.

The Crown restructured its case, and there was some delay the following morning, before the trial resumed at midday. Now the Crown would call only the school's head teacher, and the man who had taught Bobby and Jon in their first year in the same class. Bobby's lawyers were surprised to discover that the Crown was also calling on expert opinion from both Susan Bailey and Eileen Vizard. They had thought Eileen Vizard was their witness, though they had already decided not to call her themselves.

During the morning of the eighth day, Bobby's counsel and his solicitor sat with Eileen Vizard around a table in the magistrates' retiring room at the court. As they talked it appeared that she had sent a copy of her psychiatric assessment of Bobby to the Crown. Eventually she was asked directly, and said that she had indeed sent the Crown a copy. She said that she had asked Dominic Lloyd, Bobby's solicitor, if she could send the report to the CPS, and he had said it would be all right. He said he had agreed to her consulting with Susan Bailey and the other experts who had seen Jon, but she had no authority to send the report to the CPS, and he would not have given her that authority.

It was Bobby's second barrister, David Williams, who took the steam out of an increasingly acrimonious discussion. He established that Eileen Vizard would only give evidence that Bobby knew right from wrong, on the balance of probabilities. She would concede that psychiatric assessment was not an exact science. The Crown would still have to prove beyond all reasonable doubt that Bobby knew what he was doing was seriously wrong.

In the courtroom the mood was all aflutter, everyone intrigued and puzzled by the delay, and fascinated by the entrance of Bobby's mother, Ann, who had decided to attend for the first time. Ann wanted to see the teachers give their evidence, especially the head, who she felt had failed her son in some way. Ann had taken a single anti-depressant that morning, before setting out for the court. It was partially calming, but she was still shaky and distressed, her eyes permanently watery with tears. She held her head up as she walked through the court, and took a seat behind Neil and Susan Venables. They had the support of a woman from Aftermath, Ann had her psychiatric nurse.

Eileen Vizard was the day's first witness and, responding to the cautiously worded questions of Henriques, she gave evidence against the boy she had been called in to assess for the defence. On the balance of probabilities, in February, Bobby had known right from wrong, would have known it was wrong to take a young child from its mother, would have known it was wrong to injure a young child and would have known it was wrong to leave an injured child on the railway. There was no evidence that he was suffering from an abnormality of mind at the time of James Bulger's death. He was fit to stand trial.

In cross-examination by Turner, she gave her opinion that Bobby was suffering from post-traumatic stress and, although he was fit to stand trial, his understanding of the proceedings might be affected by the disorder. It was his preoccupation with what happened and the resulting distress that made her concerned about his level of understanding.

Susan Bailey gave an almost identical set of answers to questions about Jon from Henriques. She agreed with Walsh, in cross-examination, that Jon burst into tears, cried uncontrollably and showed obvious signs of distress when questioned about James's death. She had formed the opinion that, for a number of good reasons, he was currently unable to talk about the subject of the charges.

This, in summary, perhaps 20 minutes out of 17 days, was the full extent of the trial's inquiry into the boys' mental health.

The evidence of the two teachers that followed was similarly confined by carefully phrased questions. Henriques asked the head teacher at what age her pupils understood that it was wrong to strike another child with a weapon. 'I would say from when they come to school – at four or five years of age.' She had no doubts that Bobby and Jon knew in February that it would have been wrong to take a child from its mother, two and a half miles across Liverpool, and that it would have been wrong to strike a three-year-old with a brick.

The school aimed specifically to teach children how to behave towards one another. The boys' previous class teacher said that pupils were specifically taught about right and wrong, and explained the circumstances in which a class talk on the subject might occur. 'During the course of the year a child might come to me and say so and so has been pulling the legs off insects or standing on ants, and this would lead to a general discussion about cruelty to each other.'

After the *doli* evidence, the court began hearing the boys' police interviews, which were relayed through loudspeakers, with radio pick-up headphones for the jury, the judge, the lawyers and Bobby and Jon if they wanted them. Only the first of Bobby's interviews was played that afternoon, and at the end of the day's session Bobby was privately put through a dry run of cross-examination by David Turner, to see if he could be called to give evidence.

Bobby sat in his room at the court, facing Turner. His mother, his case worker, his solicitor and his second barrister were also in the room. Turner said he would have to be tough, but didn't want to frighten Bobby. It began gently and calmly. Bobby said he wasn't really frightened of Jon. Jon had never beaten him up, they had never fought. Messing about fights, not a real fight. He couldn't say if Jon was a good fighter. Bobby hadn't seen any proper fighting in the school yard. He didn't know what he was like at fighting.

On 12 February Bobby didn't know if he was frightened of Jon. There was nothing to make him frightened of him . . . well, when we were up on the railway . . .

Bobby had been happy at the Strand. He didn't notice Jon take another boy. The first time he noticed James was in TJ Hughes, when they came round to go near the steps. He couldn't remember if they went up the steps. He noticed James following, but didn't know how far behind he was. He didn't see Jon take hold of James until the top of the steps in TJ Hughes. He couldn't remember if he saw Jon hold James's hand.

I seen him hold James's hand a few times in the Strand. I didn't ask him what he was doing.

Why not?

I just didn't.

Outside by the taxi rank, Bobby said he didn't take hold of James's hand. Turner said there was evidence that they both held his hands. Bobby said, some of it is right. He didn't take hold of James's hand before the canal. It wasn't his idea to go to the canal, he just went down. He wasn't in the lead.

On the bank Jon picked the baby up and threw him on the floor face down. I was in shock.

Did you do anything?

No. I didn't think Jon was the kind of lad to do that.

Do you know what shock is?

Yes, I was nearly stiff. It lasted a couple of seconds. I went round and up and I left Jon and the baby.

Did you say anything?

I said what did you do that for? He ignored me.

Did you ask again?

No. James was crying then. Really crying. I seen a bit of a mark on his head.

Bobby thought what Jon had done wasn't really wrong, but wrong, yes.

In the room, Bobby had been looking up, and maintaining eye contact with Turner or one of the others. Now he covered his face with a wad of tissues, and kept it there, uncovering his mouth and shouting his replies.

He said he didn't tell in case Jon did it again. He was thinking, if he went and told somebody, Jon would do it again.

He just walked up, but Jon followed him. They went down near the post office and came back.

Wasn't the best thing to do to take him back to the Strand?

I don't know.

Wasn't the best thing to do to go to the security?

I never thought to do that. I didn't say anything. It was a shock for me. I'd never seen Jon do anything like that before.

Bobby was crying now. He didn't remember the taxi driver saying Jon had carried James. He didn't see that. He didn't see how James crossed Stanley Road. He didn't think where Jon was taking James, and didn't ask.

Was there anything to stop you?

No. I'm not really bothered about whether James is with us.

Did you speak to James?

I asked him what his name was. He said Tony. He was asking for his mum. I didn't say do you want your mum. I guess he would want his mum.

Bobby said they walked past the church, crossed over at the Mons. It was very busy. He didn't pick James up. He didn't have to. He didn't know what Jon did on the reservoir. Bobby hadn't played there before.

Turner. It's not a very exciting place to play, is it?
Bobby. No, it isn't.
Turner. When did you hold James?
Bobby. I had him by the hand at AMEC.
Turner. Why?
Bobby (crying again) I don't know why, we were just walking.

275

Ann. If they put him in that box they'll bury him.

Bobby. (*crying*) I'm not giving evidence. I'm not going in that box.

He calms down a little. He says when they were down at the alleyway by the police station he wanted James to go in. They didn't climb up on the railway there, they walked back to City Road. He didn't know what they were doing, they were just walking. He didn't know why.

Turner asks, why go on the railway? Bobby is crying again. I don't know. I didn't think Jon was going to hurt James.

Why not?

I'm not a mind reader.

But you're not daft either?

No. I didn't speak to Jon. You're not listening to me. On the canal I said, what did you do that for? He just said, I didn't. I just didn't ask again.

Why not?

I don't know.

Bobby is shouting, angry, interrupting as Turner tries to speak. I don't know. I don't know. I don't know.

Turner asks about the paint. Bobby sighs heavily. He agrees it was a horrible thing to do. Turner asks how James's clothes came off. Read the statement, says Bobby, sighing. He says, Jon took them off. He sighs some more. He says, I don't want to talk about it. It'll make me mum upset. Turner says perhaps it'll make you upset. Bobby shouts, if it makes me upset it doesn't bloody matter. Turner asks again about the clothes. Bobby shouts, I said, Jon took them off. It doesn't sound like you're listening to me. He did it? Yes. Don't ask me what for. Bobby sighs. I saw it.

On the railway, says Bobby, James had already been hit by bricks and the iron bar. There was loads of red stuff. He was out unconscious, not talking, on his back. Bobby doesn't know why he stayed and watched Jon do it. He never asked Jon why.

Turner asks if James's body was on the line to make it look like an accident. Bobby says how does he know. He doesn't read

276

Jon's mind. Jon never said anything about it. Bobby says he put bricks on James's head. He says it was to stop the blood coming out. Turner asks how that would stop the blood coming out. Bobby says he never said it was a plaster. Turner asks if Bobby couldn't have helped James. Bobby says, no, you ask some silly questions don't you.

The dry run finishes with Bobby emerging from behind his tissues, cockily asserting that the shoes they showed in court weren't his. The only shoes he's got with D rings are Doc Martens.

Bobby would not be giving evidence.

It took another four days to complete the playing of the interviews to the court. First Bobby's, then Jon's. There was no point in playing Bobby's last three tapes, because they had added nothing to his version of events. A précis of them was read out in court.

Jon's interviews were also edited, but his hysterical crying was still very much in evidence, and was noticeably affecting to many people in court.

Bobby seemed affected by Jon's statement, in his first interview, that Bobby was like a girl because he played with dolls. Bobby gave Jon a long hard look. Later in Jon's interviews he described how Bobby had said that they should get a kid lost so he'd go in the road and get knocked over. Jon said he had told Bobby that was a very bad thing to do. He said Bobby had replied, no it isn't. When the tape played Bobby's alleged words – no it isn't – Jon looked guiltily in Bobby's direction. It was probably just one more lie, among so many, from both boys.

The Crown seemed anxious to disprove Bobby's claim that he and Jon had taken James onto the railway line at City Broo and not, as Jon had claimed, at the end of the entry, opposite the police station on Walton Lane. A police officer was called into the box at the beginning of the third week of the trial. He had been down to City Road bridge at the weekend, and tried to get over the fence onto the railway embankment. He had his picture taken doing it, just so that the court could see how treacherous it was, and how implausible it was that the boys could have got on to the railway at that point.

It was hard to see why this mattered so much, except to highlight yet another lie from Bobby, or a truth from Jon. Most kids in Walton would have said that City Broo was an easy way onto the line. The bent fencing there was some testimony to its frequent use. David Turner and the police officer became quite fractious with each other, as Turner tried, with no great success, to undermine the officer's evidence.

The route the boys had taken to the railway line could be added to the long list of mysteries surrounding the case, which the trial could not hope to resolve while the boys kept the answers to themselves.

At the end of the prosecution case, David Turner and Brian Walsh offered no evidence. There was no defence, and all that now remained were the closing speeches.

Henriques was on his feet for just under an hour, making his final address to the jury. 'Together they took James away from his mother and from the Strand. One holding his hand, the other leading the way.

'Together they took him to the canal bank where he sustained injury, and together they took him away from the Strand where they knew his mother must be.

'Together they led him or pulled him, carried him or dragged him, injured, past and away from adult after adult, away from help and assistance which was almost continuously at hand.

'They preferred, you may think, to avoid detection, which was clearly a greater priority than James's well-being. Together they abused James. Robert Thompson delivered a persuasive kick, while Jon Venables chose to shake James. Venables led him from the Strand, with Thompson leading the way.

'Their roles reversed. Thompson carried him up on the railway embankment, with Venables leading the way. They each heard each other lie to adults.

278

'If ever a crime was committed jointly and together, then this was that crime. They were clearly both together as James sustained his terrible injuries.'

Did one defendant deliver at least 30 blows to James, with no criminal participation from the other and no active encouragement? Did one defendant build a platform of bricks to assist James's destruction by a passing train with no assistance from the other? Could one defendant have removed James's lower clothing? Would the non-partner in crime behave so coolly after the event and maintain such a lying stance, protecting the killer in interview after interview with the police? 'We submit, most certainly not.'

Both defendants had told lies in their interviews, but Robert Thompson had told the greater number. He had told lies from beginning to end in his interviews, and quite sophisticated lies at that. They had both consistently lied because they feared the truth. Those lies were themselves evidence of guilt. A verdict that either boy was guilty of manslaughter rather than murder would underestimate by some distance the gravity of this crime. This was in law a murderous attack on a small child.

Henriques referred to the *doli* issue. How could this grave conduct, he said, be described as naughty or mischievous? He cited Jon's words. I said it was a very bad thing to do. Members of the jury, said Henriques, this was a very bad thing to do.

It was Friday of the third week, Day 14 of the trial. The judge told the jury to go home and try to relax over the weekend. To try and put the case to the back of their mind. On Monday they would hear the defence speeches, on Tuesday the judge would be making his summary, and on Wednesday the jury would begin considering its verdict.

Bobby had been telling his mother that sometimes he felt like crying in the court. He wouldn't let himself cry because people would think he was a baby. Ann told him if he wanted to cry he should.

David Turner was not much more than a minute or two into

his speech on the Monday morning, when Bobby was holding a tissue to his face, evidently in tears. Turner had swapped seats with Brian Walsh so that he could be closer to the jury during his address. He had notes in a ring-pull folder, which was perched on an upturned cardboard filing box in front of him. After a break in the middle of his eighty-minute speech, Bobby came back up and took Jon's seat, behind Turner, for the only time during the trial.

The grief of Denise Bulger and her husband had dominated this trial, Turner had told the jury. Those members of the jury with children must have found the depth of their grief unimaginable. As he addressed them he could only hope to reflect the dignity that had been shown by the Bulger family in this harrowing trial.

'This case is not the tragedy of one family but three families. A tragedy for the Bulger family, yes, but also a tragedy for the families of Robert Thompson and Jon Venables.

'No one who has been involved in the trial will ever be the same again.' Many tears had been shed, but those who had been dry-eyed might also be feeling pain and misery.

Turner said the Crown's case was that a small child was deliberately abducted and that the intention from the outset was to cause at least really serious harm to James.

'If that be right then this is a most disturbing case – that children whose previous misdemeanours were mainly shoplifting and truancy should conceive and execute such a thoroughly diabolical plan is beyond belief.'

He asked if it was a mischievous prank which, in no time at all, had got out of control. 'If the plan was to cause a child to get hurt in the traffic, that never happened. If the plan was to throw a child into the canal, that never happened.'

If the plan had been to take James to a lonely stretch of railway track and to murder him, they had taken a two-and-a-half-mile route along the busiest streets in Liverpool. They had spoken to at least two witnesses, telling them they had found

James and were taking him to Walton Lane Police Station. Was not the purpose of it to invite a grown-up to intervene? If there was a diabolical, wicked plot to abduct a child and to kill him, the boys would not have spoken the truth to passers-by.

'We suggest an alternative intention. These boys were saddled by their own mischief with a little toddler who must have been tired out, as they were themselves. They had been hanging round the shops of the Strand since school time in the morning, walking with a toddler all that way, not knowing what to do with him, unable to abandon him or foist him off on a grown-up, and not having the courage to take him into a police station where they had taken him because they might have been afraid they would be in trouble. This is a far more likely scenario than the planned evil put forward by the Crown.'

Turner referred to the evidence of witnesses where Jon had taken a leading role. He asked if there could be any doubt about who was in control. 'It is our sad duty to say that the evidence points clearly to Jon Venables. You know that Robert Thompson's case is and always has been that the attack on little James was initiated and carried out by Jon Venables. It is no pleasant task for us to make that accusation against another, now 11-year-old, boy. But we say that for whatever reason, a reason that one can never know – petulance, tiredness, a sudden swing of mood of the sort that became evident in the interviews – Jon Venables unhappily and tragically carried out a sudden but sustained attack on little James.'

Turner dealt at length with the damning evidence against Jon. He pointed out that Jon had said, I did kill him, not, we did, or, Robert did. He spoke of the limited accounts from witnesses of Bobby's active involvement. He said the evidence of the van driver's persuasive kick should be treated with caution. He spoke of the alleged kick by Bobby, and the evidence that a light impact could be more likely to result in a clear mark.

A psychiatrist had said that, on the balance of probabilities, Bobby had known what he was doing was wrong. The jury would look for proof, in this case as in all cases, not on the balance of probabilities, not whether it was more likely than not, but beyond reasonable doubt.

It would have to be proved that each boy had played a part in the death of James Bulger. It meant taking a physical part in the attack. The Crown could not say, because it was not true, that Bobby had ever said that he had taken part in the attack. He always denied it. He always said, I did nothing. 'Was there active participation? What happened on the railway line? Can you say who did what? It must be proved in respect of each that there was an intent to cause death or really serious bodily harm. That there was a murderous intent.

'In this case you are asked to assess what was in the mind of a child of ten. That you may find one of the most difficult issues in this trial.'

Finally, it was appalling that a dear child, loved by all around him, should die as James did. But Robert Thompson did not cause the death of James Bulger.

Turner sat down, and the rest of the day belonged to Brian Walsh, who reclaimed his seat, placed his own notes on the upturned box, and spoke for over two hours on Jon's behalf. His speech was substantially devoted to Bobby.

Where Turner had been circumspect in his use of the cut-throat defence – straight for the jugular: it wasn't me, it was him – Walsh showed no such inhibition. He said the case had inspired widespread revulsion. It would be easy for the jury to say, let's have them both and good riddance to the pair of them. The Crown's case had given mystical significance to the word 'together'. But it was a broad-brush approach, which failed to make distinctions between the defendants.

'You are dealing with two different minds . . . two different thoughts and thought processes, and in this case dealing with a charge of murder. The Crown must prove that these two different minds had but a single thought and a single intention, namely killing or causing really serious harm to James Bulger.

'The two defendants are in fact very different boys. They have different vocabularies and different personalities. Nothing could have come over more clearly than that when you began to listen to those tapes and heard those two voices and the way they dealt with questions.'

In his interviews Robert Thompson had sounded assertive, challenging and argumentative. He had used the imagination and guile at which he was adept in a persistent campaign of lies. He was a cool, calm, collected and brazen little rogue. 'If he cried, if there were any tears, who were those tears for? They were for him.' He had treated the interviews as a debating point-scoring match, challenging police to prove it, and admitting something only if he was caught in the act or filmed doing it.

Robert Thompson was an arguing, cocky little liar, wriggling, devious and determined to say anything but the real truth: that there was blood on him because he had kicked James, beaten him and battered him.

Jon Venables, by contrast appeared as a sad, somewhat diffident boy. 'I make no bones about it', said Walsh, 'I am addressing you on behalf of the boy who told the truth, who had wanted for a long time to tell the truth, but who for the reason of the distress of his mother could not do so. He is the one boy who has shown, not just remorse, but genuine remorse.

'I am not speaking on behalf of someone who has been lying from beginning to end, through and through.'

Once the protective influence, the inhibiting influence of his mother had gone, Jon had been able to tell the police what they sensed he had wanted to tell for a long time. He had told them he had killed James, but the Crown did not suggest that this meant he killed him and no one else had anything to do with it.

'He does not pretend to be lily-white or totally blameless. He says he did intend to cause some harm to James, some little harm. He did not want him to be killed.

'If that contention is right, if it may be right, he cannot be guilty of the crime of murder, although he could be guilty of the serious offence of manslaughter.'

Jon had good reason to lie initially, since he was trying to protect the person who meant the most to him. 'He wanted to tell the truth about his limited but shameful part in it, but he could not bring himself to speak of it in the presence of his mother.'

The judge's summary started on Tuesday, and finished on Wednesday. He told the jury they should reach their verdicts on the evidence alone, and in no circumstances could they take into account what they had seen or heard or read outside the courtroom.

He said the case had aroused unprecedented media attention which had been worldwide. For the people of Bootle and Walton it had been heartrending. 'Many of the witnesses were doing the humdrum things of everyday life on that Friday afternoon when, wholly unawares, they were caught up in the last few tragic hours of James Bulger's tragic life.'

It could have been somebody taking a dog for a walk, or going to the library. It was only later, when news broke, that they realised, or thought they had seen James Bulger with two older boys.

They had been subjected to exceptional strain, arriving in court in a blaze of publicity. Many had faced a bevy of photographers, and they had come into this large courtroom, which had been packed, to give evidence. Not surprisingly, some witnesses had been overcome with emotion, and had difficulty speaking audibly. The jury would have to decide if they were accurate.

'All of those involved in this case will have been emotionally affected by the circumstances of James Bulger's death, but I am sure each of you will assess the evidence and reach your conclusions dispassionately and objectively and will not allow your emotions to warp your judgement.'

Many witnesses must have thought, if only. 'If only they had realised that it was not a case of three brothers out together, or two boys taking a little boy to the police station, but was a case of a little boy taken from his mother. They must be saying, "If I had gone to the police, James Bulger's life may have been saved." Those feelings are inevitable.

'You will probably come to the conclusion that the witnesses have given their evidence honestly, doing their best to tell the truth. But you have got to ask yourself, "Are they accurate?"' He said that inconsistencies between the witnesses' police statements and their evidence in court might well indicate that their evidence was unreliable.

Turning to the charges, and the two boys, the judge explained the law, and outlined the issues the jury would have to consider. They would have to weigh the evidence against each defendant separately, and what one had said in interview about the other was not evidence.

It was the prosecution case that the boys had jointly committed the offences. 'Where an offence is committed jointly by two people, each of them may play a different part but each can be guilty of the same offence. To put it simply, are you sure they were in it together?'

The jury might think that the evidence was overwhelming that James Bulger was unlawfully killed, and whichever of the defendants it was who inflicted those injuries intended either to kill James Bulger or to do him really serious injury. 'The crucial question is not what was their intention when James Bulger was taken from the Strand or during the long walk of over two miles to the railway line, but what was the intention of each defendant on the railway line, when the fatal injuries were inflicted.'

In deciding whether or not each boy knew that what he was doing was seriously wrong, the jury would take into account the total number of blows inflicted on the deceased, the number of blows to the head, the number of injuries to the head, the weapons used – the bricks, an iron bar or fishplate – what was done to the body after the fatal injuries had been inflicted, the moving of the body from one line to another, the removal of socks, shoes, trousers and underpants, and the placing of his body across the railway line. 'You will take into account kicking, if you find it took place, the kicking by a ten-year-old child, of a child, not yet three, lying injured on the railway line.'

The jury were reminded that neither boy suffered an abnormality of mind; they were both of average intelligence; and both attended a Church of England school where they were taught the difference between right and wrong.

There was then a meticulous resumé of the evidence of the witnesses and the boys' interviews, during which the judge highlighted various statements which the jury should consider.

Bobby's interviews: '. . . is this [a retort by Bobby] an indicator that Robert Thompson had his wits about him all the time during the interviews . . . is that a deliberate lie – maybe because Robert Thompson knew it was seriously wrong to take James Bulger away . . . is that again because he knew how seriously . . . is that the answer of a boy who had his wits about him and was trying to wriggle out of the truth . . . were they two more deliberate lies . . . it is for you to decide whether that was a deliberate lie, and the reason for making that lie . . . a crucial answer, if it be true: "I never touched him except for picking him up."'

Jon's interviews: '. . . it is a matter for you whether you think that was a deliberate lie . . . "So that's two lies you've told?" Answer, "Yeah" . . . is this the position, that Jon Venables makes admissions when faced with the inevitable, but persists with lies . . . he is still persisting with the untruth, "I never touched the baby" . . . "I did kill him", not, as Mr Turner pointed out to you, "We", but, "I did kill him" . . . is that Jon Venables admitting he was in it together with Robert Thompson to take James Bulger out of the Strand . . . is he saying there he wanted to hurt him a bit, but not seriously . . . there's that pattern Mr Turner was talking about of making an admission and then referring to Robert.'

As is becoming increasingly common in complicated trials, the judge had drawn up a list of 20 questions, to guide the jury to their verdicts. He had submitted the questions to counsel beforehand, so that all were agreed, and, at the end of his summary, he presented them to the jury.

For each question the jury would have to ask, is each and every one of us sure . . .

On Count One, the attempted abduction:

1. That Robert Thompson intended to cause or induce the child to accompany him so as to remove him from the lawful control of his mother.
2. That Robert Thompson played a part in doing something that was more than mere preparation.
3. That Robert Thompson had no lawful authority or excuse for attempting to take the child.
4. That at the time Robert Thompson was attempting to abduct the child he knew it was seriously wrong to do so.

If the answer to each of these questions was 'yes', then Robert Thompson would be guilty of attempted abduction. If the answer to any of the questions was 'no', then the verdict would be not guilty.

5. That Jon Venables intended to cause or induce the child to accompany him so as to remove him from the lawful control of his mother.
6. That Jon Venables played a part in doing something that was more than mere preparation.
7. That Jon Venables had no lawful authority or excuse for attempting to take the child.
8. That at the time Jon Venables was attempting to abduct the child he knew it was seriously wrong to do so.

If the answer to each of these questions was 'yes', then Jon Venables would be guilty of attempted abduction. If the answer to any of the questions was 'no', then the verdict would be not guilty.

On Count Two, the abduction of James Bulger:

9. That Robert Thompson played a part in causing or inducing James Bulger to accompany him so as to remove him from the lawful control of his mother.

287

10. That Robert Thompson had no lawful authority or excuse for taking James Bulger.
11. That at the time Robert Thompson abducted James Bulger he knew that what he was doing was seriously wrong.

If the answer to each of these questions was 'yes', then Robert Thompson would be guilty of abduction.

12. That Jon Venables played a part in causing or inducing James Bulger to accompany him so as to remove him from the lawful control of his mother.
13. That Jon Venables had no lawful authority or excuse for taking James Bulger.
14. That at the time Jon Venables abducted James Bulger he knew that what he was doing was seriously wrong.

If the answer to each of these questions was 'yes', then Jon Venables would be guilty of abduction.

On Count Three, the murder of James Bulger:

15. That Robert Thompson played a part in the death of James Bulger.
16. That at the time of the killing, Robert Thompson knew it was seriously wrong to act as he did.
17. That when James Bulger was being attacked on the railway line Robert Thompson intended that he should be caused serious injury or death.

If the answers to either 15 or 16 were 'no', then Robert Thompson would be not guilty of murder. If the answers to both were 'yes', then question 17 should be considered. If the answer to 17 was 'no', then the verdict would be manslaughter. If the answer to 17 was 'yes', then Robert Thompson would be guilty of murder.

18. That Jon Venables played a part in the death of James Bulger.
19. That at the time of the killing, Jon Venables knew it was seriously wrong to act as he did.
20. That when James Bulger was being attacked on the railway line Jon Venables intended that he should be caused serious injury or death.

If the answers to either 18 or 19 were 'no', then Jon Venables would be not guilty of murder. If the answers to both were 'yes', then question 20 should be considered. If the answer to 20 was 'no', then the verdict would be manslaughter. If the answer to 20 was 'yes', then Jon Venables would be guilty of murder.

The judge told the jury that the verdicts must be unanimous – 'that is, the verdict of each and all of you' – and he would give further instructions about a majority verdict at the appropriate time. If there was anything they wanted, exhibits, tea, coffee, whatever, they should give a message to a jury bailiff. Court ushers were sworn in as jury bailiffs, and led the jury out to begin their deliberation. It was 11.43 a.m., Wednesday, 24 November.

Downstairs, in his room beyond the cells, Bobby said he knew what the verdict would be. He knew he would be found guilty of murder. He was sitting there, trying to knit a pair of gloves for baby Ben. The lawyers were in the room, discussing the price of wigs. Bobby began playing with David Turner's wig. Someone joked that he could get his own for four hundred quid. Ann began knitting too and, after lunch, when the lawyers went back to see him, Bobby was sitting in his own newly completed white wool barrister's wig.

Back in court the judge was hearing applications from barristers in real wigs representing Associated Newspapers and Mirror Group Newspapers. Associated, owners of the *Daily Mail*, wanted the judge to lift his orders preventing identification of the boys in the event of guilty verdicts.

The *Mirror* wanted to identify the victim of the attempted abduction, and the victim's mother. The judge asked whether there was any contractual relationship between the *Mirror* and the child's family. Counsel faltered . . . er, in all likelihood, yes. There were smiles in the press seats, where everyone knew the *Mirror* had bought up the mother.

Associated Newspapers' application did not sound overly convincing. There was talk of the need for openness and of the fact that the boys had brought the proceedings on their own heads.

The judge said there was a rule that the interests of the child are paramount. The Crown had to bear in mind the child's rehabilitation – a task which would be made more difficult if the boys were named and identified, notoriously, worldwide.

'On the other hand this is not merely a case of ghoulish interest in the macabre. This was a ghastly crime, and unbelievable that it could be perpetrated by one or two ten-year-old boys.' It could be argued that it was in the public interest that the circumstances, the exposure of children today to films, radio, television and newspapers, video and so on may have played their part. There could be a role for legitimate investigation, which would be of interest to serious sections of the public.

The judge said he would give his decision on identification immediately after the verdict. He said he would not give any reasons for his decision.

There was a note for the court from a juror. Could a message be relayed about the collection of the juror's child from school? This seemed to be a sign that the verdicts were a long way off. At some point, towards the end of the afternoon, the judge could be expected to call the jury back and, if they had not reached a decision, they would be despatched to a hotel for the night.

It was not long after five o'clock, when the jury came back in. The judge, the lawyers and the court staff were all apparently under the impression that the jury were still talking. After the formality of asking for verdicts, they would be off to a hotel.

The rest of the court was unaware of this, and there was anticipation of a verdict. The public gallery was full. Ralph and Denise Bulger were both there, for the first time, in the front row.

Albert Kirby directed some uniformed officers to stand by the gallery railing. There was a crowd there by the doors, of barristers and others, come to see the kill.

The boys filed up the steps, followed by Neil and Susan Venables. Ann Thompson got to the foot of the steps and seized up, overcome by asthma. It didn't seem to matter too much.

There wasn't going to be a verdict. She went back through the cells to one of the small rooms in the secure area.

The jury came in and the court clerk stood to face them. The foreman, who was the man with the silver hair, stood to face the clerk.

'On the first count of attempted abduction, have you reached a verdict on which you are all agreed?'

No. The foreman's voice was brusque Lancastrian. He was very self-concious.

'On count two, have you reached a verdict on which you are all agreed?'

Yes.

'Do you find the defendant, Robert Thompson, guilty or not guilty of the abduction of James Bulger?'

Guilty.

'And is that the verdict of you all?'

It is.

'Do you find the defendant, Jon Venables, guilty or not guilty of the abduction of James Bulger?'

Guilty.

'And is that the verdict of you all?'

It is.

'On count three, have you reached a verdict on which you are all agreed?'

Yes.

'Do you find the defendant, Robert Thompson, guilty or not guilty of the murder of James Bulger?'

Guilty.

'And is that the verdict of you all?'

It is.

'Do you find the defendant Jon Venables guilty or not guilty of the murder of James Bulger?'

Guilty.

'And is that the verdict of you all?'

It was. The foreman sat down.

'Yes!' That was a punching-the-air-with-your-fist yes. It came from the front row of the gallery.

Bobby looked blank. Perhaps a trace of shock. There was a second or two before Jon reacted, pulling at his eyes with his fingers, tears falling. His parents began sobbing.

Albert Kirby walked up to the gallery, leant over, and kissed the cheek of Denise Bulger. His eyes were wet.

The jury went out to try and reach a decision on the attempt, and the boys were led down to the cells, followed by lawyers and social workers. There was a jam at the door to the secure area. Prisoners were being moved from the cells to the van, and the door had to be kept locked.

Bobby and Jon were no more than a couple of feet apart, hemmed in by adults. Jon was crying terribly and a policewoman hugged him to her. Bobby was stiff, staring ahead, not looking at Jon.

Can't we get this bloody door open, somebody shouted. And then they were through, Jon straight into the room he used, and Bobby across the courtyard to his. His mother should have been there, but wasn't. Bobby's solicitor, Dominic Lloyd, found her back in the room by the cells. She had just been told the verdict by a social worker, and was slumped over a table, distraught.

Eventually, Ann moved, and was led to Bobby. She grabbed him in a big embrace and they both began crying. The others went out of the room and left them alone. After a minute or two Ann appeared at the door. Can you get him a doctor or something, he can't breathe. So they all went back in, and Bobby was gasping for air. His collar was loosened, his tie removed. He was told to breathe deep and slow.

Dominic Lloyd took Bobby's hand and held it. There was no response from Bobby, his hand lying limp in Dominic's. Then Dominic went to move, and Bobby squeezed tightly. Dominic sat down again. All right lad, another ten minutes and it'll all be over. Bobby said nothing.

Then a warder was at the door saying the court was ready for them. Bobby began crying again and, as they walked out, some-one said, come on, here's your tie. There's no point putting that on now, said Bobby.

When they were all back in the court the foreman said the jury still had not reached a verdict on the attempted abduction. The judge said he would release them from further deliberation, and let the charges lie on file.

The judge said that in the exceptional circumstances of the case he was varying the identification orders he had made. As he spoke, a clerk rushed up the aisle to the press seats, handing out copies of a single A4 sheet containing the changed orders. It looked as though the orders had been prepared hurriedly. Bobby's surname was misspelt at the top of the sheet, and some of the wording seemed ambiguous.

There was considerable confusion among the media. Can we name them? No, said the police press officer. Yes, said the reporter from Granada Television. It was not immediately clear, though the man from Granada was right.

But the judge was moving on. He was going to speak to the boys for the second time in the trial. First he invited comments from the defence counsel. David Turner had nothing to say, but Brian Walsh stood to remind the court of Jon's confessional words. What about his mum? Will you tell her I'm sorry.

'While to someone older these may seem pathetically inad-equate words, for a child of his years they meant a great deal, and he wanted me to repeat them when I saw him a few minutes ago.'

The judge:
'Robert Thompson and Jon Venables,
'The killing of James Bulger was an act of unparalleled evil and barbarity. This child of two was taken from his mother on a journey of over two miles and then, on the railway line, was battered to death without mercy. Then his body was placed across the railway line so it would be run over by a train in an attempt to conceal his murder. In my judgement your

293

conduct was both cunning and very wicked.

'The sentence that I pass upon you both is that you should be detained during Her Majesty's pleasure, in such a place and under such conditions as the Secretary of State may now decide. You will be securely detained for very, very many years, until the Home Secretary is satisfied that you have matured and are fully rehabilitated and until you are no longer a danger.

'Let them be taken down.'

Bobby and Jon left the dock and, as they turned onto the stairs, facing the gallery, there was a shout from the front row. How do you feel now, you little bastards?

The judge then addressed the court. 'How it came about that two mentally normal boys, aged ten, and of average intelligence, committed this crime is hard to comprehend.

'It is not for me to pass judgement on their upbringing, but I suspect that exposure to violent video films may in part be an explanation.

'In fairness to Mrs Thompson and to Mr and Mrs Venables, it is very much to their credit they used every effort to get their sons to tell the truth.

'The people of Bootle and Walton and all involved in this tragic case will never forget the tragic circumstances of James Bulger's murder. Everyone in court will especially wish Mrs Bulger well in the months ahead and hope that her new baby will bring her peace and happiness. I hope that all involved in this case, whether witness or otherwise, will find peace at Christmas time.'

It was unclear why the judge had made reference to violent videos. There had been no mention in evidence of any videos. Had he too heard the rumours about *Child's Play 3*? Perhaps he was thinking of Dr Susan Bailey's report, which he said he had read, with its account of Jon watching Kung Fu films.

If he had wanted to provoke a public debate it was, perhaps, surprising that he had singled out violent videos as a possible explanation for the killing, with no mention of any other issues that might be a factor in young people committing serious crime.

The ensuing week's papers were full of Chucky doll.

Why had the judge identified the boys? This too was unclear and, as a judge, as he had said in court earlier, he was not accountable.

They could change their names, of course, in years to come. As could their families. But how would Ryan, baby Ben, Mark, Michelle and the other members of the two families who had not been convicted of murdering James Bulger be affected by the revelation of their identities, and their innocent association with the notoriety which had been thrust on Bobby and Jon?

Mary Bell had tried to live with her name when she was released but had, finally, sought the protection of the court in changing her identity and keeping it out of the tabloids.

The court emptied quickly after the judge's closing remarks. The media had copy to file, names to give, and the Merseyside Police were holding a press conference over the road.

Bobby and Jon had already gone, out in their separate vans, past a large, baying crowd, and back to indeterminate detention. The lawyers gathered up their boxes and papers and folders of files.

Dominic Lloyd and Lawrence Lee met in the otherwise deserted corridor of the court.

'Well, no surprises there, eh?' Lawrence said.

26

When this book was first published, in British hardback, the text ended at the close of the previous chapter. I had considered and dismissed the idea of adding what I am now about to write: an attempt to explain how and why Bobby and Jon came to kill James Bulger.

There had been a deluge of spurious, worthless theorising about their motives in the media and I did not feel inclined to add my own twopennyworth; I felt that all the clues, as many as were known, were already in the text. It only required a little intellectual effort on the part of the reader to piece them all together. Then I wondered if it was my own intellectual rigour that was lacking here. I had spent an unhealthily large proportion of the last 18 months turning the facts of the killing over and over in my head, trying to analyse and clarify what had happened. I had been increasingly infuriated by public and governmental response to the case. I had also had a baby, which would be irrelevant, except that it had been the constant refrain of parents while I was writing the book that I would 'feel differently' when I became a parent myself. They meant that I would identify my own baby with James Bulger and myself with Ralph and Denise and be unable to sympathise or even empathise with Bobby and Jon and their parents. Well, now I'd had a baby and did not 'feel differently' at all. Perhaps it was time to commit those thought-findings to paper . . .

David James Smith

We do not know if Bobby and Jon had planned to abduct and kill a baby but it seems to have become fixed in popular opinion, conveniently suiting the theory of the boys' innate evil, that they had hatched a diabolical plot together and always knew exactly what their mutual intentions were.

'Do you want to be in our gang – we're going to kill someone,' they told a schoolmate. Jon, in his police interviews, said it was Bobby who had proposed getting Mrs Power's son lost so that he would walk into the road and get knocked over and, again said, it was Bobby who proposed pushing James into the water at the canal.

Irrespective of whether Jon is attributing his own words to

Bobby, these sound to be condemning remarks. Perhaps, however, they are more hyperbolical than diabolical; the boastful, let's-talk-tough exaggerations of children rather than an expressed intention.

It's common enough, among adults, to talk big and threatening, without anyone seriously expecting the threat to be carried out. How often are children warned by their parents, in moments of impatience, 'you do that again and I'll kill you'?

Jon's mother, Susan Venables, tells Jon in the middle of his interviews, in front of two police officers, that she would have 'strangled' him if she had known he was in the Strand. Of course, no one imagines she would have throttled Jon; it's just a figure of speech. Perhaps a common one for Mrs Venables and almost certainly a common one for Bobby's mother, Ann Thompson and Bobby's older brothers.

Still, there was a degree of intent. Jon was identified as one of two boys tapping on a shop window to attract a child at the end of January. Their school attendance records showed that Bobby and Jon truanted together at this time. Then, in the hours before they took James, they attempted to lure another child, Mrs Power's son.

The boys roamed around the Strand for most of the morning and half the afternoon making mischief. They stole from shops, begged for 20 pence, cheeked assistants and taunted an elderly woman. They did not act with the singular purpose of abducting a child. Perhaps they had an eye to the opportunity that finally presented itself with James, wandering momentarily from his mother's care.

It does not, then, seem to have been much of a plan and, in this context, it is hard to accept that they knew they were going to go on and kill a child. One of the two boys must have first introduced the idea that led to taking James and he would certainly not have used the word 'abduct'. 'Let's get a kid . . . let's get a kid lost . . .' It probably did not go much further than that to begin with.

On the face of it, Bobby, with a point of reference in his own brother, baby Ben, is more likely to have initiated the plan and it would be neat and tidy to conclude that, say, for reasons of jealousy, Bobby did to James what he really wanted to do to Ben. But a vulnerable child – James – can, of course, represent much more than a stand-in sibling. Above all, to two ten-year-olds, a child is a person over whom they can have power. I believe that the need to exert that power lies at the heart of the case.

Whether it was Bobby or Jon who proposed taking a child, it was Jon who apparently took the lead, tapping on the window in late January, beckoning Mrs Power's son, approaching James and taking him by the hand as the trio left the Strand.

Merseyside Police believed that Bobby cunningly stood back and encouraged Jon to take the principal role. It was Bobby, by general consensus, who was the manipulative and sadistic ring-leader in the whole affair. But how much deviousness can you attribute to a ten-year-old, even one with Bobby's native acuity? There seems to be a disturbing readiness to ascribe adult guile and malice to Bobby. It may well be that Jon repeatedly took control because he wanted to.

Once out of the Strand with James the boys quickly sought the seclusion of the neighbouring canal towpath and it is not difficult to imagine their surprise, excitement even, at having 'got away with it', and their uncertainty over what to do next. We don't know how serious was the intent when they talked about pushing James into the canal, and then there was a sudden escalation, the first act of violence. One of them – each says it was the other – picked James up and dropped him head-first onto the concrete path.

It might have ended here, when Bobby and Jon then ran off, but they went back, perhaps to have a look at James, and found him coming along towards them. They pulled the hood of his anorak up to cover the head injury and set off to . . . well, to where? It was not as if they went straight to the railway line or even followed a direct route. They dawdled and meandered and it is hardly in keeping with Bobby's supposed cunning that they made their way to Walton, which both boys knew and where both, especially Bobby, were known; their final destination, the railway line, was just a few hundred yards from Bobby's home.

Perhaps they were waiting for the cover of darkness before carrying out their attack on James or, perhaps, they didn't really know what to do or where to go. A proper, artfully conceived plan would not have involved so much casual idling, messing around and wandering in and out of shops, nor offered so many opportunities to be caught in their encounters with adults. It might be stretching credulity to suggest that the boys wanted to be stopped and discovered but they certainly did not go to enormous lengths to avoid it. Of course, they lied when confronted, as children commonly do when caught out doing something wrong. Again, it is worth pointing out that Jon seems to have taken the lead in the significant exchanges.

James's fate may still not have been decided when the boys stood at the end of the entry on Walton Lane – and James was seen alive for the last time. The police station is directly opposite, across the road, and the boys were observed apparently trying to push James into the road. Just possibly, they were trying to send him off to the police station. Equally, on this busy dual-carriageway, they may have been trying to get him run over. Either way, their lingering presence here and the act of pushing James off the pavement do not suggest they had already decided to drag the child on to the railway line and attack him.

Violence had been a part of James's ordeal since his injury at the canal. Bobby had been seen to kick him. Jon admitted in interview that he had punched James while they were on the reservoir and tore the hood from his anorak when they were walking down the entry between City Road and Walton Lane.

By degrees, James's presence in their company and in their power had become a part – almost a 'normal' part – of Bobby and Jon's experience that afternoon. They had taken a boy and not been caught, they had been violent and not been stopped.

James could do nothing. He was powerless. The boys, by now, could do anything with him.

The attack on the railway line began with a casual flick of a tin of paint and escalated quickly into a very violent assault. We do not know exactly what happened or what part each boy played in the attack. My belief, which I will explain, is that Jon was responsible for the worst of the assault, though Bobby was no bystander. I imagine a great deal of nervous and exciting tension between them. Laughter, fear, aggression, anger, viciousness. The attack, once it had begun, was unstoppable.

They probably did not need to egg each other on. The experience of the afternoon and their presence together at that moment was enough. One of the boys, quite possibly both, wanted – I would even say 'needed' – to sexually assault James and this became a feature of the attack. Finally, they moved the body across the tracks and covered it with bricks. It was an obvious, but feeble, attempt to disguise the killing.

Within the hour both boys were back in their mothers' arms, Jon being verbally and physically attacked by Susan Venables for his disobedience at playing truant, Bobby sending Ann Thompson into a rage at Susan Venables by complaining that she had hit him. Both parents were oblivious to their sons' recent murder of a two-year-old boy. Both boys were immediately back in their more familiar role as victims rather than victimisers.

Nothing will ever persuade me that Bobby and Jon were born to kill James Bulger. The idea that there are people who do evil simply because they are evil has its ancient root in bigotry and intolerance. It's the kind of attitude that got 'witches' burnt and it remains a convenient, comforting means of explaining away and distancing ourselves from an event – such as the killing of a child by children.

By definition, children have been granted a special place in the history of evil and original sin. They have natural tendencies towards wickedness and need to be beaten into line. Don't do as I do, do as I tell you. I suspect that an authoritarian, repressive, affectionless approach to parenting has been responsible for producing generations of damaged children and, in its darker corners, has allowed terrible excesses of physical and sexual abuse. In turn, damaged children grow up to be parents and inflict further damage.

It used to be thought that infants and children had short memories and would not remember as adults what had happened to them at the beginning of their lives. This may be true at a conscious level but it is also apparent that they have powerful feelings. Babies, in their innocence, have primary needs and responses. They want food, love and security to thrive. A baby that is not fed when it is hungry cries and becomes agitated. If the hunger continues to be unsatisfied it becomes anxious, enraged and humiliated because it is being neglected and is powerless to do anything about it. A parent, or carer, who shouts and hits the baby to try and stop the 'fit' will make the baby feel even more resentful. The baby will eventually be fed, and the traumatic feelings, which of course the baby can't identify, will be suppressed and stored up in the unconscious because they are too painful to live with, and get in the way of the overwhelming need to love and be loved.

The potential traumas of babies and children are many and varied, from the unsatisfied needs of hunger to the extremes of physical and sexual assault. Each person will experience a trauma differently – but the worse the trauma the more extreme the later reaction to it is likely to be, up to and including killing yourself or somebody else.

This is not an exact science, but then neither is the theory of innate evil. What did the British media call Bobby and Jon? Devils, demons, monsters . . . it sounds like superstitious nonsense.

There have been few empirical attempts to prove a link between childhood trauma and subsequent violent offending and some inconclusive studies to establish the causes of delinquency. In Britain the Cambridge Study in Delinquent Development, a so-called longitudinal examination of a group of urban, working-class boys, has suggested that delinquents are more likely to emerge from large families where discipline is strict or inconsistent and the parents passive or rejecting. Intriguingly, the study also indicated that while the loss of a parent was important, it was only so in cases where there had been parental conflict. In other words, broken homes without parental conflict were not a significant predictor of delinquency and unbroken homes with parental conflict were more likely to lead to delinquency.

Current right-wing political opinion in Britain cites the 'collapse of the nuclear family as a primary cause of the rise in juvenile crime, perhaps because it deflects attention from the more obvious problem of a widening gap between rich and poor and the growing number of people living in poverty.

Certainly, families are vulnerable to the stresses and strains of low income and poor housing. The bigger the family the more extreme the hardship. The harder it gets the more likely parents are to take it out on their children. Not all parents of low-income families and not just poor parents of low-income families will abuse their offspring. But it is difficult to avoid the conclusion that the pressure of poverty in the family takes an extra toll on its children.

Liverpool's past is characterised by extremes of poverty. I was struck by the symbolically brutal scene (at the beginning of Chapter 23) of a group of adults laughing at the spectacle of children with their hands bound, fighting in the mud to catch a cock between their teeth. I though of the 'ragged street urchins' of the Victorian age, neglected and unloved. I wondered if it was more than mere coincidence that three of the past cases of killings by children, documented at the beginning of the book, had occurred on Merseyside.

As a character in a recent American novel says, 'It's the cycle of shit' (*Clockers* by Richard Price).

*

Imagine the terrible moment when Jon admits to his parents, 'I did kill him.' Not 'We did . . .', not 'Bobby did . . .', but 'I did . . .' Susan and Neil must by now suspect what is coming. Jon's burden, as is evident from his distress, is unbearable. The catharsis comes when Susan and Neil tell him, as they have been advised to do, that they will always love him. It is the trigger for the enormous emotional release of Jon's guilt.

Is it possible that the potency of those words – the expression of 'love' – was not just a result of Jon's need to hear them then, when the desire to confess had become overwhelming? Is it also possible that he had not heard them very often in the past and had doubted, or at least not always been sure of, his parents' love?

We don't know everything, or even very much, about Jon's childhood, but what we do know indicates that it was characterised by instability.

His parents first separated when he was four and were later divorced. Jon went with his mother and his brother and sister to stay at his grandmother's home. Then he moved with his mother into their own home for a short period, before they all moved back in with Neil. The parents separated again, Jon again going with his mother. Sometimes his father would come to stay, then he didn't see them very much at all for a while. Then they all began living together again for part of the week. We know that Jon's mother would sometimes send Jon to stay with his father when she couldn't cope. We know from the NSPCC case conference that Neil looked after Jon then sent him back to Susan because he couldn't cope.

Jon was 'upset and difficult' following the initial separation, and his increasingly disturbed behaviour is a clue to the feelings of confusion, insecurity and rejection aroused in him by this continuing upheaval and uncertainty. The violence and aggression he displayed at school and at home also suggest a build-up of frustration, resentment and anger.

We can only guess at the domestic conflict behind Neil and Susan's volatile relationship, but it must have been aggravated by Neil's unemployment and the special needs, first, of brother Mark and later, of sister Michelle. Being a child witness to such conflict would be distressing enough. Being a victim of it, in the stress-provoked way that Susan seems to have shouted at Jon and smacked him, could only have reinforced the impotent, powerless frustration of Jon's position.

Susan, who does not give much away, describes her upbringing as strict and disciplined. This almost certainly means the use of harsh physical punishment and, if we are looking for the root of her depressive illness, it may lie in her own childhood experience and feelings of inadequacy as an adult parent and partner.

Neil describes a happy, spoilt upbringing, despite the loss of his mother at an early age. He too has had problems with depression as an adult and there is a sense of his passive incapacity as a parent: his inability to cope with Jon, his belief that Jon being bullied is 'just part of growing up'. Even though he was living less than ten minutes' drive from Susan there was a period – a critical period in Jon's worsening behaviour – when he 'wasn't seeing much' of his family.

There are three small indicators of Jon's hostile attitude towards his father. Two occur during the police interviews after Jon's confession, when Neil has stepped in to replace Susan. Neil evidently takes a sip of water from a cup on the table. 'That's mine,' says Jon. The interviewing officer tells Jon to let his dad take a drink from the cup: 'I think he might just need one.' Later, when Jon is being questioned about the possibility of a sexual assault on James, he turns to hit his father. Jon says it's because 'me dad thinks I know and I don't'. He says he wants his mum. The third and final incident was back at Jon's secure unit after the first day of the trial when he shouted at his father.

Neil, with his own vulnerability and passivity, is perhaps unconsciously passing on those qualities to Jon: an inconsistent and fragile father figure who is adding to his son's feelings of powerless frustration.

After instability, another theme that emerges from what we know of Jon's background is a tragic tendency to denial and suppression of reality. The instinct, even before the killing, to make everything seem all right, or at least, not as bad as it appears, is so strong that it is tempting to speculate that there is something lurking in a dark corner that is too big and too difficult to confront.

In their meeting with the consultant psychiatrist, Dr Susan Bailey, Neil and Susan said they had dealt with their separation by telling Jon that they could not get on together but were still friends. They said that Neil had continued to see all the children. The implication was that everything was all right, when we know that it wasn't.

At the time, and in her talk with Dr Bailey, Susan seems to have been keen to find an external explanation for Jon's behavioural problems. Jon was simply an overactive boy who was bullied. He did not show any antagonism towards his siblings or jealousy of their special needs attention.

We know that Jon was not placated by his parents' explanation of their separation and that he was 'upset and difficult', began having temper tantrums and showed some anti-social behaviour in school. This was around the time that the police were called to Susan's home because the children had been left alone for three hours.

Jon did complain of being bullied, at school and in the street near his mother's home, and this can only have added to his vulnerability and powerless frustration.

When he was seven years old Jon was referred to a trainee educational psychologist who said that Jon seemed unable to cope with the pressures on him. Nothing seems to have changed as a result of this diagnosis. No help was forthcoming and there was continuing instability in the family. The 'pressure' must have risen inside Jon.

His class teacher noticed a dramatic deterioration in Jon's behaviour after the 1990 Christmas holidays. Did something happen during that holiday to make him so much worse? Now he begins to act out very serious internal distress, showing aggression and self-destructiveness. The consensus is that he is seeking attention. He wants attention.

His worsening behaviour – we know it is extreme because his teacher has never seen anything like it in 14 years of teaching – results in a second visit to a psychologist. Susan proposes another (denying) explanation for what she calls Jon's hyperactivity: his diet. The psychologist colludes in Susan's denial and suggests a special diet, as well as a referral to a senior colleague.

Susan tries the diet but gives up because it doesn't seem to make any difference. She does not pursue the referral. Does she give up because she does not think the problem is very serious – he'll grow out of it – or because she is afraid of the truth and finds it easier to deny?

When Jon finally nearly chokes a boy with a ruler – using such enraged strength it takes two adults to separate him from his victim – Susan attributes this to the bullying and decides he should change schools. The very action that draws him to Bobby.

All agree that Jon's behaviour improves under the more disciplined methods of his first teacher at his new school in Walton. He still butts his head against the wall in the playground, but not very often, and only the dinner lady seems concerned about this. The head teacher just wants Jon to 'behave himself' in her school and has only accepted him on the basis that he goes into a class below his proper age group – another humiliation for Jon to take on board.

Where are Jon's feelings in the 'structured environment' of his new, disciplined teaching? They cannot now be expressed in his behaviour and they cannot disappear. They can only be suppressed where they will fester. He has probably already been made to feel guilty for all the trouble he has been causing his mother. He wants to please her because he wants to be loved. He is a child and what is happening to him is not his fault, but he is being asked to carry the additional burden of responsibility.

Jon's mother notes that he seems happier playing with younger children in the street. A teacher finds him in the playground, picking on a smaller boy. He and Bobby, when they get together, enjoy a reputation for bullying. Here is Jon, vulnerable and powerless, taking opportunities to reclaim some power, and project his vulnerability and powerlessness onto somebody else.

Susan leaves Jon to make his own way to school and he begins to truant. In the new school year, with a less strict teacher, his behaviour again starts to degenerate. The teacher thinks Jon knows he is doing wrong but carries on as if he doesn't care and wants the attention. There is no uniformity of opinion about Jon among the staff. The head thinks he is 'odd'. Only the dinner lady and one teacher appear to think that there is a real problem. The truanting continues.

With the benefit of hindsight it is possible to say that, short of writing it out in big letters on the school blackboard, Jon could not have made himself plainer. If he was not helped he was going to do something really terrible. At some point, probably sooner rather than later, he would find an outlet for all that suppressed rage and powerless frustration. He would find someone vulnerable over whom he could exert absolute power. He would be abusive and very violent. It was becoming a matter of urgency.

When four detectives knocked on Susan Venables' door to arrest her son for murder she said, 'I knew you'd be here. I told him you'd want to see him for sagging school on Friday.' Sadly, tragically, I believe that, deep down, even then, Susan knew the real reason for the detectives' visit. Denial is a difficult habit to break.

If it was instability that characterised Jon's childhood, it was turbulence that defined Bobby's. Conflict and violence were an inbuilt part of life in the Thompson household. We probably don't know the half of what Bobby witnessed or was subjected to, but what we do know provides a vivid picture of a classically dysfunctional family.

His mother, Ann – like Jon, a middle child – was ill-prepared for an adult life as parent and partner. Her own childhood was dominated by the terror and tyranny of a drunken, physically abusive father and a mother who seemed to Ann to be passive, weak and unsupporting.

Who knows what historical cycle had led Ann's parents – Bobby's maternal grandparents – to play these roles or why it was Ann alone, of the three children, who felt victimised and unloved. Middle children, sandwiched between the first-born and an adored baby, can often feel isolated as the family scapegoat.

If you are denied love and affection as a child how can you express those feelings as an adult? What else could Ann do with those unsatisfied needs but, unconsciously, develop a store of resentment and anger behind a wall of truculent self-protection? Treated as if she was worthless, Ann would inevitably come to believe it. She could not live with feeling worthless, so she buried the feeling, and created a mask of aggressive defiance.

No wonder then, that she married the 'first fella who ever paid her attention'. Engaged on her seventeenth birthday, married on her eighteenth, she could not get away from home quick enough and was almost bound to step out of the frying pan and into the fire.

Her father's beating had continued, apparently unabated, into adolescence. There is something almost sexual in her father's humiliating violation of Ann's body, the beating of a teenaged daughter by a father who has just been told she is leaving him to get married.

Ann did not leave her parents' home to get married and start a family, or because she was ready. She left because she needed to. There was no hope of fulfilling the wishful, escapist fantasy she had played out with dolls. There could be no 'fairytale' marriage.

Little is known of her husband, Bobby senior, but from what we do know, the parallel between his own childhood and that of his son Bobby is extraordinary. Bobby senior, the third youngest like his son, lost his own father – through death rather than desertion – in childhood. 'The paternal role had been taken on by the elder brothers, and they were strict in imposing discipline.' This is so exact it could be a prophecy. Another turn of the cycle.

As a married couple, Ann and Bobby senior seem, initially, to have been permanently broke and unhappy. Why did they have so many children? Ann says she kept on trying for a girl and her husband wanted a football team. Perhaps the truth is that Ann wanted, or needed, the doll-like innocence of babies. A need that could never be satisfied and could only be disastrous for the children.

It is no surprise that Bobby senior turns out to be a violent drunk like Ann's father. Bobby senior, deprived of a father and subjugated to the will of his older siblings, is now in a position of power which he is only too ready to abuse.

What a good laugh it must have been among Ann and her sons, joking about Bobby senior's similarities with Peter Sutcliffe, the Yorkshire Ripper. What must the family have experienced to make that joke acceptable?

By the time little Bobby is born the family is already in trouble, Bobby senior is violent with his wife and his sons. It is difficult to believe that Ann does not employ physical punishment nor sometimes fight back at her husband. There is probably a great deal of abusive shouting and verbal conflict. There is probably very little show of love and tenderness and certainly no consistency.

The eldest boy, David, has been on and off the child protection register. Ann has attempted suicide with an overdose of Valium, not long after the birth of her fourth child. They probably thought she was suffering from post-natal depression. Don't worry, love, you'll get over it. How many truckloads of Valium would it take to dull Ann's pain? She would not expect to be helped and no help, or not very much, is forthcoming.

Ironically, family life begins to improve after the birth of little Bobby. There is more money and camping holidays. Nothing has been confronted or resolved and the construct must still be dangerously fragile but, perhaps, there is a little less pressure and conflict.

Bobby is just about two years old when his younger brother Ryan is born and he is no longer the new baby in the family. He is six years old when his father leaves and ceases all contact with Ann and the boys. (Is it possible Bobby senior was six when his father died?)

First Bobby has been displaced in the family by Ryan – at the very age of James Bulger when he is killed – and now he has been abandoned by his father. The little love and affection the family has to spare has perhaps been invested in the new-born. This was withdrawn from Bobby when Ryan came along and now his father, by his actions, is saying, 'I don't want you, I don't love you.'

The effect on the whole family of the father's departure is catastrophic. First, symbolically, the family home immediately burns down. Then Ann turns to drink, confirmed now in her role as a victim, and, unsurprisingly, incapable of being one adequate parent, never mind two.

Bobby, like his father before him, is now left to the mercies of his older brothers. The experience of conflict and violence – the deliberate and unintentional abuse of adult power – is their only model. What else can they do, when suddenly and prematurely awarded the power for themselves, but act out the same conflict and violence? We don't know what went on, while Ann was in the pub and Bobby senior was God knows where, but, at best, it was probably bullying and, at worst, it may have reached into those dark corners of excessive abuse.

At home, Ann was almost certainly short-tempered, un-affectionate and harsh. Bobby must have responded to her as a victim, wanting to please and protect his mother. He must have felt resentment too, that she was not there to protect him. He would have suppressed those feelings and perhaps projected them onto his father, who was now a convenient focus for all the anger in the family.

Bobby will also have taken on his mother's protective shell of defiance: those instincts for self-preservation that were to serve him so well in his interviews with the police and to see him wrongly perceived as the leader of the plot to kill James Bulger.

By the time Ann emerges from her alcoholic stupor, the family is in total disarray. One by one, the boys are heading into care. There is delinquency, depression and attempts at suicide (overdoses, just like Ann – another cycle).

The turbulence and confusion of Bobby's childhood could not be worse. Ann becomes pregnant and a new baby, Ben, is born. Bobby helps to feed and change the baby, perhaps enjoys helping his mother, wanting to please her. He bakes cakes in the kitchen too. It is as if he is trying to provoke some love and affection from Ann. Or, at least, some consistency in her mothering.

We know from the teachers at school in Walton that Ryan complains of being bullied by Bobby. Yet, in bed, at night they turn to each other for security, each sucking the other's thumb. It is no wonder that Bobby feels insecure or that he needs some-one to bully.

At school, no one sees a troubled child. Bobby – another Thompson in that long line of truants, bullies and general mis-creants – has expectations to fulfil and does not disappoint. His protective shell, surely only reinforced by these expectations, is misinterpreted as the demeanour of a child causing trouble. Like Jon, he is kept back in a class a year below his age group.

Neglected, resentful, betrayed by his father, bullied by his brothers, reminded at school of his poor pedigree and 'bad' behaviour, Bobby has no support.

He truants and goes shoplifting. He steals things and throws them away. He is self-destructive because he doesn't know any better and no one is there to make sense of it for him. He has reserves of anger and resentment and unsatisfied needs. He has experienced abuse of power and will one day impose his own power to abuse. Now there is no sign, other than bullying Ryan, of any urgent impulse to violence. But when the opportunity is created he will take it. With Jon he finds and makes that opportunity.

Is it possible that Jon and Bobby found each other because they were the two unhappiest and most mistreated boys in the school? Perhaps they saw something of themselves in each other. Perhaps, unconsciously, Bobby identified Jon's readiness to go to extremes.

Jon was isolated at school by his temper tantrums and uncontrollable behaviour, while Bobby was isolated by his distinction as a Thompson, with all the baggage that entailed. They were united in the humiliation of being kept down a year. Another humiliation was the last thing either boy needed.

In all likelihood, if Bobby and Jon had not got together James Bulger would not have been killed. It is difficult to imagine either boy carrying out the killing alone. I believe they needed each other's presence to bolster their nerve and maintain the 'normality' that permitted the escalation into violence. It is equally unlikely that there were other pupils in the school who were so badly damaged that they would want, or need, to participate in the abduction and murder of a child.

Many people, I know, are reluctant to accept this kind of explanation for a seemingly inexplicable, inexcusable act of such horrific violence. The will to try and understand such a crime sometimes appears to be less important than the need to find someone or something to blame. This is a kind of displacement.

The crime is so extreme and so unpleasant that it must be placed beyond all human boundaries. What will we have to address in ourselves if we seek to make a link between such violence and childhood experience which, to a lesser or greater extent, is part of all our childhoods?

Indeed, the usual response to this kind of analysis, repeated over and over in the aftermath of the Bulger case, is that lots of people have difficult childhoods and they don't all go out and kill someone. Specifically, Jon and Bobby were no worse off than lots of other children and must therefore have been driven by their innate evil.

I can only ask how many of those other children will go on to live out the disturbances of their childhood in one way or another? Delinquency, depression, suicide, domestic violence . . . I'm sure a definitive list would be much longer. You could not predict that any other boy, given Jon or Bobby's upbringing, would go out and kill a child. You could, however, predict that those boys would, at some point, be likely to suffer, or cause someone else to suffer, unless help was forthcoming.

It is also possible that Bobby and Jon were worse off than lots of other children, that because we do not know the full facts of their childhoods we do not know just how much they were asked to endure. Quite possibly, for example (though there is no evidence to support this), the sexual assault of James was repeated or acted out from Jon and/or Bobby's own experience as the victim(s) of sexual abuse.

To follow my own argument through to its conclusion, almost everything that has happened to Bobby and Jon since they killed James Bulger could be seen in the context of continuing humiliation and abuse of adult power. Their unconscious cries for help have remained unheard, except perhaps at close-quarters, in their secure units among caring staff.

It was not, in this case, just a question of apportioning blame. The guilty parties – two small boys – had to be paraded at a trial and marched through streets of newsprint. It was not, as some people have thought, the boys' lawyers who put them through this ordeal – it was the judicial process. A process which was rather like a public execution: the crowd was happy to see them drop but went home with a rather sour taste in its mouth.

Justice had to be seen to be done, and rightly so, but, with the boys so young and not yet grown, did it have to be quite so brutal? Wouldn't an informal hearing, which spent more than 20 minutes examining the boys' backgrounds and mental condition, have been better?

Was it also necessary to appropriate the boys' actions as a platform for such a variety of zealous moral crusades? Wicked boys, bad mothers, lone mothers, soft teachers, wet liberals, mollycoddled perpetrators of crime, ignored victims of crime and, most popularly, violent videos . . .

The closing remarks of the trial judge, voicing his, evidentially unfounded, suspicion that violent videos might have played a part in inciting Bobby and Jon to murder incited, in turn, an enthusiastic debate in the media. *Child's Play 3* received more free publicity than it, aesthetically, deserved.

This successfully diverted attention from what might have been a more profitable discussion about child abuse and the pressures on low-income families. And even though there was only the slightest evidence that one of the boys – Jon – might have seen a violent video – *Child's Play 3* – and even though it was difficult to see what this had to do with James Bulger's murder, the debate rumbled along, found its way into academia and prompted the publication of a 'discussion paper'. This too received more publicity than it deserved.

'Video Violence and the Protection of Children' was written by Elizabeth Newson from the Child Development Research Unit at Nottingham University, and was endorsed by a bewilderingly large number of 'psychologists, psychiatrists, paediatricians and others'.

The paper made a direct link with the Bulger case and, in the course of a preamble, stated that we should 'try to ensure that

314

Jamie (*sic*) is not just the first of many such victims'.

It went on . . .

> However, child abuse, poverty and neglect have been a part of many children's experience over the years: indeed, although neither Jon nor Robert could be said to have come from happy and nurturant homes, there was little evidence of the extremes of neglect and abuse that could be documented in any Social Service department.
>
> What then can be seen as the different factor that has entered the lives of countless children and adolescents in recent years? This has to be recognised as the easy availability to children of gross images of violence on video . . .
>
> . . . Thus it is not surprising that Mr Justice Morland speculated upon the part that such videos might have played in creating the degree of desensitisation to compassion that the children in the Bulger case showed – not only during their attack, but in comments like Robert's (before he admitted the killing): 'If I wanted to kill a baby, I would kill my own, wouldn't I?'

Maybe it was only a discussion paper, but I found this a particularly depressing document. An ill-considered remark by the trial judge had made a minor sensation in the media and was now being given the credibility of an academic paper.

Elizabeth Newson's case was founded on the precept that the phenomenon of killings by children had begun with Bobby and Jon, whereas, in fact, it was at least two hundred and fifty years old. There was the, by now, familiar argument that the two boys' backgrounds were no worse, even a good deal better, than many others. Another shaky precept. And were 'gross images of violence on video' the 'different factor' in the recent lives of children? What about poverty, the sinking life raft of the Welfare State and the consistent underfunding of education?

The argument about corrupting images of sex and violence is as old as cinema itself. It's a reasonable wish to protect children from the excesses of adult films but it is hard to accept that, without prior disturbance, children will be impelled to act out what they see on the screen.

Couldn't we find something more pertinent to discuss?

I hope I don't appear to be engaged on some moral crusade of my own. I'm only trying to offer a humane explanation for an act of apparent inhumanity. It is not outside us, it is within us. Bobby and Jon are human too. Small humans, just like James Bulger.

Since their trial the two boys have remained at the same, separate secure units where they were first held after being charged with abduction and murder. Bobby has been visited regularly by Ann and some of his brothers. He has still not had any contact with his father. Jon has had regular contact with Susan and Neil.

Though both boys are, to some extent, isolated in their units by their exceptional youth and the exceptional notoriety of their crime, they have both become part of regimes which are supposed to balance punishment with rehabilitation.

Jon's parents are said to have had concerns about the strict, disciplined approach of his unit. Early on, the Home Office advised that Jon should only move between his living quarters and the unit's recreational wing when accompanied by three members of staff. This has meant a restriction of his movements in a bigger institution with a more impersonal, less flexible style.

During the day Bobby can move freely from his room to the classroom and the lounge, which has table tennis and pool tables and a television and video, where older boys are usually sat watching music tapes.

Bobby has been working at carpentry in the woodwork shop and spends time in the communal kitchen, extending the range of dishes he can cook to curries, pizza and lemon meringue pies.

There are no plug sockets in the boys' rooms and, by day, the corridor of Bobby's unit is criss-crossed by leads that power various electrical components, including the old computer that Bobby uses for games.

Both boys have begun a therapeutic process that is eventually intended to allow them to talk openly about the killing and reach an understanding of how and why it happened. The role of therapist has fallen to Dr Susan Bailey, the consultant psychiatrist who appeared for the prosecution at the trial.

Bobby was initially unable to square the fact that someone who had appeared in court 'against' him was now going to be working for him. They now meet, together with a colleague of Dr Bailey, on a loose schedule of visits, the idea being that when the boys are ready to talk a therapeutic relationship will be in place for them.

The boys' sentences are open-ended, but the law required the Home Secretary to set the first date at which they could be considered for release: the so-called tariff date, after which they will have 'satisfied the requirements of retribution and deterrence'.

In all such cases the Home Secretary makes his decision after hearing the recommendations of the trial judge and the Lord Chief Justice and considering submissions from the detainees. There has been criticism, in the past, that a Home Secretary, who has to be re-elected, could allow political expediency to influence his decision. Bobby and Jon seemed vulnerable to this possibility: they were the objects of national loathing, there was a continuing outcry over juvenile crime and the Home Secretary, Michael Howard, was a right-wing Minister in an unpopular Conservative Government, under pressure to be 'tough on crime'.

There was some relief, among their family and lawyers, when, in January last year, Bobby and Jon received letters from the Home Office which outlined judicial recommendations.

The trial judge had told the Home Secretary that, if the boys had been adults, he would have said the tariff should be set at 18 years. Quoting his own sentencing remarks he said that, taking into account all the appalling circumstances and the age of the defendants, eight years was 'very, very many years' for a ten- or eleven-year-old. They were now children. In eight years they would be young men.

The Lord Chief Justice agreed with the trial judge that a much lesser sentence should apply than in the case of adults,

He thought ten years should be the tariff.

After the trial judge's severe comments at the close of the trial there was considerable surprise that he had not proposed a longer tariff. I understand that Michael Howard, the Home Secretary, was surprised too – the wind taken out of his sails. He had been considering a tariff of 20 or 25 years and, while he was not obliged to follow the judicial recommendations, it would now be difficult to deviate from them by so great a margin.

The recommendations had been passed from the Home Office to the boys in confidence but they were made public and became news. The family of James Bulger reacted in anger and announced a public campaign to persuade Michael Howard that the boys should never be released. *The Sun* newspaper took this up with enthusiasm and printed a special coupon which readers could complete and send to Howard.

In mid-June the boys received a second letter from the Home Office explaining that Howard would soon be announcing his tariff decision. The letter went on to itemise all the submissions the Home Office had received:

One petition, from Ralph and Denise Bulger, containing 278,300 signatures urging that the boys should never be released; one petition from the Bulgers' local MP, George Howarth, containing 5,900 signatures urging that the boys should serve at least 25 years; 21,281 coupons from *The Sun* newspaper; 1,357 sundry letters and small petitions urging a high tariff date . . . and 33 letters in support of the trial judge's recommendation that the tariff date should be set at eight years.

The third, and final, letter came in July, the message inside it delivered in person to Bobby and Jon by an emissary civil servant. Howard, having taken into account 'public concern' over the case, among other factors, had decided that the boys should serve a minimum of 15 years as punishment before they could be considered for release.

Appeals, to the English and European Courts, are pending.